# THE PARLIAMENT OF MAN

**Harold S. Bidmead** is an Englishman, born a few months before the outbreak of World War I. He was educated at Manchester Grammar School and London University, matriculating with honours – distinctions in two subjects and credits in two others. He went on to become for a number of years the Chief British Executive of a giant multinational consortium, and a founder Trustee of its British Staff Pensions Fund. On 'retirement', he joined a partnership of international business consultants.

He was for several years an elected member of the British Federal Union National Council and an Associate Member of the Royal Institute of International Affairs (Chatham House), serving its founder, Lionel Curtis C.H., on his research team.

Mr Bidmead now lives in Norway as a freelance multilingual scientific and technical translator.

He has four sons and two granddaughters.

H.S.B. –

I took this picture of you when we met in Narvik, 1947. You inspired me to go home and talk world federalism. I did, and some 500 people from Lofoten helped give birth to En Verden (One World), the still going world federalist organisation in Norway.

Your friend,

Terje Disington

# THE
# PARLIAMENT OF MAN

## THE FEDERATION OF THE WORLD

### HAROLD S. BIDMEAD

First published in 1992
by
Patton Publications
Orchard House
Swimbridge
Barnstaple
North Devon
EX32 OPL

© Harold S. Bidmead 1992
All rights reserved

BRITISH LIBRARY CATALOGUING-IN-PUBLICATION DATA
A catalogue record for this book is available
from the British Library


Set in 10 on 12 Times Roman
Copy preparation by Patton Publications
Printed and bound in Great Britain
by
BPCC Wheatons Ltd, Marsh Barton, Exeter

ISBN 1 872426 05 0

Distributed
by
Patton Publications

When the war drums throb no longer
and the flags of war are furl'd
in the Parliament of Man,
the Federation of the World.

(Alfred Lord Tennyson, *Lockesley Hall*, 1842)
He also predicted the 'rain of ghastly dew from the
nations' airy navies, grappling in the central blue.'

Dedicated to my friends and loved ones,
particularly to those without whose
discouragement I might not have
summoned up enough
pig-headedness
to complete
this
book
*

# CONTENTS

|   |   |   |
|---|---|---|
|   | FOREWORD | viii |
|   | INTRODUCTION: HOW TO ENRICH THE WORLD BY 1.5 MILLION DOLLARS EVERY MINUTE | 1 |
|   | Socratic Lullaby | 10 |
| 1 | LAW PRONOUUNCED 'LOVE' – DEFINITIONS | 14 |
|   | What is meant by policing the world? | 21 |
| 2 | A PARADISE FOR LAWYERS | 24 |
|   | The Science of Interpopular Government | 26 |
|   | A World Fit for People to Live in | 30 |
|   | The Architecture of Peace | 33 |
|   | Let's Make War Unnecessary | 37 |
| 3 | THE GENESIS OF WORLD FEDERALISM | 42 |
|   | Thou shalt not kill wholesale | 52 |
| 4 | WORLD CITIZENS No.1, No.2 and No.12,345 | 55 |
|   | Alas, We Are UN-done! | 68 |
|   | Federalist Fleet Besieges Castle | 71 |
|   | Missed one World Citizen, Found Another | 74 |
|   | Clarin Tells King of Sweden | 75 |
| 5 | DON'T MEND OLD SACKS WITH GOOD NEW TWINE | 77 |
|   | Why UNO? Because WENO no better | 81 |
|   | 'Frisco Farce | 84 |
|   | Is Peace Divisible by 55 ? | 86 |
|   | UNO Slays Bernadotte | 88 |
|   | Mass Hypnotism as Alternative ? | 91 |
|   | Sequel to the Dikbarton Hoax | 94 |
|   | Counsel for Europe | 99 |
|   | Parasols versus Parachutes | 101 |
|   | The Federation of the World | 102 |
| 6 | THE COMMONWEALTH OF GOD | 105 |
|   | Faith, Decision, Action | 106 |
|   | Trade in a Federation | 110 |
|   | A Commonwealth of Peoples | 112 |
|   | British Commonwealth as a Nucleus | 115 |
|   | The Neutrality of Eire | 121 |
|   | Domestic and Foreign Policy | 125 |
| 7 | PRACTICAL STEPS TO WORLD UNITY | 129 |
|   | War, the Recurring Decimator | 132 |
|   | Are the Allies Federating? | 137 |

Squaring the Globe:
   I Danger of Deadlock     142
   II Bretton Woods — or just 44 trees?     144
   III A Museum Peace     146
   IV First Aid, then Cure     148
   V Edward I and George Washington     151
   VI Will War End Before Peace Begins?     153
   VII How Green are our Allies?     156

8     FEDERALISTS ON PEACE PATH     159
   Federal Europe is conceived     163
   Citizens of the World Unite     174
   I meet a Future President of India
      and half-win the Nobel Peace Prize     176
   Good News from Ghent     181

9     PAX OR PACTS?     183
   Pax Atlantica?     186
   Women and the Atlantic Pact     193
   Dragons' Teeth     195
   Mandate Madness     196
   The British Ministry of Peace     198
   Open Letter to General Eisenhower     200
   Voters of the World, Unite!     202

10     I MEET AN ATOMIC BOMB MAKER     207

11     BOOK REVIEWS AS PROPAGANDA:     212
   Psychology and World Order     213
   The World at the Crossroads     215
   Soviet Policy towards Disarmament     216
   The Great Rehearsal     216
   Peace or Anarchy     217
   The Last Trump     218
   The North Atlantic Pact     219
   Searchlight on Peace Plans     220
   The World Must be governed     222
   The Pilgrimage of Western Man     224

12     UNCLE SAM     226
13     SOME OBJECTIONS ANSWERED     228
14     A HOUSE OF MANY MANSIONS     235
    BIBLIOGRAPHY     241
    INDEX     243

# FOREWORD

'World government is not only possible; it is inevitable, and when it comes it will appeal to patriotism in its truest, in its only sense, the patriotism of men who love their natural heritages so deeply that they wish to preserve them for the common good'

Sir Peter Ustinov, *PlanetHood**

Not a small part of Sir Peter's fame is due to his work for UNICEF. In that capacity he is no doubt well aware that this organization, depending as it does on voluntary contributions, would be a thousand times more effective if it were to become a Ministry of an international federal government. Although the world is but one village, it is still a vast place, inhabited by myriads of people, and in that context U.N. and its organs constitute but a puny organization capable of applying only a thin smear of cosmetic over some small parts of the Earth's face.

In his speech accepting the presidentship of the World Federalist Movement, Sir Peter equated Britain to a federal union. This shows that, like many other brilliant and charismatic world thinkers, he has nevertheless gone only part of the way towards studying the data sheet of federalism — its technicalities — as readers of this book will quickly discover.

The setting up of the 'United' Nations after World War II was a step in the wrong direction, a move away from world anarchy towards *legalized* anarchy, a realm where national sovereignty reigns supreme.

Any physician who offered to eradicate a disease without harming the germ or virus that causes it would be laughed out of his profession. There is a consensus among political scientists to the effect that national sovereignty is the prime cause of war, yet national sovereignty is the overriding principle on which the United Nations is founded. Stripped of its verbosity, the Charter of the United Nations is an instrument for keeping the peace by making war, a contradiction in terms and a monstrosity in practice.

## Foreword

Yet most current proposals for a new world order are based on the vain hope of maintaining peace without harming its arch enemy – national sovereignty. Even Willy Brandt's *Stockholm Initiative\** states that the new world order 'must' be built on the principles of sovereignty, and goes on to say 'the U.N. organization must fully respect the sovereignty of its member nations.'

It is true that the authors of the Stockholm Initiative specifically state: 'This will require a new concept of sovereignty' though they do not go as far as to admit that the sovereignty should vest in the individual citizens , not in the nation state.

President Bush obviously believes that in his new world order, international law will continue to act on nations, not the individual men and women of whom they are composed.

The many federalists who allowed themselves to be enslaved by the United Nations Association ('Don't rock the boat – give this second League of Nations a chance!') now put their trust in proposals which without exception (so far as I can see) would leave the germ of national sovereignty alive and kicking, free to increase and multiply at the first opportunity. My question is, therefore, 'Why waste one's time, money and energy on a manoeuvre which, even if it becomes a tactical success, will still be a stategic failure?'

Even the letterhead of Sir Peter's World Federalist Movement states that it stands for a 'Just World Order Through a Strengthened United Nations.' All the schemes outlined in its collection of twenty *Essays on Restructuring the U.N.\**, contain the seeds of their own destruction, a fatal reliance on the pernicious principle on which the U.N. is founded. Those who do not make the mistake of pinning their hopes on national sovereignty are deluded into thinking that one only has to *promise* not to exercise it and it will not be used – that indeed it will cease to exist.

There is one ray of hope in the situation. Some of those who pay lip service to national sovereignty are its secret enemies, but suffer from a syndrome well known to psychologists. They are reluctant to show their true colours for fear of antagonizing their colleagues. If they were to admit that it was their intention to seize the first opportunity to stab national sovereignty in the back, there might be hope for the world. However, as this book shows, I prefer the honest approach.

Let me here utter a warning. As an enemy of national sovereignty myself, I would not agree to the British parliament abandoning national sovereignty if this meant that, e.g. the Falkland Islands would not longer feel protected. Men will abandon their security to a new order only if they can trust it to defend them better and less expensively than can the present system of keeping the peace by making war.

National sovereignty is today, like Hitler's national socialism of yesterday, Public Enemy No.1. Why do the current proposals for a New World Order fail to recognize this fact?

In the course of its long fight against disease, the medical world continues to identify and eliminate malign agents that are recognized as causing specific ailments, and attempting to wipe them off the face of the earth for good. In this regard, some significant successes have been achieved. If national sovereignty could be eradicated from the world's body politic, war could be added to the list of irrevocably extinct species. This may not happen in our lifetimes, but it is our duty to point the way. This book tries to do just that.

Harold S. Bidmead<br>
Oslo<br>
May 1992

\* See Bibliography

# ACKNOWLEDGEMENTS

For the cover I am indebted to Dr Gerald Moore, environmentalist, physician, dental surgeon, actor, painter, sculptor, author and lifelong friend. As I interpret his painting, it depicts the world citizen, trapped in the martial entanglements devised by well-meaning but blind politicians.

I also owe thanks to Gerald for much useful advice and help, and to John Coll and Mrs Brit-Eline Larsen of Forenede Translatører, Oslo, for invaluable technical assistance.

Thanks, too, to my longstanding federalist friend Terje Disington, of Svolvær and Oslo, whose aid is much appreciated.

# INTRODUCTION

# HOW TO ENRICH THE WORLD BY 1,500,000 DOLLARS EVERY MINUTE

(What would your share work out at?)

Even before 'Desert Storm', the world was wasting USD 1,500,000 every minute that passed, day and night, on mass killing machines. In the USA alone, this was costing an average of USD 3,500 *per annum* for every American household.[1] Imagine what social improvements could have been accomplished throughout the world for these vast sums, the wise spending of which could conceivably remove any wish for any nation to go to war anywhere at any time.

The foregoing figures are taken from *Defense Monitor* for 1987, quoted in *PlanetHood* by Benjamin B. Ferencz and Ken Keyes, Jr.

It was perhaps ironical that, at the time when huge quantities of Western armaments were, we hoped, becoming redundant by reason of the dissolution of the Warsaw Pact, the process of their destruction was used to remove, simultaneously, the superfluous military might of Iraq. Waste is sinful! Unfortunately, however, much more than surplus military equipment was destroyed at the same time.

[1] I am told that only bankers and other experts understand USD – US dollars, but as I doubt whether the various computers dealing with this book will be able to convert the conventional dollar sign, I have to remain modern and up-to-date!

## The Parliament of Man

The Arabian Gulf crisis was a classic example of the shortcomings of the United Nations, even though — laboriously and slowly — the UN did succeed in reaching decisions which the designers of its Charter apparently never intended it to be able to make. Otherwise, why did they insert the veto?

Observant readers may notice that, of the two names for the Gulf, I prefer to call it by the one preferred by our Arabian allies, for whom the USA showed little consideration by calling it the 'Perzjan' Gulf. (During World War I, President Wilson was careful not to call the North Sea the German Ocean).

As will be seen from the historical evidence quoted throughout this book, the author was not the only federalist who regarded the UN from the outset as a blundering giant which, *if* it embarked on war (having with difficulty ordered 'open fire') might never be able to agree on giving the 'cease fire' signal. In the event, at the end of 'Desert Storm', the U.N. Leviathan did manage to resolve on an armistice, but refused to permit the allies to resume hostilities in the event of Iraq breaking the truce. It is obvious that if Iraq does violate the armistice, the allies will cast aside their UN mask and take matters into their own hands — in which the war had actually been ever since it commenced.[2]

In a letter to a Norwegian daily paper, an opponent of the Gulf War complained that it was not, as claimed, a surgical operation, since it was throttling Iraq. My view is that if a mad dog's fangs have been embedded in my vital organs from August to January, I welcome the surgical operation entailed in cutting the creature's throat.

---

[2] Whilst writing, this prediction has come to pass. On 20 March 1991 the US shot down one of two Iraqui aircraft which took off north of Baghdad. But now, tied (though loosely) and hampered by the Security Council's resolutions, the UN ('coalition') forces stand idly by while Saddam Hussein bombs his 'own' people with chemical weapons. Genocide and human rights in Iraq are obviously not the concern of the U.N. Of the so-called 'Great' Powers only France differs from this view. (Still later note: US forces have now entered Iraq to defend some of the genocide victims. British commandoes have also been in action for the same purpose. The UN is left to sign on the dotted line, or not, no matter what the Charter may say or its other members may say or do.

## Introduction

To those who still think along the lines of reforming the 'United' Nations, I still say that there is no future in darning a worn-out sack with good new twine. The U.N. 'Security' Council must be replaced by a *government*.

We must not blind ourselves to a fact pointed out in *PlanetHood*, to which have referred earlier:

> The U.N. Charter ... was deliberately put together with non-binding loopholes that made it unable to preserve peace. There have been about 130 wars since 1945 with an estimated 16 million dead in which the Security Council did not use the power given it in the Charter to stop the agression and killing.

(Note, however, that the authors use the word 'power' when they mean legal duty, not *de facto* ability!).

The undemocratic voting procedure of the UN not only results in unjust decisions, but provides excuses even for miscreants to throw doubts on the fairness of all its other decisions, no matter how right these may be.

The only proper objects of government are not governments but human beings; supranational law must be made to act against the individual lawbreakers, not against any of their innocent fellow citizens. Justice has no use for weapons of mass destruction.

We must make the law stronger than any entity that might break it; in other words, arm the law and disarm the litigants. This would ensure obedience to supranational law without the need for violence, because it would act on *individuals*, not on states or nations.

Weapons do not cause war, nor can they prevent it. But men will not give up their weapons until they are sure they have an international organization that can protect them and their rights better and less expensively than they can do this themselves.

So long as there are nations that do not at first participate in the parliament of man, a second U.N. (a third league of nations) may still be necessary as a Bourse or 'change to facilitate meetings of diplomats, but such a debating society cannot possibly *guarantee* peace.

In a world where the 'peacekeeping' authority can do so only by

## The Parliament of Man

warlike means, any decision made by a statesman may be a choice between wrong and wrong. Whether the reader considers war to be worse than appeasement, or vice versa, this book will I hope provide food for thought, as it suggests a cure for both evils.

Trial by ordeal (you were 'guilty' if you could not hold your hand in the flames without burning) is long out of date. So is trial by combat. But in a world where the 'peacekeeping' organization keeps the peace by waging war, justice is determined by the question who can afford the best bomb sights.

President George Bush, broadcasting on 16 January 1991, stated:

'We have ... an opportunity to forge ... a new world order, a world where the rule of law, not the rule of the jungle, governs the conduct of nations.'

(Note that he apparently intends the law to act upon nations.)

Bush is not the only politician talking of creating a New World Order after the Gulf war. Will they make the same mistakes again, by trying to make war impossible instead of making it *unnecessary* as a means of settling disputes? In this book I try to indicate how democratic justice could provide the answer.

The main argument of the book runs as follows:

◆ The world needs a democratic world-embracing federation that will be so powerful that nobody will dare to threaten it, so just that none will wish to challenge it, and so successful that all who had at first stayed outside will clamour to join.

◆ A supranational authority must be scientifically designed. In the past, the 'statesmen' have given us parasols when we needed parachutes. We must devise a system in which hooligans like Noriega or Saddam Hussein can be arrested right away for conspiring to commit a breach of the peace, rather than *after* they have precipitated a war and committed nameless atrocities.

◆ From now on, world affairs should be in the hands of the common man. International law must act directly on individuals. Democracy must leap the frontiers. We need to make representative and responsible government world-embracing.

## Introduction

World unity has never before been so vitally necessary, but our 'global village' is tending to break up into scores of nationalist communities. These two needs – unity and diversity – can be met *only* by a *federal* system. There is much popular misunderstanding of federalism, but in this book I have tried to explain the idea in simple terms.

I also include some hints and encouragement to the ordinary man and woman in the street who wants to work for peace in a realistic manner, wishing to make sure that the statesmen do not make the same mistakes again.

I try to show how the federal principle of international organization can prevent the formation of a super-state, which one of the first federalists, Alexander Hamilton, called 'an execrable tyranny'. Federation is an antidote to the super-state, ensuring that people will not be bossed around by the central authority in matters that are of purely national and local concern. Federation enables ethnic and national independence to co-exist with world *inter*dependence.

The book will, I hope, be of interest to all peace lovers (not only the pacifists, nuclear disarmers, etc.) whether organized or not. It does not offer an instant recipe for future peace. However, it argues that we must set up signposts showing the direction in which we must go – away from the destructive idea that international law must be made by states, for states. We must make a model of the new world society, plant an acorn from which will grow the oak that will one day shelter the earth. This model will be a worldwide federation, founded on a democratically elected Parliament of Man – a step towards the realization of Tennyson's dream of The Federation of the World.

This nucleus might be provided by the EC, once it has federated. Potential new members are already queueing up, some from the old Warsaw Pact Bloc. Even Switzerland is showing willing. The next batch of applicants to appear on the horizon might conceivably be the other members of the British Commonwealth of Nations, followed perhaps even by the USA itself. Minorities feel safer in a federation where each member state is in a minority.

One danger, of course, is that the EC may already contain too many members for them to be able to reach agreement on a federal constitution, unless it is decided that some of the powers now assumed by the European Parliament shall instead be left with the national parliaments.

Another possible nucleus may be provided by some or all of the powers that allied themselves to prosecute the Gulf War, including perhaps in due course Israel, if the USA is a participant.

The question naturally arises: why has international federalism so far failed to consolidate the enormous gains it made in the middle of this century? In my view, there are two main reasons:

◆ Once the United Nations had been formed, most people told federalists not to rock the boat, but to give this second League of Nations a chance. Many lukewarm federalists heeded this admonition, were submerged, and some never showed their light again.

◆ The federalist movement, like many other progressive forces, became fragmented into various little groups. They, the realists, thus became confused with the idealists and woolly pacifists.

Nevertheless, there is tremendous federalist potential lying just below the surface, on the basis of which very little would be required to set off a chain reaction of peace that could transform the world.

\* \* \*

The foregoing was written after the Gulf War. The rest of this introduction was written partly before the invasion of Kuwait and partly during the course of the war. It is left unedited, not only for its curiosity value but because it demonstrates that federalist principles do not depend on circumstances but on scientific facts.

This book ought, by rights, to have been written and published in 1987, to mark the birth of inter-state federalism 200 years previously, but I was at that time too busy trying to survive.

The reader will find that it is, in essence, a series of 'letters to the editor', starting with the articles written in 1787 and 1788 by Alexander Hamilton, James Madison and John Jay for the *Independent Journal* and *New York Packet* in their campaign to persuade the

## Introduction

people of the State of New York to ratify the American federal constitution and thereby bring it into operation. Those letters and articles have been preserved for posterity in, e.g. *The Federalist* (Everyman's Library). Inspired by their example, I too contributed my mite, with some modicum of success so far as concerns worldwide publication. One purpose of this book is to awaken similar inspiration in present-day readers.

The blossoming of the federal idea which took place toward the end of World War II and shortly thereafter did not bear much fruit, unless one counts the slow and laborious progress of the European Community towards a true federal union open to other democratic peoples, (though the more who join before this end is achieved, the less prospect there is of success).

Partly because no-one is a prophet in his own country, I have lived the past 20 years in voluntary exile. It was, at times, a hard struggle for existence, and my federalist activities were, I am ashamed to say, left dormant for some time. However, apprehension has been growing within me lest the world become too indifferent to the dangers that still beset it. Perhaps, I thought, belief in the evil and paradoxical idea that the atom bomb will protect the world from another holocaust has become strong enough to prevent our even setting out toward the goal of world order through law. The strange thing about this thought is that wars of various kinds have been, and still are,[3] proceeding in various parts of the world, yet there is a widespread feeling that the atom bomb will prevent them from becoming worldwide.

(Nobody, not even those most closely concerned with the 'United' Nations, seems to trust this 'peace-keeping' organization to do anything worthwhile in the matter, except to provide premises, round tables and interpreters for discussions and − eventually perhaps − the sealing wax and red tape to be applied to the various dictated 'peace' treaties.[4])

---

[3] Whilst writing, Iraq has invaded Kuwait.

[4] Despite recent events involving the U.N. I have left this passage as originally written, since the fact remains that the 'United' Nations is a snare and a delusion, lulling the world into a false sense of security, and blinding its eyes to the true cure for world war. See Chapter 5.

## The Parliament of Man

During my active phase, apart from writing letters and articles for the press of five continents, I also organized and addressed public and private meetings and debates. For this purpose I took a modicum of tuition in public speaking. All I can consciously remember of this coaching is the dictum that most audiences (even if they consist of Members of Parliament) are capable of absorbing only one idea at a time.

However, the federal idea is really composed of three ideas, plus one essential qualification:

◆ International law must act directly on individuals.

◆ It must therefore be enacted by a legislature directly elected by individuals.

◆ The international authority must be an authority; i.e. it must have full governmental power. However, (and here is the essential qualification, the federal element of the formula) the sphere in which its authority acts can be limited to a specified list of powers.

What originally fired my imagination when I first heard Dr. William Curry expound the federal idea was the discovery (to my mind) that the necessary international authority could have *full* governmental power in a *limited* sphere. This not only kills two birds with one stone; it solves the problem of how to avoid a world despotism, my main objection to the ideal of world unity. It seemed to me that people needed only to be told this gospel to become fanatical believers, and the world would be saved.

Ah, the naivety of youth!

Nevertheless, I was happy if I could get just a few members of just one audience at a time to go home with the one idea in their heads, that an international authority must be directly elected, not composed of representatives of governments.

Perhaps, I thought, after a second meeting they would go home with the conviction that the international authority would have to be responsible to an international parliament.

It might take a third meeting (or newspaper article) to persuade them that the international authority need not be a despotism; to

## Introduction

convince them of the truth of Hamilton's remark (in words slightly modernized):

> If the federal idea is betrayed and rejected, the probability is that we shall be induced to confer supplementary powers upon a revived League, and either the machine will, from the intrinsic feebleness of its structure, moulder into pieces in spite of our ill-judged efforts to prop it up; or by successive augmentation of its strength, as necessity might prompt, we shall finally accumulate in an undemocratic body all the most important prerogatives of sovereignty, and thus entail upon posterity one of the most execrable forms of tyranny that human infatuation ever contrived.
>
> *New York Packet*, 14 Dec.1787

I still regard this rightful fear of despotism as the most potent weapon in the anti-federalist armoury. However, federation is an antidote to despotism. Nevertheless, the danger that the federal constitution, no matter how well and carefully drafted, might be perverted and manipulated by crooks and scoundrels can never be entirely eliminated. In any commonwealth, protection of the Constitution is a sacred task. The Constitution must be made difficult to amend (though making it difficult to destroy also makes it difficult to improve).

An essential element of a federal constitution is a Federal Supreme Court, to interpret the constitution. Nevertheless, the Supreme Court Judges are merely the spearhead of the defence of the Constitution, to which all jurists, ship's lawyers and even the man-in-the street should be devoted. The price of freedom would continue to be eternal vigilance.

Compared with present circumstances, the federation would be a relative heaven, not only for its ordinary citizens; it would also be a hotbed for lawyers, though this is surely better than our present paradise for arms kings.

Since the truths about federalism, though simple, require constant reiteration if they are to gain general acceptance, I make no apology for repetitions of the tenets of federalism in the following pages. I should like to believe that, by expounding the federal idea in different words and with varying analogies, metaphors and similes, I shall reach more understanding in my readers than if the notions had been presented but once, in only one formula.

## The Parliament of Man

Cookery books are written and published that are devoted entirely to dishes concocted from one specific ingredient, e.g. potatoes, milk or kiwi fruit. Collections of sermons appear in print, conveying but one message: 'God is good.' And yet they seem to find their respectively satisfied audiences. I hope this book will find mine. In my youth I had a manual: *Glove-making with Illustrations*. I used it to tease the girls, keeping my thumb on the initial 'G'.

This book is not written with a view to the market, any more than were my letters and articles on which it is mainly based. Its purpose is to spread the idea. Therefore, I do not ask you to recommend your friends to buy it. Rather, pass it round among them and, above all, urge them to pass the idea on to all their acquaintances and members of parliament. The chain reaction of peace may at last gather momentum, and eventually sweep all before it.

\* \* \*

## SOCRATIC LULLABY

Vaguely recalling a psalm to the effect that common sense comes 'out of the mouths of babes and sucklings', and remembering that Socrates taught by asking questions, I penned the following, which is based on an actual conversation: (My first son Christopher Hamilton was then seven years old, and Ernest Bevin was the British Foreign Minister). My second son Gregor considers it to be the most simple and suitable introduction to the theory of federalism. I therefore include it here as part of the Introduction. It was published in eight periodicals in English and French.

**Christopher Hamilton:**
        Daddy, is Mr. Bevin a foreigner?
**HSB:**    *No, old man.*
**CH:**     Then why is he called the Foreign Minister?
**HSB:**    *He's the British Foreign Minister.*
**CH:**     How can he be British if he's foreign?
**HSB:**    *He's not foreign.*
**CH:**     Ooh, Daddy, you just said he was!

## Introduction

**HSB:** *I didn't; he's called the Foreign Minister because he looks after foreign affairs.*
**CH:** Why are they called foreign affairs, Daddy?
**HSB:** *Because they concern people from other countries. Our Foreign Minister has to meet other people's foreign ministers to decide what to do about the world.*
**CH:** And do they?
**HSB:** *Do they what?*
**CH:** Decide?
**HSB:** *Not very often.*
**CH:** Why not?
**HSB:** *Because of human nature.*
**CH:** Does human nature mean not being able to decide?
**HSB:** *I didn't mean that. I meant human beings are different from each other, and often disagree.*
**CH:** Hmm ... Daddy, have you got a Minister for your affairs?
**HSB:** *How do you mean?*
**CH:** Have you got somebody to meet other people to decide what to do about us?
**HSB:** *Yes, in a way. I have a Member of Parliament to represent me at Westminster, to help run the country's affairs.*
**CH:** And does he decide?
**HSB:** *He helps in getting things decided.*
**CH:** Does that mean he isn't human?
**HSB:** *Of course he's human!*
**CH:** But you said it's human nature not to be able to decide, and he can!
**HSB:** *What I said was that human nature makes people disagree when there are several of them trying to decide.*
**CH:** Is your Member of Parliament the only human being at Westminster, Daddy?
**HSB:** *Goodness me, no, there are hundreds more in Parliament.*
**CH:** Then how can they all decide?
**HSB:** *They vote.*
**CH:** Why can't the Foreign Ministers vote?
**HSB:** *They can, and do vote.*
**CH:** Then why can't they decide?
**HSB:** *They could decide things by voting, but it is seldom much use because the ones who don't agree to a decision will not do what the others want them to.*

## The Parliament of Man

**CH:** Hmm .. S'pose lots of the people at Westminster don't agree to the voting there, and don't do what the others want them to do, why do they bother to vote, anyway?

**HSB:** *But they do. They do do what the majority want them to do, or rather the Government does it and nobody stops them.*

**CH:** Not even the Members who voted against it?

**HSB:** *No.*

**CH:** Then why haven't the foreign ministers got a government of their own?

**HSB:** *They have, or rather, each of them has his own government. We have ours, the American Minister has the American Government, and so on.*

**CH:** Then why don't the governments make the foreign ministers all do what the voting tells them to do?

**HSB:** *Because it's usually the governments that tell their foreign ministers which way to vote, and those governments that told their ministers to vote against a thing won't want to obey if that particular thing is decided upon.*

**CH:** Then why don't the foreign ministers have a government of their very own, to make the other governments do what is decided?

**HSB:** *Because, old man, you can't make governments do what they won't do, except by making war on their countries, and we don't want any more war, do we?*

**CH:** Do the people in Parliament have to make war on some of the people to make them obey the voting?

**HSB:** *No, Christoff.*

**CH:** Why not?

**HSB:** *I suppose it's chiefly because the separate Members of Parliament haven't got armies or air forces of their own.*

**CH:** Then why don't the foreign ministers take the armies and things away from the different governments?

**HSB:** *Because they haven't the authority, or power, to do so?*

**CH:** Hasn't anybody the power to do that?

**HSB:** *No.*

**CH:** Not anybody? Not even the people who gave the governments their soldiers and guns and bombs and things?

**HSB:** *Well, yes, perhaps the people could do it.*

**CH:** Then why don't they?

## Introduction

**HSB:** *They could be strong enough only if they were organized.*
**CH:** *Then why don't they join the World Movement for World Federal Government?*
**HSB:** *That's quite enough talking for this evening. It's high time you were asleep . . . Bless me! He is!*

\* \* \*

# CHAPTER 1

## LAW PRONOUNCED 'LOVE'
## – DEFINITIONS

In any discussion it is important to define the terms used. There would be fewer misunderstandings in everyday life if people would first begin their counter-arguments by saying: 'It depends on what you mean by . . .'.

Despite what I have written above, more knowledgeable readers may prefer to skip this chapter, at least for the time being, but before they do so I would urge them to read its Appendix (Policing the World).

Before the leading spirits in the formation of the present United States Constitution, George Washington, Benjamin Franklin, Alexander Hamilton, James Madison and John Jay, really knew what they had discovered, they used the terms federation and confederation as practically synonymous, whereas in this book, if I use the term confederation at all, I shall mean a league, not a union, despite the fact that, e.g. Canada describes itself as a confederation, though virtually a federation.

Translation of terms into other languages also presents difficulties, as I have found at federal union conferences abroad. Even simple statements like the following from an American are apt to be misunderstood:

'This guy was a trader, and was finely shod. Even in this new error he made it easier for the Ruskies to send missals into our country.'

Strangely enough, far from being a reference to a merchant with good

*Law Pronounced 'Love'*

shoes, recently assisting the Soviet-US postal service, the meaning of this remark was:

'This man was a traitor, and was finally shot. Even in this new era he made it easier for the Russians to send missiles into our country.'

## DEFINITIONS

*Federal:*

Of a commonwealth in which several States unite under a common parliament and government, but remain independent in their internal affairs. Hence 'federation'.

In a federal government there is a division of governmental functions between one authority, usually called the Federal Government, which has power to regulate certain matters for the whole territory, and a collection of authorities, usually called State Governments, which have power to regulate certain other matters for the component parts of the territory. The allocation of functions between Federal and State Governments cannot be altered either by the Federal Government acting alone or by the State Governments acting alone, and the exercise by the Federal Government of its allotted functions cannot be controlled by the State Governments, or vice versa. Federal government means a division of functions between authorities which *in no way are subordinate to each other*, either in the extent or in the excercise of their allotted functions.

K. C. Wheare, *What Federal Government is*

If the central government has power to interfere in State matters, the system is not federal but is a unitary State with subordinate (municipal) authorities.

If the decisions of the central body have to be ratified by the States parliaments or governments, the central body is obviously not a government at all, and the system is a *con*federation or league.

*Unite:*

There is no real political union unless the *electorates* are merged.

*Government:*

A government, to be a government, must be capable of making decisions that it is capable of carrying into effect.

As Curry said in *The Case for Federal Union:*

## The Parliament of Man

Government is the only alternative to solution by combat that mankind has discovered, and democracy the only safeguard of freedom. But only some problems are world problems; others are local problems. Hence the need for a federal structure with a democratic basis, taking the individual human being as a unit.

It is no more illogical to arrest and imprison only the right hand of a man, accuse it of theft, try it and punish it, than it is to make war on an entire nation because its leader is a tyrant or homicidal maniac, or both.

If (as the pacifists seem to think) world peace depended solely on men's willingness to 'sit round a table and thrash things out' we would have achieved perfect tranquillity long ago. Mere debating societies, diplomatic discussions, cooperation, agreements, pledges, promises, papal prayers, solemn pacts and mutual understandings are of no avail unless backed by law, law in the sense of national and federal law ('interpopular' law), not mere international 'law'.

The idealist believes that people have only to be pursuaded to agree, and strife will cease. The realist knows that people will always tend to disagree. Decisions must therefore be arrived at by voting, and by some method of ensuring that the decision will be adhered to. Only a governmental system can achieve this.

*League:*
Footballers know that this has several meanings; in this book the word refers to an agreement, treaty, compact, etc. among states which, even if the treaty asserts that they are surrendering part of their sovereignty, still retain sovereignty *de facto*, since there is no real impediment to their breaking the agreement at any time.

The United Nations is a league, the old League of Nations with the booby traps more skilfully disguised.

*Parliament:*
Although the word parliament literally means 'somewhere where talking is carried on', in other words a hot-air factory, it must here be understood to mean far more than that. Throughout this book, the word 'parliament' is to be understood in the normal English sense, a legislature, i.e. (literally) a law-making body.

## Law Pronounced 'Love'

*Blockade:*

Act of indiscriminate warfare against guilty and innocent, men, women and children. Favoured instrument of U.N. policy. Very occasionally, a league like the U.N. can decide on a blockade, but cannot decide to lift it, just as it can sometimes resolve to order 'open fire' but cannot be certain to vote for a 'cease fire' in due course!

*Sovereign:*

In a true democracy the individual voter is sovereign. National sovereignty is for authoritarians and fascists who believe that man exists for the state, and not the state for man. It is true that democrats speak of parliament as being 'sovereign'. Admittedly, members of parliament are not required to appeal to their constituencies for ratification of the laws they enact, but the sovereignty of parliament is but temporary, lasting until the next general election; then sovereignty returns to the individual voters in whom it ultimately resides. In the sense that the individual voters are thus no longer sovereign until they can again exercise their vote, the delaying effect of this is salutory, limiting the evils of mob rule, and giving the electorate time for reflection and popular debate.

In a democracy, sovereignty is vested in the electorate. It can thus be delegated, partly to a common (federal) parliament, partly to national parliaments, the rest remaining with the electorate.

*Law:*

In the first conversation I had with Edgar Gevaert, the editor of *Parlement*, Ghent, he insisted and constantly reiterated the view that the cure for world war was 'love'. I was appalled. I had come all the way to Belgium to visit a federalist, a realist. But I seemed to have landed up with an idealist, a pacifist! In a last desperate attempt to save the situation I switched to French, and was relieved to find that, far from relying on *'l'amour'*, dear Edgar put his trust in *'la loi'*. He merely believed that 'law' was pronounced 'love'.

> Federal law does not drive the innocent to support the law-breaker as League law inevitably tends to do. Federal law is able to act against offenders more quickly than can League law.
> W.B.Curry, *The Case for Federal Union*

Note that in this context Curry speaks of 'League law'.

## The Parliament of Man

Actually, the English language needs three different words for law:

◆ One word for *natural law*, which cannot be broken, and does not require any parliament or legislation.

◆ A different word for *national law*, which can be broken only at the risk of detection, arrest and punishment; law which in democracies requires the prior consent of parliament.

◆ A third (and radically different) word for *international 'law'*, which is frequently ignored with impunity and which, despite its extreme fragility, is immensely difficult to set up and maintain.

*Supreme Court:*

The union must have a Supreme Court, which unlike the Hague Court, would be able to enforce its decisions — by peaceful means.

*Constituent Assembly:*

New forms of government originate in some kind of Constituent Assembly, to which delegates come to plan a constitution which they will then submit to their constituents to ratify. Such new systems should preferably have a constitution (a fundamental law) providing for a parliament (a legislature), the members of which are not delegates (i.e. persons whose acts would require the subsequent approval of those for whom they claim to speak) but representatives who are already vested with authority from their constituents to make laws that do not require ratification.

*Ratify:*

Consent to (e.g. to a treaty that was made subject to ratification).

*State:*

A nation organized for war. In the context of federation the term is usually employed in the sense of, e.g. the constituent states of the United States of America, the cantons of Switzerland, the provinces of Canada; Westphalia, Bavaria, etc. in the Federal Republic of Germany. In this sense such 'states' are 'nations' organized for peace.

*Power:*

When you hear talk of 'power' or 'powers', ask yourself, or the

## Law Pronounced 'Love'

speaker, what he means by it. One does not need to have read [1]Bertrand Russell's *Power* to realize that some supporters of the old order suffer from the delusion that to confer duties on an international organization is tantamount to giving it the power to perform them. Even the most powerful locomotive in the world must have a means of getting off 'dead-centre', otherwise it cannot move itself, let alone a train.

Especially when drafting an international constitution it must always be borne in mind that the voting system should reflect the power behind each vote. In a limited liability company, the voting reflects the capital invested and the risks run by each voter. It might be argued that a more democratic principle would be 'each shareholder, one vote', but such a system would soon result in chaos in the commercial world. Let us be realists, not merely idealists! We are out to *diminish* chaos, not increase it.

*International:*

In the context of federal union, I dislike the word international, as it literally means 'between nations', whereas the idea of world government is that governmental authority shall act directly on individuals, and not on nations or states. Even in disputes between member states, or between a state and the federal authority, the law acts upon individual officers, not on entire communities, which may be largely innocent. The Scandinavians have a word for international (*mellanfolklig* in Swedish) which literally means inter-popular, and which perhaps deserves greater currency.

So-called international 'law' rests on treaties, pacts, covenants and conventions, which come into existence only through the patient exertions of delegates who (even if they succeed) thereafter have to return home to plead for ratification. Many such conventions are

---

[1] My friend Edward Clements and I were once received by Bertrand Russell in his Richmond (Surrey) home, when we took the opportunity to ask him to support Federalism openly. His reply at that time was to the effect that he preferred not to limit himself by concentrating on the bare mechanics of peace-keeping. In one sense his reference to mechanics was apt: If you want something to pull a train, a study of mechanical engineering is necessary if you are to devise a locomotive that will stay on the rails and harness its power so that the entire mechanism pulls in one direction.

## The Parliament of Man

stillborn for lack of the necessary number (sometimes 100%) of ratifications, so that the 'law' applies, if at all, only to those potential delinquents who have agreed to abide by it, and not to other offenders; in other words, a 'law' that applies in or to parts of the world but not in or to others. How many would honour a tax 'law' if their competitors in the same country were exempt?

*Force:*

Used in the scientific sense: something which if applied to a stationary object tends to make it move, or if to a moving object, tends to give it acceleration or deceleration.

(Force can be positive or negative: promotion or prevention, explosion or implosion, etc.).

A government enforces the law with the minimum of force required to do so, and avoiding injury to innocent persons. Such coercion seldom reaches violence, and even then, great care is taken to minimize damage to innocent persons or property.

*Violence:*

A federalist friend of mine (who erroneously believes it is possible to federate, successfully, dictatorships and democracies), points out that violence differs from force only in degree, and therefore the assertion that a union uses force and a league uses violence is merely a play on words. In a sense he may be right, but in *political* science we wish to convey a difference in essence as well as in degree; it is only necessary to compare the force exerted by police and the violence exerted by soldiers. (See Appendix to this Chapter).

An Arab might say that American troops defile a holy city, but many would say that troops defile *all* cities. It may be 'in' to dislike policemen, but the general public would not say that police defile a city – quite the contrary. Policemen may not always behave like gentlemen, but there are laws and regulations to ensure that they shall, and to punish offenders against this rule *without penalizing the entire Force* or the community it exists to serve.

Police enforce laws, whereas armies implement policy by violent means. Though a 'peace-keeping' army may try to enforce local law, the soldiers are not conversant with it. Soldiers, when called upon to enforce law, are more likely to enforce martial 'law', which often

## Law Pronounced 'Love'

entails indiscriminate reprisals against those who are merely suspect, or 'guilty' by association or by kinship; it may entail the burning of houses or thatched huts; in extreme cases martial action has entailed the dropping of atomic bombs on cities. (See also Appendix to this Chapter).

There is no such thing as indiscriminate justice. Mention of the word indiscriminate reminds me of the fact that during World War II the BBC announced that German planes had dropped bombs at random. The following morning, the Nazi radio reported that Random had been totally destroyed.

*Cooperation:*

Literally 'working together'. In international affairs this is no substitute for union, which entails a merging of electorates.

*Nucleus:*

Not to be confused with nuclear, an adjective reserved for the atomic energy sphere. To mark the difference, when we need to describe the kernel around which something grows, like a snowflake or raindrop round a speck of dust, or a wider federation around the first model, we use 'nucleus' as an adjective, e.g. a nucleus federation.

*Democracy:*

Representative and responsible government. In this book I do not use the term 'democracy' in the sense of mob rule.

*Politician:*

Someone who is willing to help old ladies half way across busy streets.

\* \* \*

## WHAT IS MEANT BY POLICING THE WORLD?

When discussing their 'New World Order,' the politicians make great play of the idea of policing the world, whether by NATO, the UN or the USA either alone or assisted by a coalition of its allies, stooges and bribed lackeys. It is therefore essential to be aware of the nature of a police force and of its design requirements if we are not to be left at the mercy of yet another execrable form of world tyranny.

As published in *Federal News* for November 1943, the following resolution was passed by the Federal Union National Council earlier that year explaining:

**THE VITAL DIFFERENCE BETWEEN A POLICE FORCE AND THE MILITARY**

In view of the expressed desire of Allied statesmen to create a permanent organization of the United Nations, coupled in some quarters with proposals for an international police force, the immediate task of the Federal Union Movement is to point out at every opportunity:

★ Such an organization can hardly hope to succeed unless some, if not all, of the nations within it unite to form an international government, which must of necessity be federal in type.

★ There is danger of confusion between a *police* force, which deals directly and individually with the citizens from whom its powers are derived, and *military* force, which is directed not against individuals as such, but against communities and states. Federal Union holds that this distinction is fundamental, and that ultimately a world police force alone can provide a stable basis for an orderly and peaceful world.

★ Since a police force can be administered only by a government or its organs, the only authority competent to control the proposed international police force would be the federal government.

★ The powers of the international police force would thus be legally applicable only within the federation and only in federal matters as defined in the federal constitution. (The enforcement of state laws would be the concern of the state police.)

\* \* \*

I was one of the originators of this resolution. I have come across fragments of correspondence with Barbara Wootton (Baroness Wootton, a prominent member of the Federal Union National Council) from which it is clear that she gave me invaluable help in drafting it, and I feel sure that if any influence was needed to get it passed, it was her efforts that must be given the credit.

\*

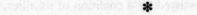

## Law Pronounced 'Love'

*1992 Note:*

A significent contribution to the 'New World Order' debate was 'The Stockholm Initiative on Global Security and Governance' held at Saltsjöbaden in April 1991, supported by 36 famous statesmen such as Willy Brandt, Benazir Bhutto, Harlem Brundtland, Jimmy Carter, Vaclav Havel, Edward Heath, Robert McNamara, Julius Nyerere and Edouard Shevardnadze. Note that they were modest and truthful enough to call it 'Governance' and not 'Government'. The proposals were published in a Report: 'Common Responsibility in the 1990s' (issued by the Swedish Prime Minister's Office), and consisted of 28 points (twice as many as President Wilson's, and nearly three times as many as Moses'). Point 27 proposes a new San Fiasco/Bretton Woods conference. Point 1 calls for *'improved* United Nations capabilities...', and Point 2 for 'a global law enforcement arrangement, *in line with the U.N. Charter*, focussing on the role of *sanctions* and on *military enforcement* measures' A pessimist would regard these proposals as the tired old tatters of the same tired old ideas of tired old men. An optimist would regard them as a disguised plea for world government, without which the aims outlined are unlikely to be realized. It is my belief that many of the signatories would have declared openly for world government, but abstained only in the interest of unanimity.

Not in so many words, but in effect, Point 28 does call for an international constitutent assembly to draft a constitution of 'Global Governance' and should be vigorously supported. But if a mistress is something between a mister and a mattress, governance is a cross between government and influence. As George Washington said: 'influence is not government'.

# Chapter 2

# A PARADISE FOR LAWYERS INSTEAD OF FOR ARMAMENT KINGS AND DIPLOMATS

**HOW WILL IT HAPPEN?**
The most probable way in which a nucleus world government will come into being is that a grand constituent assembly will be held, comprising delegates from all nations interested in the idea. It is easy to fall into the temptation of guessing what kind of constitution will emerge, and listing what powers will be assigned to the federal parliament, and what powers will be agreed as common to both the federal government and the states governments, though it is obvious that *all the remaining power* will continue to vest in the national governments, parliaments and electors.

As the Bibliography indicates, many writers have yielded to this temptation. The results are interesting, instructive and useful, provided it is borne continually in mind that such draft constitutions are illustrative only. We cannot dictate or predict what the constituent assembly will decide. To some extent this will depend on the time when the Assembly is held.

For my part I shall confine myself to supposing that the number of states that initially join the federation will be inversely proportionate to the amount of power conferred on the federal government. If it is set up solely to protect, e.g. the environment, and to tax sufficiently to provide the finances necessary for that purpose, there will no doubt be several states willing to join. If on the other hand the federal government is given powers over a very wide field, e.g.

## A Paradise for Lawyers

population control, citizenship, defence, free trade, foreign policy, space exploration and exploitation, federal currency, inter-state communications, atomic energy, civil aviation and shipping, fisheries, ocean-bed mining, suppression of terrorism, drug trafficking and A.I.D.S., and protection of the democratic constitutions of the federation and of its member states, and of the Rights of Man, there will be fewer volunteers for founder membership. In any event, students of human nature will expect the new constitution to be a compromise, granting the federal authority an optimum degree of power, and ratified by an optimum number of founder nations. However, provided there is a *clear understanding that the new Union is a nucleus*, open to all nations willing and able to accept and uphold the constitution, we should be content with this — for the time being!

Realists will also expect some nations to hesitate to ratify the new constitution, or not to ratify at all in the lifetimes of most of us. (This would be more of a loss to them than to the federation, since unwillingness to join might often be tantamount to inability to live up to obligations.)

Admittedly, there would be little point in establishing an international federation to provide only environmental protection. A viable federation must surely have powers over foreign policy (until all the 'foreigners' have joined it), defence, and the power to levy federal taxes to finance its existence. Many would-be constitution drafters will think of other powers that could appropriately be conferred on the federal legislature. However, rather than no union at all, it would surely be preferable to start with a nucleus that is capable of surviving and expanding as and when it proves its viability and success. Subject to constitutional safeguards, the way should also be left open for the federal power to be extended over a greater (but still restricted[1]) sphere, as and when it proved its efficacy.

It is important to stress that the Constitution will always be under attack, and must be defended. Any tendency of the federal authority to decide issues outside its sphere must be resisted. The abuse of power will be fought by lawyers, publicists and the man-in-the street, not by war but by constitutional means. The price of freedom will still be eternal vigilance. Federation will not cure all the political ailments

---

[1] If this sphere was not restricted, the union would, of course, not be 'federal'.

that man is heir to. But fighting such evils will be less violent and destructive.

A Federation is a paradise for jurists, no place for arms kings.

✾ ✾ ✾

## THE SCIENCE OF INTERPOPULAR GOVERNMENT

Mankind owes an immeasurable debt to science. It is all the more astonishing, therefore, that so many politicians, let alone men-in-the street, throw science to the four winds when they turn their minds to international affairs.

As Clarence Streit so cogently pointed out in *Union Now*, the sciences use convenient units for their respective purposes, volts, amperes, joules, grammes ... but statesmen use a most unwieldy and inconvenient unit, the nation. The only appropriate unit, the individual, is left to the national politician to manipulate. We have comparative peace when the individual is treated as the unit; individual law-breakers can be halted and punished when the law is enforceable on the individual delinquent. In contrast to this, we have conditions of economic or even military war whenever the statesmen use only the state as the unit of world government.

Foresters may fight fire with fire, but a peacekeeping organization must not use war as its instrument.[1]

◆ This brings us to the first principle of democracy:
The individual is the only proper unit of government. Only by applying this rule can law be enforced without violence, without war.
This principle is true both within and beyond national boundaries.

◆ The second principle of democracy (representative and responsible government) was discovered by King Edward I of England. It is this:

---

[1] The use of 'armed force in the general interest' is enshrined in the United Nations Charter; indeed, it is the prime factor in its mythical peacekeeping 'power'.

## A Paradise for Lawyers

The elected representatives of the individual units must be empowered to pass laws without having to ask their constituents to ratify them. Otherwise, there is little likelihood of the laws ever coming into effect.

◆ The third principle applies when we come to interpopular or world government. It is this:
The individual voters, each of whom remains sovereign, divide the functions of government between
(a) their national parliaments for national affairs and
(b) their common federal parliament for their joint (inter-popular) affairs.

By ignoring the difference between a league and a government, the statesmen caused the failure of the British Commonwealth of Nations to prevent World War I, the failure of the League of Nations to prevent World War II, and the failure of the United Nations, which like its mirror-predecessors, merely prevented all the wars that were unlikely to break out, and failed to prevent any of the others.

◆ There is of course a fourth principle, namely:
Any government, to remain a government, must have the power to tax to sustain its own existence.

It should be noted, however, that the sum of federal and state taxes would be immeasurably less than the total of our present burdens. In fact the immense saving involved is one of the main arguments in favour of federating. The choice facing us is as easy as that between a gift of ten dollars or a gift of ten thousand dollars, all other things being equal.

In contrast to a federation, a league depends on voluntary contributions. Some members pay, others omit to do so (including some who never intended to do so).

Just as there should be no taxation without representation, it is unreasonable to expect to enjoy representation in the federal parliament without being taxed by it.

No country in the world is too far away to belong to a union, no matter where the capital may be, whether fixed or peripatetic, provided the union has a federal constitution, thus precluding any interference by the supra-national government in national affairs.

## The Parliament of Man

Where do we want to go?

Before we can make progress in anything, we must decide in which direction progress lies.

The ideal, to my mind, is a world that is both united and divided; united on world affairs, yet leaving individuals free to run their own private affairs as it suits them, or to group themselves as may be appropriate for matters relating to, e.g. family, business, hobby, religion, municipality, country, nation, state, and the like.

Here I would add a proviso:

> The state has been defined as 'a nation organized for war'. In that sense there is no place for state nationalism in the future world order.

A world both united and divided would of necessity have to be a federal union.

Once having decided in which direction progress lies, we should endeavour always to move only in that direction. The French speak of 'reculer pour mieux sauter'[2]; it is alright to retreat if this will later help you to reach your goal more quickly, but otherwise one must always realize that movement in the wrong direction is not progress but regression. It is also important to bear in mind the dictum of Admiral Mahon regarding the supreme importance of correct strategy.

At the time of writing, it has been announced that the Ukraine has declared itself an independent state with the right to its own defence force and monetary unit. This lengthens the list of similar declarations from, e.g. the three Baltic States, and from Russia, Georgia, Usbekistan, Moldavia, Armenia, etc.

In addition, states such as Czechoslovakia and Yugoslavia are displaying the same tendency to disintegrate, and/or leave the Warsaw Pact. Hungary is applying to join the European Community. By the time this appears in print the list will no doubt be longer. Twenty years of living abroad have removed me somewhat from British politics, but it may be that Scotland and Wales still hanker after separate parliaments for their local affairs. This would be no problem in a federal union, in which many of our current international prob-

---

[2] (Roughly) to move back in order to take a running jump.

## A Paradise for Lawyers

lems would fade into insignificance (and the others would not trouble the union!).

Even those who are now rejoicing over the dismemberment of the Soviet Union can hardly welcome the idea of many separate Soviets, each with its 'fair' share of the USSR's stock of atomic and other weapons. There was a time when the Balkanization of Europe was regarded as an evil, bound to lead to war. And so it did, since the states, rather than the individuals of which they were composed, were sovereign. On the other hand, of those of us who at one time rejoiced over the division of Germany into two parts, some who are still alive are now welcoming the reunion of East and West Germany. But would it not be preferable to invite the various German states: Prussia, Bavaria, Saxony and so forth, to become separate member states of a Federal Europe, open to all other democracies willing to uphold the Rights of Man? The very size of the new united Germany may scare away potential members of Federal Europe, e.g. Norway.

Norway, where I have been living for the past 20 years (though I am still a citizen of England, a British 'subject' and World Citizen No.12,345) is an interesting example of the differences between democracy, mob rule, and representative and responsible government. In Norway, they succeed in mixing these three almost inextricably.

In 1972, the Norwegian government, believing that Norway ought to enter the European Community, held a 'consultative' referendum. The isolationists[3] gained a 53-47% 'victory' (77.7% participation), well organized as they were under the lawyer[4] who subsequently defended (and still defends) an influential spy convicted of selling Norway's secrets to the Russians and to Iraq. The isolationists used various propaganda tricks, such as the slogan 'No to the sale of Norway!', and telling old people that their pensions would stop if Norway joined the Community. But instead of reiterating that the

---

[3] Composed mostly of the less educated sections of the population, according to an article in *Aftenposten* 10 January 1991 by Tore Nedsbø, of the Norwegian Embassy in Bonn.

[4] Even this lawyer seems to be changing his mind. According to *Aftenposten* of 23rd July 1991 he is quoted as saying: 'If Sweden and Finland join the EC, and if the EC opens itself to Eastern Europe, we shall see a world different from 20 years ago ...'

referendum was consultative only, i.e. non-binding, and rejoicing that so few of the untutored[5] masses had voted against its enlightened idea, the government and indeed Norwegian politicans of all sides, almost without exception took this exploratory vote as a signal to shun for eighteen years the very idea of joining a European Community. However, they now seem willing to approach Europe as if it were a rich uncle, doling out largesse to a supplicant nephew. There are still many Norwegian politicians who do not dare to invite the electorate to express its currently more educated views on the subject.[6]

In my opinion, we have mob rule when the people are encouraged to make their views binding on the nation even when they have little knowledge of the facts, and we have ideal democracy only when the voters' elected representatives use their knowledge and experience in a responsible manner.

To one living in Norway as a foreigner, precluded from participation in the country's politics, it is galling to see how they tolerate as head of the state broadcasting authority a man who, defying a western boycott, joined the despots in Red Square to salute the invaders of Afghanistan, an admirer and supporter of Jaruzelski in the throes of Solidarity's struggle against him. Similarly, it was exasperating to see how the Norwegian Nobel Committee decided that Comrade Gorbachev was more deserving of the 1990 Peace Prize than was a Chinese anti-communist heroine. The award of the 1991 prize to Aung San Suu Kyi to some extent atoned for this gaffe, perhaps partly because it may seem less dangerous to annoy a military junta in Burma than to antagonize a military clique in a huge communist country like China.

\* \* \*

## A WORLD FIT FOR PEOPLE TO LIVE IN

President Bush's infamous alliance with Syria, one of the many bribes paid for 'unanimity' in the U.N. on 'Desert Storm', was a decision

---

[5] I first wrote 'ignorant', but do not wish to give the impression that I equate knowledge with intelligence.

[6] At the time of going to press, there has at last been a dramatic change in this situation.

between wrong and wrong. In the article below, published in English and French years ago by fourteen editors, but still topical, I referred to the need, in this imperfect 'League-type' world, to make decisions between two evils.

### A World Fit for People to Live in
### Plan for individuals – not governments

Permanent peace can never rest upon the basis of agreements between Governments. Furthermore, in any international security system resting primarily on the continual collaboration of proud and powerful Powers, justice will prevail only on those occasions when it coincides with expediency. Wars have often resulted from the fact that men are prone to consider injustice too high a price to pay for peace.

The administration of justice frequently involves a choice between right and right. Many of the expedients to which statesmen are now being driven in their search for world security face us, however, with a choice between wrong and wrong. Of this nature is the controversy over the Yalta decisions on Poland. In a region where boundaries between politically independent States cannot be drawn anywhere without causing injustice and misery to millions of human beings, even the best frontier is no better than a grey veil over a black outlook.

Similarly, to attempt to improve the San Francisco proposals might seem like building a palace upon sands which could scarcely bear the weight of a tent.

The world is confronted with a dilemma: whether to create a world-wide international organization that cannot possibly be a government, or to create an international government which cannot at the outset be world-wide. The purpose of this article is to suggest that we do both. Attempts by the protagonists of either to discredit the other may lead to the rejection of each. In the post-war world, divided whether we like it or not into at least three major and many lesser political blocs, dominated by governments which derive their powers and owe their allegiance to separate communities, we shall need a table round which the interplay of power politics can proceed without bloodshed, and across which the guns can be pointed without the triggers being pulled. The alternative to that table is the battlefield.

## The Parliament of Man

But any hope that the world can be peacefully and justly governed by a cartel of sovereign governments is as vain as it would be to expect the Government of Britain to preserve the peace of the Realm if that 'Government' derived from an assembly of nominees of the County Councils, whose 'laws' could not pass into effect until ratified by the fifty-two separate Councils, and if such 'laws' even then did not act directly upon individual citizens but only on and through the County Authorities.

International law can never mean what it purports to say until it operates directly upon individuals. Police action cannot be taken against a whole nation. The perverted principle of legislation upon States, as the only subjects of international law, has invariably failed. Throughout history, attempts to coerce dissentient Powers have split the comity of nations into two — usually equal — camps and led to wars whose outcome has seldom borne much relation to the merits of the case, and which have inevitably punished the innocent with the guilty.

The weakness of the San Francisco Charter lies not so much in any minor imperfections, for these would exist in any scheme propounded by fallible human minds. The fundamental principle on which it is based is false: it is not possible to govern governments even by governments. Individual men and women are the only proper objects of government, and they are the only subjects from which an international authority can properly derive its powers. An authority that derives its powers ostensibly from governments finds in practice — as do all Leagues — that in an emergency it is left with only duties and blame for failure to perform those duties, whilst the power indispensable to their performance remains in other hands! It follows therefore that the world community needs an elected parliament to make binding (personal) law in purely international matters, whilst leaving the various national legislatures full power in their separate national spheres. Only thus can we ensure at the same time the safety and the independence of nations.

Most idealists would agree with the realists that such an ideal can probably not be accomplished, in our generation, on a global scale; but we owe it to posterity to start the world in that direction. We must create forthwith a working model of the future international community, a 'regional arrangement' which, furthermore, might prove to be the dynamic without which the San Francisco scheme could not operate at all.

Such a working model might be created by, for example, the peoples of the British Commonwealth of Nations and the countries of Western Europe who in matters of safety and prosperity are so interdependent, and whose democratic mode of life provides the basis of mutual trust so necessary for such a step. In such a Union, each national community would have a minority share in the defence and foreign policy of the whole. The system should be open to all other like-minded nations as and when they are able and willing to accept the same constitutional conditions binding the founder members.

From such an acorn will spring the oak that will one day shelter the earth.

\* \* \*

## THE ARCHITECTURE OF PEACE

Whilst on the subject of scientific government, the following article, published in several countries in English and German, is still relevant:

### The Architecture of Peace

The ancient art of architecture owes much to Science. A building must be designed on scientific principles if it is not to collapse under the first strain and bury beneath its ruins those whom it was intended to shelter.

The progress of civilization owes much to Man's ability to learn from experience, profit from past mistakes, and formulate for his future guidance sundry collections of rules-of-thumb that have ultimately converted his every activity into some semblance of a science, this one relying on certainties, that on modest probabilities, others on empirical formulae. Admittedly, in some fields logic has been carried so far that it may seem to have reached a phase comparable with second childhood. Aldous Huxley, writing sometime between the wars, averred that 'the physicists are at present involved in such difficulties that some pessimists have suggested that the universe is fundamentally irrational'.

## The Parliament of Man

True, the social sciences may never reach the maturity attained by mathematics; economics and psychology may never become respectable in the eyes of the Exact Scientists. Nevertheless, the world would be a more ignorant, squalid, hungry, fearsome place than it is already, were it not for the Royal Society. Prudent men plan their buildings, their commercial ventures, their agriculture, their campaigns against pestilence, their wars. But they abandon the dictates of good sense when they go in for lotteries, and take elaborate precautions to ensure that the art of politics remains uncontaminated by scientific principles except when absolutely unavoidable. The apparent failure of political experiments has too often been taken as 'proof' of the futility of making political experiments at all. (Consider, for instance, the ill-fated attempts to sow English parliamentary government in untilled ground. Their failure has been widely attributed to some alien quality in the soil!). Apart from the singular success that attended the transfusion of the American system of inter-State government into the Swiss, Canadian, Australian and Russian constitutions, there are few notable instances in history of Man having drawn the correct inferences from the lessons of history. Even the American constitutional experiment cannot be regarded as having passed the laboratory stage, since it has always been confined within the boundaries of the respective nations and has not so far been applied to any attempt at international government.

In the international sphere, in those fond realms of cloud-cuckoo make-believe, the statesmen live in the Stone Age, in the era of the big club, where the Scientific Epoch appears to them as but an anxious dream. And so, led from the rear by politicians who are led by the nose by the diplomats, the caravan of humanity divides its ranks into those who shout 'My country, right or wrong!' and those who cannot even conceive of the possibility of their country ever ceasing to be right.

The practice of politics appears, indeed, to engender in its votaries a romantic attitude towards Truth; the facts accommodate themselves to theories in a manner indebted more to Art than to Science. How often one is regaled with a stream of generalizations based on irrelevant particulars, in support of a favourite 'ism' or a pre-conceived and prejudiced conclusion; when the actual facts of the case are shrouded in obscurity! Seldom do we see a politician pursuing the slender thread of truth to the bitter end, and acting on his conclusions no matter what the cost to himself. Disillusionment, jettison of false beliefs, is often a painful but necessary alternative to a sojourn in a fool's paradise.

Harold Nicholson, whom *The Listener* styles a skilled observer of many conferences, writing in that paper (29 August 1946) on the Paris Conference, declared that:

> All of us who have watched this Conference would agree that as an experiment in open diplomacy it has already failed ... They have reduced the Conference to the level of a charade ... They do not believe in what they are doing.

He called for 'a voice which will recall the pledges ... the pledges in the Atlantic Charter ... pledges ...'.

But can an experiment be said to have failed if it has illustrated a fact? If the fact passes unnoticed, does not the failure rather lie in the eye of the 'observer'? One might feel justified in regarding the Paris Conference as a valuable and successful experiment in that it tends to disprove something the diplomats and skilled observers hoped it would prove. Paris has revealed the futility of pledges, the bankruptcy of diplomacy, open or shut, folded or flat, as a means of attaining peace with justice. In the words of Señor de Madariaga:

> 'The atomic bomb has made three imposing ruins: Hiroshima, Nagasaki and the San Francisco Charter.'

It is easy to dismiss such a verdict as the irresponsible cynicism of a subversive spectator. But even Trygve Lie, Secretary-General of the 'United' Nations organization, has admitted its intrinsic impotence, in his summary of its operations to date, published in August 1946.

> 'The United Nations is no stronger than the collective will of the nations that support it. Of itself it can do nothing.'

It should be obvious to any skilled observer of inter-national affairs, provided he is not permanently blinded with the dust that he or his colleagues helped to throw into the eyes of the public concerning the previous League, that Mr Lie's apology errs heavily on the side of optimistic understatement. The most cursory study of the United Nations Charter reveals that it formally confers upon the new League the same debilities as have been revealed in practice. The General Assembly has not even the right, let alone the power, to do anything else than 'discuss' matters and 'make recommendations', either to the

States Members or to the so-called 'Security' Council. The 'Security' Council cannot even arrive at a decision, let alone take action on any matter affecting international law and order, unless the Big Five are agreed, and two of their puppets vote with them, in which case of course there would be no need for an organization to prevent war, anyway. If they disagree, the 'collective will' of the nations is revealed as the myth that it most frequently is.

It should not be necessary to underline the conclusions reached by skilled observation from three such different points of view. A more laudable undertaking would be to inquire into the possibility of improving the United Nations Charter or, if this be impracticable, of supplanting it with a construction better designed to stand the stresses and strains of world politics. The inquiry would lead us back through English history to the first principle of effective and permanent government discovered by King Edward I:

> 'The members of a legislature must be empowered by their electors to make laws that do not have to be referred back to the constituencies for ratification.'

We should have to re-discover the principles of inter-State government that have proved their own validity whenever and wherever they have been applied:

◆ Representatives to the supra-State body must be elected not by the State governments but by the citizens, thus minimizing the disintegrating effect of bloc-voting.

◆ International law must act directly upon the individual citizen, not through the intermediary of the constituent governments.

(The only way to enforce 'laws' upon States as such is by war, or threat of war. We cannot keep the peace by waging war.)

◆ The supra-national government must have full governmental power in its own sphere, but this sphere can be restricted to a limited number of specified fields, e.g. defence and foreign affairs.

The United Nations Charter completely perverts every one of these vital desiderata. As a result, the nations are disunited and – what is worse – an ever widening gulf has been flung between the citizens of every nation and those of every other.

It would have been too much to expect the Charter to apply these principles on a global scale in the present state of the world's political development; this will have to wait for world-wide self-government at national levels. But the statesmen should at least have attempted to set up a working model – no matter how limited in extent – of the future world commonwealth of nations.

The idealists had set their revived hopes upon a universal friendly society in which bitter rivals would lick each other's wounds. It would have been more realistic to recognize that the formidable imperfections of the New World League render it nothing better than temporary accommodation. We must lay elsewhere the foundations of the permanent structure that will one day shelter the Earth.

\* \* \*

## LET'S MAKE WAR UNNECESSARY

In order to 'spike the guns' of self-professed experts who still adhered to the principle of national sovereignty, I entitled the following article ' Peace by Sovereignty', by which I meant the sovereignty of the electors. It was accepted by several eminent journals throughout the world (eleven in all), in English and French[1]. As regards details, the text of my article clearly reveals that it was written half a century ago, by a much younger and rather more arrogant man. But I still consider the dogma to be valid.

### Peace by sovereignty

To regard war merely as evil is to betray ignorance of what we are really up against. War is a force which men set in motion in the hope of mitigating or removing some still greater evil. War is waged in order to establish a more perfect state of peace. 'Blessed are the peacemakers!'

---

[1] The French translation was made by Monsieur Laurent Galarneau, editor-in chief of *l'Avenir National*, New Hampshire, USA, to whom I am duly grateful, as also to all the other translators into the various other languages whose names the respective editors (typically) failed to specify.

## The Parliament of Man

But the peace-*keepers* will be blessed by few unless their strategic objective is not to prevent war but to render war redundant as a possible instrument for the progressive attainment of more perfect peace and prosperity. If armed conflict between nations had been, by some magical dispensation, abolished, Hitler would on 3 September 1939 have crowned his bloodless conquests of Austria and Czechoslovakia with a pacific absorption of Poland, leading on to the leisurely subjugation of every country in the world. War is not the only weapon in the Nazi armoury. Fortunately, when the time came to declare war upon Germany as the only remaining means of establishing a less imperfect state of peace, there was no magic rust to keep the sword of Britain locked in its scabbard.

To render war unnecessary, some other means of changing the *status quo*, as and when necessary, must be found. In the past, peaceful change in the international sphere has been narrowly interpreted as formal changes of frontiers. As Professor D. Mitrany points out in his new book *A Working Peace System*: 'The true task of peaceful change is to remove the need and the wish for changes of frontiers.'

If disputes between men and parties of men cannot be settled one way or the other, there comes into being a state of deadlock, leading eventually to complete social paralysis. Disputes can be settled either by violence or by recourse to the intellectual force of reason; when the pros and cons have been adequately thrashed out by the interested parties, one yields to the other, or both accept the decision of a disinterested arbiter, chosen in advance. Through the medium of laws, disputes can often be settled by reason before they arise.

In this imperfect world, a community can remain peaceful only by compelling its members, by force if necessary, to settle their disputes by peaceful means. The ultimate arbiter of disputes within a community is the 'sovereign power'. In an authoritarian community the government is sovereign. ('The State is all.') In a democracy the government exercises sovereignty only as agent for the people, from whom its powers are derived. National sovereignty is a conditional trust, not an irrevocable Divine Right.

The alternative to Anarchy is Government; Anarchy sometimes seems preferable to authoritarian government, but popular self-

## A Paradise for Lawyers

government is an ideal before which anarchy pales into the negation that it really is.

If the nations of the world are to settle their disputes peacefully, there must be established an authority to exercise sovereignty in world affairs, whilst the national governments continue to exercise sovereignty in national affairs. Sovereignty involves the making of judicial decisions, tending to build up a body of Case-Law; but it does not necessarily involve legislative action in the sense of making laws by which to settle disputes before they arise. In practice, however, a government cannot function smoothly if, for lack of a Statute Book, every conceivable issue has to be settled by litigation. Furthermore, a sovereign authority is obliged to take executive action, if only to ensure that its decisions are duly enforced. Such action involves the framing of regulations having the force of law. Though we may properly limit the legislative field over which the authority is sovereign, undue limitation leads to impotence.

Sovereignty in world affairs includes the power to decide, in the last analysis, whether a question falls on one side or the other of an agreed line drawn between world affairs and national affairs. If the world authority were autocratic there would always be the danger that — having this power — it would degenerate into the worst despotism our planet has ever experienced. It is obviously preferable that world sovereignty should vest ultimately in the people of the world, in the governed, particularly in those citizens of the world who are competent to manage their own common affairs.

'Government of the people, by the people and for the people' cannot be guaranteed by any mere paper constitution. Confer a democratic constitution upon a community of fools and their government will become autocratic before the ink is dry. Despotism is not so much the antithesis of democracy as the absence of it, an expression of the people's inability to govern themselves. Let us say, more optimistically, that it is proof of their need for protection, education and encouragement in the Art of self-government. Men learn best not from books but from experience, from the example of others, from working models.

Popular self-government will embrace the Earth by degrees — not through decrees.

The best polity is one in which the powers of the government are derived from the widest electorate compatible with adequate government. Its citizens practise how to govern themselves, and their ability to do it well grows with exercise. The competent electorate widens in consequence. Democracy nourishes what it feeds on.

It is essential that the body exercising sovereignty should be so constituted that it never itself suffers from deadlock – that main element of anarchy that it exists to abolish. It must be able to reach decisions, to reach them so expeditiously that the disputants are given no pretext to resort to violence as a more speedy arbiter, and it must be able to translate decision into action without having to rely upon co-operation from the party against whom judgement may be pronounced.

It follows therefore that the decisions of an international authority must not have to run the gauntlet of all the separate national legislatures before being put into effect. Laws made by the central legislature within its allotted sphere must not require ratification by any other parliament.

It also follows that the force behind the law must be permanently at the disposal of the legislature, and must be of such magnitude as to ensure the relative disarmament of all possible litigants in the face of the Law. This principle must be applied in both the national and international spheres.

If the world develops towards this ideal, and the results of the Moscow Conference suggest progress – real or illusory – towards it, events will probably follow the natural trend of evolution. Government came before popular self-government. World government will come before democratic world government. Vertebrate animals developed from the jelly-fish type of organism. Constitutional political forms may follow the development of functional organs described by Professor Mitrany in 'A Working Peace System'. Such a system, however, could not by any stretch of the imagination be called a Durable Peace system until the backbone of a sovereign international authority had been formed within it. This Professor Mitrany does not deny, but fails to give it the emphasis it demands.

The world is thus faced with a challenge. Evolution is too slow. World government on jelly-fish lines cannot sustain the strain of modern politics. For too many decades we have been marking time in politics, whilst forging ahead in technics, thus creating a paradise for

## A Paradise for Lawyers

fools and rogues. Man must consciously accelerate evolution, taking two stages in one big stride. We must establish an international government that is also democratic, and then extend it as rapidly as practicable to include all countries; it must at least embrace the whole world in the sense that even in democracies a proportion of the population has for the time being no vote (e.g. young people) and in the sense that even in the British Commonwealth law and order is imposed from without on dependencies as yet unable to govern themselves from within.

I have already pointed out that constitutional forms are alone insufficient to ensure self-government. But a good constitution can be one of the most powerful means of accelerating evolution. For ten years after 1777 the thirteen American States struggled to work the Covenant of their League of Friendship, but became ever more deeply bogged down in a spreading morass of anarchy and despair. In 1787 they drafted a federal constitution.

> Look at the immediate results. In the first ten years of Federal Union the American people quadrupled their trade. The standard of living in every one of the thirteen States went up and up. The States that were so indebted in 1787 that they could no longer borrow a nickel were soon piling up a surplus. The various territorial and trade disputes threatening war between them – who can recall any of them now? Some people say we cannot follow this example now because we can't change human nature. But they did not change human nature then. All they did was change their form of government, gear it through Federal Union to the best instead of the worst in human nature. That done, the very people who had failed with a League in 1787 began at once in 1790 to succeed astoundingly with Union.
>
> Clarence K. Streit, *Union Now*

We, in our generation, can lay the foundations of world peace. They will rest upon courage, wisdom, and patience, judiciously blended with optimism.

# CHAPTER 3

# THE GENESIS OF WORLD FEDERALISM

'We have more need than ever for "Federal Union", with its fifty-year history of gentle persuasion, to teach us imaginative sense.'
Lord Jenkins of Hillhead – *Federal Union, the Pioneers'*, 1990

In the Autumn of 1938, when, in the Munich crisis, democracy seemed to have plumbed the very depths of self-abasement, two significant things happened which did much to put democratic prestige once more in the ascendant.

An American journalist in Geneva, Clarence K. Streit, commenced to write a book entitled *Union Now*, which aimed at preventing the outbreak of war by the federation of fifteen specified democracies. At the same time a spontaneous movement – 'Federal Union' – started independently in Great Britain to canvass support for a federation of free democratic peoples under a common government, elected by and responsible to the peoples for their common affairs, but leaving national self-government for purely national affairs. This was intended to be a first step towards ultimate world unity.

The proposal was that the federal government would control foreign policy, armed forces and armaments; it would have substantial constitutional powers over tariffs, currency, migration, communications, international public works and similar matters. It would also have power to ensure that colonies and dependencies were administered in the interests of the inhabitants, and not for the benefit of any particular member state, In other words, some powers

## The Genesis of World Federalism

would be vested exclusively in the federal authority, some vested exclusively in the member states, and some would be shared on specified formulae.

An organization formed in America to further the recommendations of *Union Now* – 'Interdemocratic Federal Union' – and 'Federal Union' in the U.K. worked in close collaboration, their ramifications covering the entire world. 'Federal Union' alone had several hundred branches throughout Britain and Northern Ireland, and contact was maintained with similar organizations in Holland, Eire, Switzerland, France, Australia, South Africa, New Zealand and with representatives in forty other countries. In common with other democratic movements, it did not entirely lose touch with anti-Nazi elements in German and Italian Europe.

'Federal Union' adopted as its badge an anti-Nazi device, three symbolic arrows, slanting upwards to the 'right'. (Heralds knew they were ascending towards the left, so that both political trends were satisfied.)

**A collecting tin label on which the 'three arrows symbol' was used. It was designed by the author's father.**

By April, 1940, *The Case for Federal Union* by W. B. Curry, published the previous winter, had sold 100,000 copies. By that time the average weekly increase in membership of 'Federal Union' was 400. Among its members and supporters the movement boasted many eminent authorities in all spheres of life and of diverse political creeds, and its influence rapidly permeated the government. The offer of Federal Union to France, made in 1940 and reiterated by

Churchill in the spring of the following year, showed that the vital importance of the federal principle was fully appreciated by the Prime Minister and the British Commonwealth and Allied Cabinets.

Sir William Beveridge, technical adviser to the Minister of Labour, and member of the Federal Union National Council, stated:
> 'Federalism carried beyond national boundaries presents itself each day more clearly as the means by which international order can be combined with preservation of national cultures and individualities.'

Sir Archibald Sinclair, Secretary of State for Air:
> 'An essential principle of modern social policy is that we are all members of one another, and the same principle must be applied in the life of nations if we are to succeed in outlawing war. The principle of federation supplies an obvious line of approach.'

Lord Lothian, when British Ambassador to Washington:
> 'Some form of federation ... at any rate for part of Europe is a necessary condition of any stable world order.'

Duff Cooper, Minister of Information:
> 'We hope to see in Europe a unity based on the free will and consent of the various nations who will pool their resources, share their responsibilities and combine their armed forces while retaining their own liberty.'

Arthur Greenwood, War Minister without Portfolio:
> 'In our view a lasting peace is obtainable only by the establishment of a commonwealth of states, whose collective authority shall transcend, in its proper sphere, the sovereign rights of individual nations.'

(Note that the 'collective authority shall transcend, in its proper sphere, the sovereign rights ... '. This is pure federal theory.)

Similarly, Lieut.-Col. Moore-Brabazon, a newcomer to the Cabinet, broadcast a few days before his appointment an exhortation that individual states should never again be permitted exclusive ownership and control of air forces. This view was subsequently endorsed by Herbert Morrison, Minister for Home Security, R. A. Butler, Chancellor of the Exchequer, and Harold Nicholson, Parliamentary Secretary to the Ministry of Information.

Apart from a large and rapidly growing volume of literature of its

## The Genesis of World Federalism

own, including a weekly newspaper *Federal News*, 'Federal Union' influenced to a marked degree other contemporary literature, and the daily press. The movement claimed hundreds of press notices a week.

In December 1941 the *New York Times* published a full page advertisement urging the President of the USA to submit to Congress a programme for the constitutional union of the democracies. Among the group signing the petition were Justice Owen Roberts of the U.S. Supreme Court and Mr Harold Ickes, Secretary of the Interior. At the same time, the magazine *Fortune* reported that a public opinion survey showed that 30 million American adults believed that after the war the U.S. should join a union of democracies in all parts of the world 'to keep order'.

Somewhere among my press cuttings (mislaid at the moment) is a record of a resolution (proposed by Henry Usborne, M.P. and seconded by me) passed by 'Federal Union' to the effect that a World Federation of Federal Union Movements should be established, This led to the formation of the World Movement for World Federal Government, which held its first World Congress in Montreux, Switzerland, in August 1947.

Also in August 1947 appeared 'The Plan in Outline'. This document, wherein the ideas of the Crusade for World Government were first proposed, originated as a Report of a Parliamentary Committee of the House of Commons. Sixteen M.P.s constituted this Committee, chaired by Henry Usborne. 'The Plan in Outline' was published in August 1947, and was then signed and supported by seventy-eight other members of the United Kingdom Parliament.

The intention of the Plan was to implement the aims of the World Movement for World Federal Government by arranging an unofficial World Constituent Assembly consisting of one delegate per million inhabitants from as many countries as possible. The purpose of the Assembly would be to draft a federal constitution for the participant countries. The elected representatives would be paid, out of funds to be voluntarily collected, not less than the current national parliamentary salary (to ensure good calibre delegates!).

Such a constitution would be subject to ratification by the various parliaments. If ratified by legislatures representing at least one-half

## The Parliament of Man

of the population of the world, the Constitution would come into effect in respect of those states that had ratified.

The Plan suggested that the minimum powers that would probably be allotted to the federal government would be armed forces, atomic energy and the power to tax for its own finances. However, it hinted that the convention might propose powers over large-scale economic planning under the ægis of a World Food Council.

By May, 1948, Henry Usborne, M.P., on returning from a trip to the USA, announced that the Americans would be electing 140 representatives by the votes of more than 30 million Americans in the summer of 1950, and that the World Constituent Assembly would be held in Geneva in the autumn of that year. He predicted:

> 'From this Peoples Convention will issue forth a Charter of World Government. And this Charter will be ratified and world peace will be permanent by 1955 at the latest. This is the prophesy that is now being made; and events, I believe, will justify it.'

Sceptics on the Parliamentary Committee, and other federalists, had doubted whether American support would be enough to ensure the success of the Plan. (Response from other countries was extremely encouraging). Henry Usborne had therefore volunteered to address meetings of the most conservative groups in all the difficult towns across the American continent: New York, Washington, Cleveland, Detroit, Chicago, Ann Arbor, Memphis, Denver, San Francisco, and Los Angeles[1].

Usborne reported:

> 'In every place the reception was the same: the idea caught on; it captured the imagination.'

The Emergency Committee of the American Atomic Scientists, headed by Dr. Albert Einstein, contributed $3,000[2]. The United World Federalists, with 20,000 members, adopted the Plan unanimously at its annual general meeting that month. Usborne's report concluded:

> 'And so it is in other countries. All over the world the beacons of world government are being lighted. We may yet see a Peace in

[1] The 'Un-American Committee' was then at the height of its rampage!
[2] Worth nearly double this sum today.

## The Genesis of World Federalism

our time[3], a real and permanent peace through World Government. Tennyson's "Parliament of Man" is no idle dream. In a very few years — by 1955 if all goes well — it will become a reality.'

It is a tragedy that this prophesy failed, and those cheering beacons faded and died.

In the months that followed world federalists took samples of the electorates in various parts of the world, notably Chelmsford (England), Nivelles (Belgium), Silkeborg (Denmark), Bad Kissingen (Germany), Gosford (Australia) and New Lynn (New Zealand). The British vote showed well over 80% in favour of the plan of the Crusade for World Government, and the New Zealand 67%. In all other cases the vote was between 90 and 94% in favour and, except for Denmark, between 60 and 79% of the electorate voted.

In the General Election, Henry Usborne fought on the Crusade for World Government platform and won over 22,000 votes for World Federal Government, being returned to Parliament with a 4,000 majority in a total poll of 44,000. In the neighbouring constituencies, candidates who had pledged support for the Peoples World Constituent Assembly were returned. Of the nineteen Scottish M.P.s who had committed themselves in advance for or against the Assembly, twelve were supporters. In the London boroughs, of the eleven Government candidates who pledged their support, six were elected. In addition, one Conservative candidate gave specific support and two (Mr R. Carr and Mr Duncan Sandys — Mr Churchill's son-in-law) promised 'general support.' The two last-named were elected. Twenty-six out of the twenty- eight Liberal candidates who were signed-up supporters polled many votes because of their advocacy of world government.

Due mainly to the efforts of my friend and colleague [4]Fyke Farmer, the Tennessee State Parliament passed, in April 1949, with one dissentient vote, a law providing for the election of delegates in August 1950 to the World Constituent Assembly in December 1950, and for the payment of their salaries and expenses.

Similar bills were introduced in Kentucky, France, Western Germany and Sweden, and others were in preparation for Britain, Hol-

[3] Chamberlain's infamous words on returning from Munich, taken from the Czarist national anthem.

[4] On the next page is his correspondence with Prof. Albert Einstein.

## The Parliament of Man

```
        A. EINSTEIN,
       112, MERCER STREET
          PRINCETON,
         NEW JERSEY, U.S.A.

              December 5th, 1950
```

Mr. Fyke Farmer
Hotel New Willard
Washington D.C.

Dear Mr. Farmer:

        I am sending you enclosed my statement in behalf of the Geneva Convention which I have drafted in your presence last Saturday. You may use this statement at your discretion.

                With best personal regards,

                        sincerely yours,

                        *A. Einstein*

encl.                  Albert Einstein.

**Professor Einstein was an ardent supporter of federalism. The statement on the right was drafted by himself with Fyke Farmer in December 1950. It was was for use in the Peoples' World Constituent Assembly Campaign. Above is corresponponence accompanying the statement.**

48

# The Genesis of World Federalism

A. EINSTEIN,
112, MERCER STREET
PRINCETON,
NEW JERSEY, U.S.A.

The mounting danger of a totally devastating conflict is rapidly convincing the whole world that World Federal Government must be created. But up to now there has not been in existence, to serve this goal, a forceful, permanent body, truly international in its composition and supra-national in its thinking, enjoying the confidence of like-minded people in all countries and recognized by them as their true representatives. To give birth to such a representative body is the main objective of the Geneva Convention.

The Geneva Convention must also decide the question how far the United Nations can form the basis of our efforts to establish World Federal Government. We are convinced that the United Nations can only become a World Government if the Assembly consists no longer of representatives of governments but of representatives directly elected by the people. Because only direct representatives of the people themselves can be expected to serve, according to their own judgement, the interest of supra-national order and security.

*A. Einstein*

Princeton N.J.
December 5th, 1950           Albert Einstein.

land, Belgium and Italy. In official State referenda, the voters of Connecticut and Massachusetts endorsed the world federation idea 11 to 1 and 9 to 1 respectively; referenda were also authorized in Florida and Oklahoma. Twenty-six State legislatures in the USA passed legislation favouring world government. Six directed Congress to convene a constitutional convention to propose amending the U.S. constitution (if necessary) to expedite American participation in a world-wide federation. Of the various resolutions to this end placed before the Congress itself, HCR 64 — aiming at transforming the United Nations into a world federation — was gaining new sponsors every month, the total reaching at least 111 in the House of Representatives alone.

**WORLD CITIZENS MOVEMENT**

On June 19, 1949, a report by Jean O'Donnell appeared in *The Freethinker* under the heading 'Davis and Goliath', of a mass meeting held in the Vélodrome d'Hiver in Paris and attended by 15,000 people to hear Garry Davis, World Citizen No.1. The article claimed that all newspaper readers were aware that Davis, an American by birth, had renounced his American citizenship in favour of the ideal of world citizenship. The previous September he had camped outside the Palais de Chaillot, headquarters of the United Nations General Assembly, to agitate for World Government. In November he had interrupted the futile proceedings of the General Assembly.

Before being hustled out, all he had time to say was:

'In the name of the people of the world, who are not represented here ...'.

From another part of the gallery his speech was finished for him by Robert Sarrazac, former French resistance leader:

'We the people want the peace that only a world government can give ... I appeal to you to convene immediately a world constituent assembly which will raise the flag of one government for one world.'

After the Vélodrome mass meeting, another one, held in the Salle Playel, accommodating 2,500 people, was jam-packed and thousands had to be turned away. With written and telegraphed greetings from

## The Genesis of World Federalism

Dr. Albert Einstein, Sir John Boyd-Orr[5] and a number of British Members of Parliament, Davis was supported on the platform by Albert Camus, André Breton, 'Vercors' and other prominent French writers.

'My need of peace is the same as yours,' he told the cheering audience in his 'American' French. 'We believe the fatal crisis is approaching. Are we going to wait and hope, until it is too late?'

A week later, 15,000 people attended a meeting at the Vélodrome d'Hiver to hear the reply of Dr Evatt, President of the United Nations General Assembly, to questions put to him by Davis.

The audience booed Dr Evatt's assertion that 'it was not the prerogative of the United Nations to make peace, but to maintain it once the Great Powers had made it.'

Davis had asked the United Nations to devote time in the current session of the General Assembly to examine the possibility of convening a World Constituent Assembly to prepare a world government.

Shortly thereafter, Davis and his supporters declared that the hope of obtaining the organization of world peace through the 'United' Nations would have to be abandoned. Thus Davis arrived at an agonizing decision by laborious pragmatic ways, a decision which many federalists had already reached by pure reasoning.

Instead, it was decided to set up the World Citizens Registry, which I and thousands of others hastened to join[6].

✳ ✳ ✳

This similarity may have given the fatal stab to the World Citizens Movement, confusing the public into thinking that federalists believe

---

[5] At a meeting with Sir John at his club, the Athenaeum, I once offered, as organizer of the Federal Union Press Committee, to provide him with federalist articles to sign. He vigorously protested that he never used 'ghost writers'!

[6] See Chapter 4. The symbol they adopted was a 'matchstick' man/woman within a circle, representing the world. See the illustration on page 54. The Campaign for Nuclear Disarmament later adopted a symbol very reminiscent of this, suggesting a figure (within a circle) signalling in semaphore: 'N.D.'

that weapons cause war. Weapons do not cause war, any more than disarmament causes peace. They are merely a symptom of war.

The ND people are trying to scrape off some of the spots in a vain hope of curing the disease that causes them.

\* \* \*

Since the above was written, I have read the recently published *Federal Union: The Pioneers* (see Bibliography) which shows how Federal Union went underground, so to speak, and continued to permeate British public opinion, particularly in bringing about British participation in the European Community. Their success in making the EC a federation still hangs in the balance.

\* \* \*

## THOU SHALT NOT KILL WHOLESALE

I referred above to my friend Fyke Farmer of Nashville, Tennessee. The message he brought is still relevant today. Of any publicity I obtained for him I can find only an article published in Luxemburg, in German, which I have translated as follows:

### Thou Shalt not Kill Wholesale
Interview with Fyke Farmer, Elected Delegate to the
Peoples' World Convention
From our London Correspondent

'I should never have believed that I would ever be obliged to live in a world like the present. I was born in a Christian country, and I was of the opinion that Christians would, as such, try to live in obedience to the ten commandments. I was trained as a lawyer, and lawyers are accustomed to prosecute people who sin against the commandment that states:

"Thou shalt not kill!"

Spiritual leaders and politicians, and generals who accept the office of Supreme Commanders of international armed forces before there is an international civil authority competent to appoint them, are now trying to persuade us to believe that this commandment merely states:

"Thou shalt not kill *retail*!"

To my mind, there should be a new commandment:

## The Genesis of World Federalism

"Thou shalt not kill *wholesale!*" '

These words were uttered by Mr Fyke Farmer, former District Attorney of Nashville, Tennessee, which city he designated as Atom Bomb target No.1. One bomb would be enough, he thought.

'Russia,' he says, 'has never said how many atom bombs it possesses. Its spokesmen merely content themselves with saying that they have enough.' 'As far as I am concerned,' says Fyke Farmer, 'this "enough" is as good as a feast.' Despite his earnestness, Fyke Farmer never overlooks the humorous side of a problem, and when he laughs he laughs heartily. He gave up a very lucrative law practice in order to devote his entire time to the idea of world government. He is one of the three delegates elected by the citizens of Tennessee to represent them at the World Constituent Assembly, first held in Geneva in December 1950 and adjourned to 9 November next in Paris.

He arrived in London by air after a short visit to Belgium to give support for a draft law, which is now before the Belgian parliament, and which has been signed by two Belgian M.Ps from each party, calling for national elections of Belgian delegates to the Constituent World Assembly. He seemed optimistic about the outcome of the parliamentary debate.

'Under the auspices of the United Nations', says Farmer, 'my country recognized the Declaration of Human Rights as the supreme law of the United States. Several judgements handed down by the American courts have confirmed this. Furthermore, the Nürnberg verdicts have established the principle that no-one who incites or commits a crime against humanity may invoke as an excuse orders from above or his own national laws, if at the time of commission of the crime there was a moral choice open to him. Neither the diplomats nor the United Nations themselves have so far been able to define an aggressor. Measures which one party regards as defensive are regarded by another as aggressive preparations. Thus, my own country – like other states that have signed the Universal Declaration of Human Rights – is preparing for war in gross violation of international law.

Most of the taxes levied by the state are used for armaments, and to this I must take exception. Since a moral choice remains to me, I have resolved not to pay federal taxes. There should be an international court to deal with appeals from private citizens wishing to disassociate themselves from any act of their respective governments that violates international law.'

Article 28 of the Universal Declaration of Human Rights states:
'Every person is entitled to a social and international order in which the rights and freedoms contained in this Declaration may be fully enjoyed.'

Mr Farmer pointed out that this pre-supposed an international court of law before which individual citizens could appeal against any violation of Human Rights, and an international government with the ability to carry out the decisions of this court.

'International law must act directly on individuals, otherwise it cannot be enforced peacefully', said Mr Farmer. 'It is absolutely vital that war criminals be prosecuted *before* they start a war. If we wait until *afterwards*, the Nürnberg verdicts will be self-contradictory, as they would merely ensure that politicians have to deploy every weapon — even atom bombs and germ warfare — to avoid being defeated. Because, after a war the Nürnberg principle would then be applied only on the vanquished.'

The World Citizens' Movement membership card showing their logo

# Chapter 4

# WORLD CITIZENS No.1, No.2 AND No.12,345

Though I had long felt myself a cosmopolitan (as well as English and British) it was in 1950 that I first became an official 'World Citizen', by enrolling as a member of the World Citizens' Movement. Garry Davies, an American federalist, was the founder, and I seem to remember my Swedish friend Anders Clarin, the founder and Chairman of the first Swedish Federalist organization, Världsfederalisterna i Sverige, claiming to be No.2. Be this as it may, 12,342 other people must have enrolled before me, for my membership card (dated 1950) dubs me World Citizen No. 12,345. It is illustrated overleaf.

Of course, this was long before the advent of the European Community and its Community Citizenship. I had great fun with my World Citizen membership card, flourishing it at frontier posts in (several successful) attempts to use it as a passport. That it is stamped by nine immigration authorities is the result of some officials having been misled by my ploy.

I ought to emphasize here that I was by then a Federalist, a member of the Federal Union Movement, and had indeed been elected to the National Council of Federal Union in 1941. I was not a 'joiner' in the sense of the term in those days applied to those who would join any association that claimed to stand for a good cause. I had resolved not to compromise my status as a federalist by enrolling in any party-political body or indeed any society that might delay my direct work for federalism. In this light I regarded membership of the

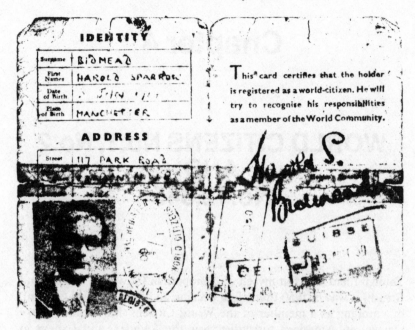

**The author's membership card of the World Citizen's Movement**

**The author's press card of the Federalist Press Association**

## World Citizens No. 1, No. 2 and No. 12,345

World Citizens Movement from the point of view of its publicity value, merely a peg on which to hang discussion about international federal government.

I once mentioned this to an elderly Swedish lady on board ship, and she confided that her only tease of immigration officials, when completing her landing card, was when she filled in the space provided for 'Sex?' She customarily replied 'Yes.'

The first time I encountered the federal idea was in 1940 when my first wife and I went to a meeting at the 'Q' Theatre (run by Jack de Leon, who, with his enthusiastic and energetic daughter Jean, were keen federalists[1]. The speaker was Dr. W. B. Curry, Headmaster of Dartington Hall School, and the title was the same as his book: *The Case for Federal Union*, published in 1939.

The effect on us was the same as must have been experienced when the first wheel was demonstrated. 'Why did we not think of this ourselves, and long before this?'

This book of mine claims to contain little original thought, though I hope it will contribute new ways of looking at the problems of international government and world peace. It will in many places seem to be a series of quotations and recommendations to read this or that book, in particular Dr. Curry's book and also, *Union Now* by Clarence Streit, to which a whole chapter and several appendices in Curry's book are devoted.

The present book will contain many echoes from other federalists, past and present, often without my being conscious of the fact, just as many people today seem (to me) to be echoing my own remarks of half a century ago, without their realizing it. Such experiences are, I find, occasions for satisfaction, not to say self-congratulation. Whilst offering my apologies to any whom I may have unwittingly plagiarized, I hope they will experience the same feeling of gratification as I have when I find my own 'gospel' returning to me, with improvements and embellishments.

At this great distance of time I cannot of course recall details of Curry's address, though I feel sure he covered most of the essence of

---

[1] They helped to convert artistes such as Robert Donat (whom I also interviewed), Alistair Sim, Sybil Thorndyke, Claire Bloom, Roger Livesey, Ursula Jeans, and Miles Malleson, to name but a few.

his book. However, the main theme has remained ever since firmly entrenched in my mind:

◆ Firstly, the world needs an international government that will eventually grow into a world government.

◆ Secondly, the new order must be federal, in that international affairs must be entrusted to the federal government, national affairs being retained by the national governments.

◆ Thirdly; the only proper units of government are individuals, not states or communities, and the international laws they are called upon to obey should be made by the individuals themselves (not by the states to which they belong) through the medium of an international federal parliament.

Perhaps for the first time, I realized the meaning of federation: that only a limited range of powers need be granted to the federal government, and yet it would still remain a government, with true governmental capability.

The first thing we did on returning home was to read Curry's book and to join the Federal Union movement, which had been founded by Charles (now Sir Charles) Kimber, Patrick Ransome and Derek Rawnsley[2] in 1938.

The three objects of the movement were:

◆ To obtain support for a federation of free peoples under a common government, directly or indirectly elected by and responsible to the people for their common affairs, with national self-government for national affairs.

◆ To ensure that any federation so formed shall be regarded as the first steps towards ultimate world federation.

◆ Through such a federation to secure peace, based on economic security and civil rights for all.

These aims seemed to me self-evident, though it was often necessary to explain — to new members as well as to sympathizers — that the

---

[2] Derek's parents, Noël and Violet Rawnsley (who, incidentally, had founded the National Trust) later initiated a vigorous correspondence with me on the basis of my published articles. One of the regrets of my life is that I never found the opportunity to accept their warm invitation to visit them at their home — 'Dil-aram' (Pyramids) — on the island of Anacapri.

## World Citizens No. 1, No. 2 and No. 12,345

united democracies would retain their own parliaments for the 'self-government' mentioned in Object 1, as well as their constitutional monarchs, state presidents, and the like.

It was also necessary to point out that, as the experience of history teaches, the formation of the new federation would probably take place by means of some kind of Constituent Assembly, where delegates (who would require to go back to their constituents for ratification of what they decided) holding various kinds of mandate — some, perhaps, with no authority beyond that conferred by their own reputations among their fellow men — would meet together to thrash out or edit a draft constitution.

Television has now made such strides, and has become so popular that millions of viewers all over the world can be glued to their sets to watch and listen to, e.g. Melodie Grand Prix. Furthermore, over a thousand radio stations were recently linked to enable more than a thousand million people to listen to a posthumous broadcast by John Lennon from the United Nations (!) Thus there is a good chance that one day soon some such link-up will be used for a worldwide appeal for support for a world constituent assembly. The chain reaction of peace could start.

Once such a constitution was ratified by a sufficient number of nations for the union to come into being, the next step would be for the peoples to elect a federal parliament, consisting of representatives who would not have to go back to their constituents for approval of the legislation they enacted.

Subsequently, as an ordinary member, later as a locally elected member of the Federal Union National Council, then as a national councillor, I strove consistently to keep these aims 'pure'. I and my likeminded colleagues were opposed by the advocates of communism, socialism, Beveridge-ism (womb-to-tomb social insurance) and various other enthusiasts and cranks who were constantly attempting to add subsidiary or competing aims to these three.

My argument was that it would be harmful to confuse the issue by, e.g. enumerating the powers that would have to be held by the federal authority, or adding, e.g. proportional representation, free trade, adoption or abolition of the gold standard, specific lists of nations who should be invited into or excluded from the federation, or any of the other pet hobby-horses ridden by some factions of our supporters, or by those who had joined in the hope of capturing us.

## The Parliament of Man

In my enthusiasm for the federal idea I deluded myself into thinking that other people must be like my wife and myself[3], that all they needed was to have the federal idea explained to them: their eyes would then open and they would clamour for a nucleus world federation to be set up without further delay.

One element of pressure we exerted was to write to our Members of Parliament. I told mine, a Member who had sat for so long he had almost forgotten his own name, that irrespective of party loyalties I was determined not to vote for any candidate who did not support the federal idea, which of course I explained. The reply I received in due course was the sort of answer that might have pleased both the Angel Gabriel and Mephistopheles, but was not suitable for Purgatory or for planet Earth.

Due to some kindness (or devilry) on the part of the Member's secretary, however, the envelope also included a letter from the Conservative Central Office telling him what reply to give me. The two texts were identical!

I was therefore not surprised when Mr Churchill's party lost the General Election after the war. His Party let him down, though in this connection it must be remembered that Mr Churchill himself had, more than once during his political career, crossed the floor of the House (i.e. changed party).

During the war years I made contact with many expatriates and several exile governments, making friends among the Belgians[4],Czechs, French, Hungarians, Norwegians, Poles, Slovaks, Yugoslavs[4], etc.

I wrote letters to editors and articles for any press that would print them, whether anarchist[5], atheist, socialist, quaker, zionist, catholic,

[3] My first son was christened (Christopher) Hamilton, after the pioneer federalist Alexander Hamilton.
[4] E.g. on my International Federal Union Press Committee. In June 1942 I organized a public meeting in Chiswick Town Hall for Dr Rudolf Bicanic, Vice-President of the Yugoslav National Bank, General Marcel de Baer, and Lord Wedgwood. After the war, Dr Bicanic (rhymes with Itchy Bitch) took back with him as his wife a beautiful English girl who had attended one of his Federal Union lectures. A similar adventure happened to me, but did not lead to the altar; my fiancée believed in short engagements, and broke ours off when it had gone on long enough.
[5] Federation means less government and less onerous government.

## World Citizens No. 1, No. 2 and No. 12,345

masonic, imperialist or pacifist (though I was anxious not to be classed as a devotee of any of these).

The result was I had over 700 items published, some quite lengthy, in about 200 newspapers and journals in forteen countries on all five continents, in English, French, Spanish, Swedish, Dutch, German, Czech, and Esperanto (and in Braille). The range was from the sublime to the ridiculous, from *The Times* (under three banner headlines), *Manchester Guardian, Scotsman, Fabian Quarterly, Time and Tide, Tribune, Truth, Cavalcade, The Economist, Picture Post, Dalhousie Review, International Affairs* (Journal of the Royal Institute of International Affairs − Chatham House, in London), *Australian Quarterly* (Journal of the Australian Institute of International Affairs), *International Affairs Journal* (organ of the Indian Institute of International Affairs) and *Pakistan Horizon* (Journal of the Pakistan Institute of International Affairs) to *Ethiopia News, Lloyd's Log, Metal Bulletin, Market Grower, Salesman and Fruit Trader, Outfitter, Tailor & Cutter*, and my old school magazine! Of course, I use the term 'ridiculous' not in a sense derogatory to these worthy journals, but in the sense that they may seem unlikely channels through which to introduce the elements of international political science to the public.

Including about sixty to seventy book reviews (all dealing of course with international federal government) my articles and letters were printed in periodicals ranging from daily and local U.K. papers, a front-line infantry bulletin (T.T.), magazines in Sydney (Australia), Ceylon, Nova Scotia, South Africa, New Zealand, Sweden, Belgium, USA, India, Luxembourg, Germany and Holland, They appeared in French and German papers in the USA, and, during the war, in English and foreign language papers published in England by the allies (e.g. *Message*, a Belgian magazine, which through the good offices of my friend General de Baer, Member of the UN Commission for Investigation of War Crimes, also published, in full, my pamphlet *The Parliament of Man*).

The fact that, despite the dire shortage of paper, so many editors considered my articles fit not only for publication but (frequently) for translation, provided much encouragement. With the rejection slips alone, using only the letterheads, I was able to paper one whole wall of my study!

## The Parliament of Man

The foregoing boasting is primarily intended to encourage younger enthusiasts to try, try again, and again and again, and again. Next time round, I hope they will concentrate on television.

I even received, from a Japanese woman who had apparently approved my message, a set of chopsticks, and a knife and fork, all engraved with prayers for my good digestion. (Whether this explains my unfailingly good metabolism remains an open question).

Despite all the efforts of the federalists at that time, the anticipated irresistible revolution in world opinion failed to occur. But we persisted. Besides writing, I organized and addressed private and public meetings, and attended federalist conferences in Montreux, The Hague, Luxembourg, Geneva, Stockholm, Ghent, etc. I converted my Income Tax Assessor, who became Chairman of the Federal Union Lunch Club which I organized. (There was another one in Fleet Street.)

I might also mention that during the war, federalists in reserved occupations like myself (in armaments[6] and with a gamé leg) engaged in other activities besides propaganda.

My family, being offered evacuation to federalist homes in California or New York, chose Oxfordshire, England. Finding a way from Chiswick to London EC3 (and back) five or six times a week was at times problematical. All through the war I had a regular job (including firewatch duties) in the City of London, (I saw it burn around me), and also assisted the Ministry of Economic Warfare through Sir Eldon Manisty and his staff. On Sundays I firewatched at home or worked on one of the eight farms 'adopted' by the Federal Union Movement, where – on my first day – knee-deep in cow dung I learned to sympathize with Hercules in his stable, and – when engaged in the comparatively cleaner task of harvesting tomatoes – gained some appreciation of the reason why I now have to pay such an exhorbitant price for the Norwegian-grown variety.

One Bank holiday, to assist ailing Federal Union funds, Norman Stoddart, a fellow Council Member, offered a generous supply of ice cream, which I helped him and other enthusiasts to sell on Hampstead Heath. For weeks afterwards I imagined I smelled of vanilla, but the result was substantial enough to be recorded in this year's history book: *Federal Union, The Pioneers.*

[6] Iron ore.

## World Citizens No. 1, No. 2 and No. 12,345

In gratitude for having been given the use of the local church hall for meetings of the Chiswick branch of 'Federal Union', I promised the vicar, the Rev.W.J.Simmons, B.A., that 'one of these Sundays' I would attend one of his services[7]. He later became chairman of the branch[8]. At the time of his decease this promise was still unfulfilled, and it has occasionally troubled my conscience ever since. On the other hand, a rather more heinous offence gives me no qualms. Once, during World War II, seeing a white shirt − a rarity − in the window of a Military Tailor I went in to order and was told that they were all reserved for naval officers.

'Was I connected with the Navy by any chance?'

'Not directly,' I reluctantly admitted[9] 'but I am an Associate Member of Chatham House.'[10]

'Ah, Chatham!' he replied, 'Certainly, sir, I could let you have one, but no more.'

The thought that I had by nefarious means misappropriated to myself a clothing ration that belonged to our fighting forces never troubled my sleep thereafter, I am sorry to admit.

The first Federal Union National Council to which I was elected included national figures such as Professor Norman Bentwich, Sir

---

[7] The intended christening of Christopher Hamilton came to naught because of two letters in a three-letter word. I stubbornly protested at the orthodox description of the child's conception; the vicar steadfastly refused to amend the word 'sin' to 'fun', adding that neither would he have agreed to change the Lord's prayer to ask for our daily Kellogg's corn flakes!

[8] The Hon.Treasurer was Eileen Goldsworthy, whose stalwart work for the Cause amply justified her name.

[9] I was tempted to boast of the part I had played in the capture of a cargo of iron ore in the first week of the war, but thought of Chatham naval dockyard instead!

[10] Colloquial name for the Royal Institute of International Affairs, housed in the former home of William Pitt the Elder, first Earl of Chatham. Incidentally, Pitt knew Britain had no right to tax the colonies; if he had remained in power until the time of the Boston tea party, this would probably not have happened, and the US and the entire British Commonwealth might now be joined in Federal Union. The great wars of the past 200 years might not have occurred! Nor would there be an Irish Republican Army, as Pitt's Irish policy was tolerant.

## The Parliament of Man

William (later Lord) Beveridge, Professor George Catlin, Dr W. B. Curry, Sir Robert Grieg, Professor C. E. M. Joad, R. W. G. Mackay (author of *Federal Europe*), Alan (now Lord) Sainsbury[11],Sir Drummond Shields, Dr. Olaf Stapleton, Francis Williams, Barbara (later Baroness) Wootton, and Miss Monica M. Wingate (sister of General Orde Wingate, of the Chindits). Older readers may remember the latter from the Burma campaign, World War II. Battle conditions permitting, he used to lecture his troops on federation.

In preparation for the annual election for the National Council for 1942, I and my fellow council members Cyril Joad and Cyril Moore collected proxies for the annual general meeting, with a view to removing members of the Council who were agitating to add further Objects to the aims of the society. Unfortunately, our efforts came to the attention of the opposition at any early stage, with the result that they collected more proxies than we did. Thus Moore and I were unsuccessful in the ballot, though Joad scraped through. The outcome was a popular outcry from the floor of the Conference, compelling the new Council to exercise its powers to co-opt two additional members (making sixty in all). I was co-opted, but not Cyril Moore. With his consent I accepted office, and in my maiden speech to the new Council I warmly thanked 'the dog which, having been disinfected, de-bugged and de-loused, was now asking one of its fleas to come back and continue to bite it!'

Early in 1942 Federal Union produced a programme entitled 'Peace Aim; War Weapon' in the hope of encouraging anti-Nazi forces in Germany to overthrow Hitler. There were some strange reactions to our arguments. Several serious-minded persons whose views I might otherwise have respected argued that traitors were traitors, even if they were traitors to Hitler, and that association with such people was not to be encouraged. I thought of my young friend Ruth, a student nurse whose parents had been murdered and incinerated in Auschwitz, and whose hatred of her fellow countrymen had escalated daily as she viewed the mangled bodies of babies and little children dug out of the ruins of their homes. I recalled my friend

---

[11] Capitalist who, at prices his customers can well afford, stocks, in his London supermarkets alone, more than enough goods to supply every grocery store in the entire Soviet Union.

## World Citizens No. 1, No. 2 and No. 12,345

Ludwig Wachtel,[12] fleeing from Hitler via Norway and then the North Sea, because of his book documenting Adolf's insanity. I remembered Wenzel Jaksch, then a member of the Federal Union National Council, and technically a traitor to Germany merely because he was Chairman of the Sudeten German Social Democrats, who had been swallowed up by the Nazis with Chamberlain's acquiescence at Munich.

I had heard of the co-respondent who refuses to marry the unfaithful wife on the grounds that she would do the same to him, but this was carrying the argument too far!

It was about this time that Federal Union was approached by two individuals who claimed some connection with MI 5 (or 6 or some such number – or was it the KGB?) and an interrogation was held at the Federal Union Club in Piccadilly. Presumably the suggestion was that we would prefer this venue rather than one behind closed and possibly locked doors in some padded cell!

The attitude of our guests was not so much collaboration as opposition, and suspicion that we were a subversive organization! I no longer recall why I was one of the few Federal Union representatives, but I assume I was there in my capacity as organizer of the Brentford and Chiswick Branch. This was the constituency of the M.P. who had asked Parliament to ban Federal Union.

Although I drank only grapefruit juice, I have but a hazy recollection of this no doubt hilarious meeting. But it occurred to me how jealous of its prerogatives is the sovereign state, and how much time, brainpower and money is wasted in its defence. Non-productive activity of this kind (including, of course, all types of war preparations) is a major cause of inflation. More profitable employment could surely have been found for these counter-espionage intellects!

To celebrate Victory in Europe on VE-day, a Czech federalist friend, Ota Adler, later to be awarded the C.B.E. for his stalwart efforts to bring Britain into the European Community, threw a very cosmopolitan party at his West End home. The genuine Pilsner beer,

---

[12] Once when I was taking tea with Ludvig and Mary Wachtel in their home on the top floor of our block of flats, one out of a stick of bombs exploded above our heads. Fortunately it burst in the water tank, resting on a steel girder. Except that we were peppered with glass and other débris, we all survived.

*The Parliament of Man*

kept all those long years in his cellar just for the occasion, had an unforgettable taste, never equalled by any of the many imitations, made in Scandinavia and elsewhere, that I had or have since encountered. Maybe sentiment played a part in the flavour!

The first time I set foot in Norway after the war (in Narvik), I was informed even before the ship berthed that a federalist then unknown to me (Terje Olsen, now named Disington) had undertaken the long boat voyage from Svolvær, and was waiting on the dock-side to greet me. Thus my visit was converted into a minor propaganda campaign. As the frontispiece of this book shows, Terje went on to found the current federalist organization in Norway. (The picture was taken in 'Bromsgård', a guest house whose visitors' book included the names of famous Swedish painters as well as Bertha von Krupp, who had given her name to a record-sized German field gun in World War I. Note that I am wreathed in palms!). A casual acquaintance made on the train to Stockholm insisted on arranging meetings with radio and newspaper contacts, resulting in a long interview being published in an influential Stockholm daily.

I remember another incident in the winter of 1950. I was working late in the City when there came a frantic call from Margaret Richards, the hardworking secretary of Federal Union. Could I take the place of Henry Usborne, M.P. in a debate with Sir Ted Leather, M.P. on a motion 'That this House would surrender National Sovereignty to World Government'?

I had an appointment early the following morning at Aldeburgh in Norfolk, a hundred miles away, but ...

'Yes,' I said, 'Where and when?'.

'At Lloyds, in about a quarter of an hour,' she replied.

Knowing where Lloyds was (!) I got there on time, and found the library packed, some people standing, and some in the gallery.

Though he was opposing the motion, it turned out that Leather was as keen a federalist as I, as is borne out by his later pamphlet *The Commonwealth, Federation and Atlantic Union*. In other words, the debate was not *whether* Britain should federate, but *with whom*. In the circumstances it was unfair of the editor of *Lloyds Log* merely to report, a fortnight later, that the motion was defeated. It was 'defeated' by only one vote, and was a 'victory' for federalism – incidentally, the type of federalism that *I* supported, since I regard *World*

# World Citizens No. 1, No. 2 and No. 12,345

federation as a *distant* ideal. But such is the power of the suppress!

Afterwards, – I think it was the chairman of the meeting, Mr E. C. T. Carden, President of the Chartered Insurance Institute, invited Mr Norman Tremellan, (Chairman of the Insurance Debating Society) and myself to dinner at the Savoy.

My host decreed that we should start with oysters, and he would show us how to tell whether (at the Savoy!!) they were fresh.

After an enjoyable dinner and stimulating conversation I reminded our host that he had not initiated us into the secret of freshness in oysters.

'They shrink when you apply the lemon juice.' he explained.
(*Mine had not flinched!*)

Half way on my trip north, long past midnight, it became apparent that I am allergic to dead oysters. I really thought my last hour had come, and that I would expire lonely and unnoticed by the wayside, with no Samaritan in sight.

However, I recovered once I had discarded my passengers and could greet Christopher Hamilton (a border at Sizewell School) with genuine smiles the following morning.

Following up Federal Union's contacts, I used to make house calls. I asked one woman who answered a doorbell in one of the less salubrious parts of Kensington:

'What do you think of Federal Union?' She replied: 'I don't really know. After all, it's bad enough if cousins marry, isn't it?'

Victor Hugo once remarked:

'There is one thing greater than armies – an idea whose time has come.'[13]

The time did not yet seem to have arrived for the triumph of the federal idea!

But the battle with ignorance and apathy continued. I was not discouraged, though the cares of providing for a growing family eventually led me to hand over the torch to younger and more vigorous followers of the Cause.

---

[13] He also said: 'I represent a party that does not exist – civilization. This party will make the twentieth century. There will issue from it first the United States of Europe, then the United States of the world.' It is a pity that this prediction seems to have been about one century too optimistic!

## ALAS! WE ARE UN-DONE!

On 15 October 1948, under the above headline, the *Leeds Weekly Citizen* courageously published the following 'report from our Specious Correspondent in Paris,' Harold S. Bidmead:

> The Third Session of the General Assembly of the Untied Nations has opened here in a blaze of glory, the U.N. having, at long last, gone into action. At least, it requested the French Government to take action on its behalf, by evicting from United Nations territory Mr Garry Davis, self-proclaimed Citizen of the World.

It is significant that this eviction was an act which the Charter does not authorize U.N.O. to take. As a spokesman explained to me, however, here was clearly a case for immediate action; there was no time to wait for the matter to be discussed by the General Assembly, and for that body to 'make recommendations' (Article 17). This would probably have involved recommending the 'Security' Council to make recommendations (Article 37, paragraph 2) or to decide (if it could decide, which is doubtful) to take action under Article 36. This Article, too, authorizes the 'Security' Council to make recommendations.

\* \* \*

Mr Davis had already announced that he was no more interested in recommendations than were the Jews or Arabs, the Russians regarding Korea and Berlin, the Bulgarians, Albanians and Yugoslavs concerning Greece, the Indians over Hyderabad, the Dutch over Indonesia or the South Africans in the matter of South West Africa or discrimination against Indians. Under Articles 42 et seq., explained my informant, U.N.O. had the 'power' to 'take action by air, sea or land forces ... Such action may include demonstrations, blockade, etc.' but, in the words of Mr Trygve Lie, UN's Secretary General, [1]'deadlocks have blocked all progress in the Military Staffs Committee' and the UN has nothing to demonstrate with. Even if it

---

[1] 1992 note: The Joint Military Staffs Committee has been in suspended animation for 45 years. The reason is obvious. Its duty is to counter the machinations of potential aggressors. Yet any committee member who divulges such plans is a traitor.

## World Citizens No. 1, No. 2 and No. 12,345

had, the probability was that the demonstrators would neutralize and paralyze each other's efforts.

The presence of a World Citizen on UN soil was clearly 'a situation which might lead to international friction ... or likely to endanger the maintenance of international peace and security', since Mr Davis was disseminating dangerous thoughts.

Twenty-six year old Garry Davis has officially renounced his American nationality and handed in his passport to the American Consulate here.

'This is the only way to save our civilization.' he says, 'Abandon narrow nationalism and outdated hypocritical diplomacy, which perpetuates quarrels instead of healing them. All men of good will should demand an international government. We should unite under just law, instead of splitting into national enmities which bleed each other white.'

In diplomatic circles here, such remarks are considered rank heresy.

'UNO, with its system of one state one vote, is the most democratic body in the world,' said Monsieur Protocol, sipping his apéritif and holding a Corona Corona between his elegant gold-filled teeth. 'After all,' he added, 'the war was fought for democracy, was it not?'

That the little Grand Duchy of Luxembourg has the same voting strength as the USA on unimportant matters he described as proof that the rules of cricket were not unknown outside Britain. He pointed out, too, that on important matters, particularly those likely to endanger the peace of the world, equality also prevailed, since nobody had any voting power whatsoever, or at least, no state had any voting power that could not be completely nullified by the vote of another.

Monsieur Protocol was bitter about Citizen Davis' notion that international law should operate directly upon individuals. If that were the case, Mons. Protocol pointed out, war criminals would be arrested before the war, instead of afterwards, and the world would be robbed of such historic war guilt trials as were held, for instance, at Nürnberg. The very idea that international law should be enacted by an international parliament, elected for the purpose by an international electorate, M. Protocol denounced as undemocratic.

## The Parliament of Man

'How could people be expected to obey laws they had made themselves?' he pertinently asked.

UNO had been based on a belief in men's natural and inherent tendency to agree. That was realism. Mr Davis was not only a dangerous idealist; he was a pessimist, spreading the doctrine that men are prone to disagree, and that decisions must therefore be taken by majority vote in a voting procedure that truly reflects the political power behind each vote. Davis had actually repeated a slogan that 'it is better to stand up and be counted than to be counted whilst lying down under rows of little wooden crosses.'

\* \* \*

In Paris, UNO will be asked to approve the Secretary General's annual report, reporting failure in Palestine, in Indonesia and Kashmir, in Greece and Korea, the collapse of the Atomic Energy Commission, the paralysis of the Commission for Conventional Armaments, the one advisory opinion given by the International Court of Justice and its one (unfinished) case, the failure of the Military Staff Committee to create a law-keeping force, the failure of the U.N. Charter to provide a law-making body, and the proposal of the Interim Committee that the Charter be amended.

A resolution has been tabled to the effect that it was not the United Nations that failed the nations, but the nations that failed the United Nations. This represents an appreciable step forward since 1919-1939, when the League of Nations did not fail the nations − the nations failed the League of Nations.

A spokesman pointed out that Mr Lie's opinion is that the Charter is 'more than sufficient to deal with every situation which has come before the Security Council to date ...'.

It is not considered propitious to make any change in the present set-up. Delegates are having quite a gay time in Paris, and hope to be back next year.

\* \* \*

*World Citizens No. 1, No. 2 and No. 12,345*

## FEDERALIST FLEET BESIEGES CASTLE

On one occasion I received a phone call from the Immigration authorities at Tilbury asking whether I would put up warranty for Anders Clarin – 'lacking obvious means of support' – who claimed to be a federalist. At that time I was living alone in Southway, Hampstead Garden Suburb (practically next door to another federalist, Harold Wilson, the British Prime Minister). I took Clarin on as my 'au pair' for some time, the ensuing exchange of ideas being mutually beneficial.

In the Summer of 1949 the press was full of the exploits described below. I assisted with fourteen articles, in English and German, in the more popular papers.

**Federalist Fleet Besieges Castle**
**Dinghy Campaign for World Government**

My Swedish-born 38-year-old friend Anders Clarin, founder Chairman of Världsfederalisterna of Sweden, arrived at Northolt Airport on 17 May without a passport, having torn it up over the Channel. Friends of five nationalites were waiting to greet him, but the British authorities were unsympathetic.

He declared himself a World Citizen, informing the immigration officers that he had merely tried to make Bevin's words come true, so that people could go down to Victoria station and buy a ticket to travel anywhere at will, without passport formalities. He was obliged to return to Brussels by the same 'plane.

Heatedly denying that he is an idealist, Clarin contends that: 'we world federalists want others to federate with us because we want to establish a relationship that will be profitable to ourselves.'

Clarin is one of the first members of the World Citizens Movement, founded by Garry Davis. When I reminded him that even his own father had described him as being 'as idealistic as a new-born babe,' he laughed and said that babies were no more idealistic than he was.

*1992 note:*

At this distance in time, I cannot for the life of me recall how I managed to interview him when he was technically not permitted to land!

## The Parliament of Man

'I say that world federalism is not idealism, definitely not,' he declared emphatically. 'It is extreme egoism. We do not need to go so far as psychoanalysis to understand this. When we want others to federate with us we want to establish a relationship which we consider will be profitable to ourselves.'

Asked to explain, he went on:

'The same motive is common in all efforts to establish good relations when people live together – in law-making, town-planning, community building, programmes of social benefit, party politics, and so on; even the rules of good behaviour demonstrate it. Likewise, egoism is the motive for world federalism.'

Warming to his theme he continued:

'Don't try to make me believe that you want the Eskimoes, the Germans, the Greeks, the Norwegians, the Chinese and the Argentinians to federate under world government because you want to help them to live in peace and freedom and be for ever happy. And don't try to fool yourself that your kind heart is your motive. Most important of all, don't try to make others accept the plan of world government on an idealistic basis. We are realists who base our actions on the belief that men will always differ, and that they must therefore institute government among themselves.'

Hardly pausing to draw breath, and seldom knowing which language, English or Swedish he was speaking, Clarin continued:

'The federation of states and nations is a political matter - consequently the way to effect it must be by the political method. Politics have very little to do with idealism, except when idealism is used as a persuasive instrument for a political end. Be frank about it; be honest about it; federalism is egoism. It can't be made too clear to ourselves and to others that we want world government for the benefits which we shall all derive from it.'

It seemed to me a great pity this ebullient visitor was not enabled to interview any of our tired politicians, particularly those in the Cabinet.

At 4.45 p.m. on Friday 3 June I learned that Clarin was imprisoned in the Petit Château in Brussels for landing without a passport, and that other prospective world citizens were rallying to his aid. I immediately decided to go to Brussels and see for myself what all the fuss was about. I did not go down to Victoria station. In fact, once I

## World Citizens No. 1, No. 2 and No. 12,345

was in Tilbury I did not need to buy a ticket at all. We could all travel more freely if we had more friends.

I arrived in Belgium the following evening, after eight hours in a little ship[1]. Belgian currency is not one of the things which Mr Bevin's government issues along with his courteous request 'to allow the bearer to pass freely without let or hindrance and to afford him every assistance ... ' but the first Belgian (a Flamand and a stranger) to whom I explained my mission, bought my ticket as far as Ghent, where I contacted Edgar Gevaert, editor of *Parlement*, the multilingual federalist monthly.

I was told that Clarin had been liberated already, owing to the efforts of 19-year-old Evan Cameron, a former staff member of Federal Union, London. Cameron had spent sixty-two sleepless hours in his rubber dinghy in the moat surrounding Clarin's prison – fed by voluntary gifts from the populace which were conveyed to him by a young American girl, Ruth Allenbrook. Through a megaphone he had tirelessly informed the public of the issues at stake, and suggested that Belgium might offer to Clarin the hospitality that France accorded to Garry Davis.

After the release, all three disappeared, and although Clarin had been expected to avail himself of facilities offered to him by the French authorities, the Belgian Douane had no trace, when I enquired, of his having crossed the frontier.

The exploit resulted in a huge volume of comment – mostly favourable and approving – in the Press and from the 'man in the street.' Comparisons were made between the suffragettes and what

---

[1] The little ships I used on this and subsequent visits to Ghent as a member of the editorial committee of *Parlement* were all named after precious stones: *Améthyste, Rubis, Eméraude*, etc. I once asked the Master why the ship was flying a red flag, when the owners were capitalists. He replied that they had to, 'because we carry ammunition!' No wonder the fare cost me only half-a-crown a time! (I was told that for five shillings I could have had a laundered blanket.) The other members of the Editorial Committee of *Parlement* were: Noël and Violet Rawnsley, Abbé H. Grouès, Henry Usborne, J.de Smedt, Mary Lloyd, G.B. Devos, Marie Gevaert, Robert Lindsey, M.R. Cosyn, Victor E. Van der Eeken, Fyke Farmer, Henri Koch, John Popper, Jean Diedisheim, Dr M.J.Mitchell, Knud Nielsen, Arthur J.Grenfelder, A.R.Brent and Ingvar Sigurdsson.

*The Parliament of Man*

the Belgian Press dubbed the 'Direct Action Corps (Naval Branch) for a World Federal Government.' The new Lionheart and his new Blondin were the topic of conversation in all the Flemish pubs, and even a popular weekly like *Pourquoi Pas?* gave Clarin a whole page of good-natured encouragement. The Belgians did not mistake them for cranks, trying to become citizens before they had built their city. But it cannot be too highly stressed that neither Davis nor Clarin wish or expect others to follow their example.

\* \* \*

## MISSED ONE WORLD CITIZEN – FOUND ANOTHER

*Brussels:*
Having failed to catch the flying World Citizen, Anders Clarin, after his release from prison here, I took advantage of the situation to visit Edgar Gevaert, whose monthly review *Parlement* is published in six languages and distributed throughout the world.

### They admire Garry Davis

His home and studio is in the village of Laethem St. Martin, world famous as the centre of a Flemish school of painters.[1] Today it has added fame of another kind: though he and his family tend, unaided, a farm of 22 hectares (54 acres), they yet have found time to make the whole neighbourhood and the town of Ghent so world-government conscious that their home is a positive hive of activity in that interest.

If you appear on the streets of Ghent with a pamphlet bearing Garry Davis's photograph you are mobbed by the local gamins for possession of one.

Save for the luxury of a home decorated with their own paintings, the Gevaerts live the lives of simple farming folk, yet such is Madame Gevaert's hospitality and campaigning zeal that it is nothing, I was told, for them to seat forty guests at table.

Their prodigious achievements have been made rather less onerous by the assistance of their ten children – four fine boys and six comely

---

[1] Another Belgian painter whose hospitality I and Christopher Hamilton later enjoyed was Baron Antoine Allard, an influential and energetic federalist himself.

# World Citizens No. 1, No. 2 and No. 12,345

girls — all artists, musicians and linguists, in their 'teens or thereabouts, but most of them old enough to have worked as lumberers in the French Maquis when fleeing the Nazis as political refugees. One of them, Thérèse Gevaert, will, I venture to predict, one day make a name for herself as an author and illustrator of children's books.[2]

Having studied Gevaert's anti-Hitler pamphlets dating from 1933, I could easily see why Adolf was so anxious for a *tête-à-tête*!

I came away cheered by an invitation to return soon, and greatly encouraged by the memory of a team of federalists working unceasingly together in single-hearted devotion to a great cause.

\* \* \*

## CLARIN TELLS KING OF SWEDEN

Later that year, I was able to report as follows, in English and German:

**Clarin Tells King of Sweden; 'I give up my citizenship'**

Anders Clarin, thirty-eight-year-old Swedish born federalist, who hit the headlines in the Belgian and British press last summer as a world citizen, has just created a stir in Sweden with a personal application to the King of Sweden for permission to relinquish his Swedish nationality. It reads:

> Your Majesty,
>
> I enclose my identity card and respectfully request to be unconditionally relieved of my Swedish citizenship. The following are my reasons for this request; I consider that it is morally unjust to be bound in loyalty to a special ethnic group in preference to loyalty towards all mankind. Consequently, I am unwilling to allow citizenship in any fully sovereign nation to compel me to obey or to share responsibility for any of its decisions which may be likely to lead it to wage war. Such decisions are inevitable so long as Humanity is divided into fully sovereign states.
>
> Circumstances would be different if the nations were to place themselves under a communally constituted and directed authority, and live together under law, as the individual citizens do in a democratic community. This would provide a framework for peaceful international col-

---

[2] She has, in USA, as Treska Lindsey; she married a Federalist.

laboration[3] under international law – the basic principle of world federation, to which idea I am wholeheartedly devoted.

I cannot therefore, in conscience, remain a citizen of any sovereign nation whatever, not even of Sweden.

So far as I am aware, Swedish citizens are not legally entitled to relinquish their Swedish citizenship at their own request, unless they are in process of adopting another nationality, which is of course not my intention. This fact has necessitated my present application.

I shall be grateful for an expeditious disposal of this question, since it concerns my personal status.

The Chancellor at the Ministry of Justice who is dealing with the application stated that it would receive attention in due course, but that he doubted very much whether it could legally be granted.

Clarin's gesture is purely personal, and does not commit the World Movement for World Federal Government.

\* \* \*

I met Anders Clarin again many years later in Stockholm. He was then in receipt of a state retirement pension (unsolicited), and so I presume he remained a Swedish subject. But the letter from the Chancellor shows that, so far as concerns Sweden at least, 'subject' is a more correct term than 'citizen', since an element of slavery is involved in the relationship.

---

[3] Unless there is a translation error here, my friend Anders uses a word in a sense which, for the purposes of this book, I do not accept. The *citizens* of a federation can collaborate in the strictly Latin sense that they 'work together', but 'international collaboration under international law' is no basis for peace. It is not their collaboration that unites them; it is their allegiance to a common law. Collaboration, cooperation, joint efforts and the like, are no basis for world peace, and have no permanent success unless they lead to a merging of electorates.

# Chapter 5

# DON'T MEND OLD SACKS WITH GOOD NEW TWINE

'There have been many attempts to combine the abolition of war with the retention of sovereignty. All have proved futile, and ... they will continue to prove futile.'

Curry, *The Case for Federal Union*

The preamble of the San Francisco Charter, the Charter of the 'United' Nations, reads: 'We, the peoples ...'. These three words constitute the only part of the Charter that should be retained in the unlikely event of the 'United' Nations being adapted and converted into a constitution for inter-state government, apart perhaps from those other sections of the Preamble that do not refer to equal rights of nations, to international 'law' or to the use of armed force 'in the common interest'.

Contrary to the impression given by most of the Preamble, the Charter was not a covenant among peoples, but among governments.

Right from the outset, I and many of my friends were bitterly opposed to the idea of a new league of nations being used as the new instrument of purported world 'government'.

Our main objection was, of course, its unreliability. We saw the allies as a team of mountaineers, setting off with a safety rope which we knew to be defective in its every fibre. We saw their crampons or griffins (or whatever it is to which they entrust their lives) as being made of cast iron with crystalline flaws in every angle.

I myself regarded as completely irrelevant the question whether or not a new league of nations should be set up as a debating society for states unwilling to be governed. A league would make diplomacy perhaps a trifle less slow and difficult for the diplomats, but not a jot less futile.

'If all the diplomats in the world were to be placed head to toe across the Pacific Ocean, it would be a good idea.'

'The so-called "Security" Council provides no more security than an ordinary safety-pin.'

'There is more security in the United Dairies than in the United Nations.'

Such remarks must of course be taken with the pinch of salt that accompanies most jokes. I was always pleased to encounter opposition in our work to spread the federal idea, since a spirited debate attracts more public interest than mere apathy. One objector in a local paper plaintively pointed out that my opposition to the League of Nations was destructive, since the League had so much experience and such expensive premises. To my mind, if he had included the beautiful and efficient secretaries and the skilful translators his argument would have doubled in weight, yet still remained as light as a feather.

Actually, of course, he had missed the point. Just as we federalists felt we were fighting evil ideas rather than evil Germans, Italians and Japanese, so we were not fighting the noble men and women who had so valiantly tried to make the League of Nations work (and, later, to unite the untied nations); we were fighting the evil principle that had defeated and was bound to defeat much of their effort. Indeed, the United Nations has succeeded admirably in many aims, *apart from the primary aim for which it was established*!

Far from demolishing the magnificent palace occupied by the League of Nations, now used by some organ of the 'United' Nations, I hate waste, and would propose that it be converted into the Federal Ministry of the Environment. The able staff of the United Nations, or those who did not prefer to continue to deal with those parts of the world that still refused to be governed, would no doubt find better and more rewarding employment with the new Federal Union, where their efforts would be efficacious, and would not be continually defeated by the vicious principle of government of states by states and for states.

Apart from my objection to this principle as a blueprint for the new

## Don't Mend Old Sacks with New Twine

world order, I felt most strongly that if a new league were to be brought into being, especially as part of the war settlement, its very existence would provide a serious obstacle to world peace. People would say: 'Don't rock the boat. We have the new League of Nations. Let us give it a chance!'

Even today, when by a fluke the Security Council has succeeded in reaching an agreement, some commentators are remarking that this indicates that the organization is at last beginning to succeed. *Must we wait another half century before it gives its next sign of life?* Even now, it has voted sanctions against Iraq, but at the time of writing[1], weeks after the first decision, it refuses to give the states members the 'legal' right to implement them. Is this the efficiency required of a peacekeeping organ? The UN Military Staff Committee has done nothing for 45 years!

If you had a watch that told the correct time only twice daily, you might conclude that it was not working. Must we trust a 'peacekeeping' organization that functions adequately only once every half century?

At its inception, there were many, professed federalists among them, who proposed revision of the San Francisco charter into a federal constitution. But can a mouse evolve into a horse? Perhaps it could do so if mutation came into operation. Maybe a mouse has a better chance of evolving into a horse than a lump of inert inorganic matter has of developing into a living organism.

It was this train of thought that led me to oppose the San Fiasco Charter. In principle I could see the propaganda value of federalists urging revision[2] of the Charter, provided they explained why a nucleus federal union would be preferable. But the notion that a world-embracing league could convert itself into a world-embracing

---

[1] The 'Security' Council has at last, three weeks after the decision to impose sanctions, voted to permit them to be enforced. The USSR, however, declined to use force to implement the decision for which it originally voted! This was later amended to permit 'a UN force' to enforce sanctions.

[2] So far as security is concerned, the only amendments were made in August 1965, increasing the membership of the 'Security' Council by four states (Art. 23) and making it even more difficult to reach decisions (Art. 27). Merely cosmetic amendments! However, those who consider it dangerous to allow a league to make decisions will consider them improvements!

federation, and still be viable and democratic seemed to me utopian, and waste of effort to promote it.

Revising the San Francisco Charter seemed to me like trying to cross an abyss in two leaps.[3]

Similar objections can, of course, be raised against NATO and against the European Steel and Coal Community, which has since developed into the European Economic Community and shows signs of evolving into a federal union. Though I vigorously pointed out the disadvantages of an Atlantic Treaty compared with an oceanic federation[4], I felt it strategically preferable to concentrate on the failings of UNO. As regards the EEC, however, my sympathies have in the main been in favour.

One reason for this was that at the Hague Conference in May 1948 I realized from the outset that the Europe we were building would be a functional entity, driven mainly by federalists who were determined to convert it into a nucleus Federal Union open to all nations that are able and willing to join. This motive force consists of men and women who fully realize that they are trying to bridge a gulf, and that until the keystone of federalism is in place there is always the danger that the whole edifice will collapse and crush us beneath its ruins.

For instance, it may accumulate so many members before becoming a fully fledged federation that it may be difficult to reach agreement on any federal constitution.

During an inter-Scandinavian debate on television recently a Danish woman member of the European 'parliament' claimed that she had sought election merely for the sake of the information she could bring back from that 'undemocratic' body (as she described it). She complained that the European parliament had no power, and could pass legislation only with the approval of the Council of Ministers.

This may be true, but pressure from Members of the European Parliament will result in that body, since it is popularly elected, winning its due powers in course of time. Admittedly, this puts the

---

[3] There is, of course, what I choose to call the Chinese method of bridging an impassable river. Build both legs of the bridge on your side, and divert the river under it!

[4] A Norwegian proverb states that 'the ocean unites'. On heavy cargo, a voyage round the world costs less than a trip across a small continent.

## Don't Mend Old Sacks with New Twine

cart before the horse, but — for lack of a more promising approach — the movement towards a nucleus Federal Union still has my support.

The television debate was spoiled by the spectacle of an embarrassed young man who described himself as a 'federalist', but being completely unable to define the term or explain what federation means. The nearest he got to the federal idea was to say that federalists wanted decisions to be made at the appropriate levels, e.g. minor affairs at low levels and major matters at high levels. Even this did not come across very clearly.

I was acutely distressed on his behalf, and resolved to press on with this book with the utmost despatch. At any rate, the incident served to convince me that the simple elements of federation cannot be reiterated too often.

\* \* \*

## WHY UNO? BECAUSE WENO BETTER

Eight periodicals, including the *Twentieth Century*, published in Allahabad, considered the following criticism of the United Nations as suitable for publication, with its sometimes disrespectful allusions to the Dumbarton Oaks and Bretton Woods Conferences, to Paul-Henri Spaak, Belgian P.M. and Foreign Minister (who was a federalist), and to the San Francisco (U.N.) Charter.

### Why UNO? — Because WENO no better

If preserving the peace involved nothing more than wrapping it safely in cotton wool we shouldn't have to worry much about whether the Museum's Council of Curators were elected or nominated, and by whom; and about their rules of voting and whether they actually had the power, authority and money they needed to do their job without bungling it.

But this new world of technical efficiency is heading fast for disaster if it is being built on the criminal political inadequacies of the past. The machinery of international collaboration just won't work if constructed on unsound lines. To argue that the old 60-horse power League was alright but that the Members would not allow the contraption to work, is like saying that as long as the engine is in working order it doesn't matter if it is connected to the wheels with paper chains inscribed 'cooperation'.

Our new 5-cylinder 50-h.p. 'United Nations' League is the old chassis with bran-new Dumb Arton Hoax coachwork. Its engine will run on gas generated from Breton wood fuel mixed with hot air, ignited by a Spaak. The engine will not fire unless the Big Five cylinders synchronize – and they are designed to function independently. The horse power is so harnessed that the horses can, at a moment's notice, all pull in different directions.

To change the metaphor, does a house of cards gain stability by having two more stories added to it, even if each is as big as the USSR or the USA?

That this description of the San Fiasco Charter is not unfair can be seen from a study of its text, and the way in which it is functioning in Paris. Extraordinary care was taken in drafting it to deprive the Organization of the ability to perform its main duty – 'to maintain international peace and security'.

Its creators were faced with the alternatives of setting up an organism with the power to decide and act, or creating a sort of world conscience capable of neither, with powers no greater than a glorified debating society. By an ingenious compromise we now have a delightful mixture of both. Decisions will on occasions be arrived at and not carried out; on other occasions, by way of compensation, action will be taken without waiting for UNO to make up its mind. Although the voting procedure may too slow for the merits of a dispute to be decided before hostilities commence, it is hoped to be able to decide who should by rights have won the war by the time it is all over.

Voting procedure has been based upon the following denials of democracy:

◆ Disenfranchise all who do not support their Government for the time being in power.

◆ Distribute voting power among the member Governments on the basis of one Government one vote, even if this means that 150 million Americans south of the Rio Grande outvote 150 million Americans north of it by ten to one.

◆ In compensation, disenfranchise entirely the 150 million South

Americans and all other members of small nations when it comes to making decisions likely to affect the peace of the world.

### Loose False Teeth

The General Assembly does not even possess the right, let alone the power, to do anything else except 'discuss' matters and 'make recommendations', either to the States Members or to the so-called 'Security' Council.

The 'Security' Council cannot even arrive at a decision, let alone take action, on any matter affecting international law and order unless the Big Five are all agreed[1], and two of their stooges vote with them, in which case of course there would be no need for an organization to prevent world war, anyway. On the other hand, most disputes likely to disturb world peace will arise by reason of a disagreement between members of the big Powers. If the Big Five disagree, UNO is paralyzed. The new World League may have teeth, but they are false ones that will drop out the moment the jaws are opened.

Mr Ernest Bevin, British Foreign Secretary, estimates that UNO will cost the fifty-one nations, for a year, less than half the cost to the U.K. alone of one day of war. And even this paltry budget will be raised by voluntary contributions. The 'United' Nations Organization has no Treasury, no troops, no government of its own. Armed only with duties, it will speedily be made to look ridiculous by its failure to perform them.

It is no wonder that the British Foreign Minister, speaking in the House of Commons on 23 November, remarked:

'I am asked to re-study San Francisco. I have not only restudied it but, when it was being developed I was gravely concerned whether we were really finding the right solution. ... We are driven relentlessly along this road: the necessity for a new study for the purpose of creating a world assembly, elected directly from the people of the world as a whole – a world assembly with a limited objective; the objective of peace.'

Let us not reject UNO until we have something better. But let us make it quite clear to the statesmen that we demand something more inspiring than a ten-year diary inscribed 'Peace on Earth based on Goodwill to all men.'

---

[1] Decision making has since been made even more difficult; see Chapter 6.

## The Parliament of Man

International law will be meaningless until it is made by directly-elected representatives of the people, and acts directly upon people, through laws that do not have to be OK'd by fifty-one different parliaments before they are anything better than pious recommendations. So might our children survive to see the realization of Tennyson's vision of the Federation of the World.

\* \* \*

## 'FRISCO FARCE

Long after it had been written, the *Weekly Telegraph for Waltham Abbey, Cheshunt & Districts* (Mr Winston Churchill's constituency) published on 24 January 1947 the following letter from my lifelong friend G. E. I. Clements, LL.B.:

### The 'Frisco Farce
### By Flying Officer Edward Clements, R.A.F.

The soldier and the citizen home from the wars is being indoctrinated. Having fought so hard to win the war, he believes that the statesmen are fighting equally hard to win the peace. His governments, his press and all his means of learning what is happening in the world outside foster the idea that a sane world is being shaped upon sound international principles. Dumbarton Oaks, San Francisco, and the Paris Conference are placed before him as the grand preliminaries to a new international order.

But what is really being done? At the meetings of UNO so far held, Government delegates have all the time shown that they are not prepared to step out into the future, but are clinging to the old conception of alliances, mutual understandings and the League idea. It is clear that no greater international security has been achieved beyond that which would exist in any case so long as the Allies remained united in their determination to be the upper dogs. Once the coincidence of interests disappears there will be nothing left with which to secure the peace of the world. Already there have been squabbles over Poland, bickering over voting rights, disagreements over dependent territories, and many other demonstrations of the overriding consideration given by all to national as against international interests.

## Don't Mend Old Sacks with New Twine

Instead of this make-believe we should face the facts squarely. Whilst the devastation of man's bombing has been demonstrated and the potentialities of super-atomic weapons tasted, there has been no change in the traditional approach to the maintenance of international security. It has been clearly shown that whether the 'new' international order which came out of the San Francisco deliberations be called the Covenant of the League of Nations, the Charter of the Commonwealth of Nations or the Charter of Rights, it is still nothing but a formal expression of the intentions of the Great Powers, charter or no charter.

Charters do not keep the peace, nor do armaments. Only the genuine expression of the world community can keep the peace. And there is no world community. Yet the war itself has demonstrated the inter-dependence of all upon each other; the radio, the aeroplane and other means of rapid communication have made the world one. Every man, woman and child are today firstly 'Earthonians' and only secondly British, Americans or Russians. To achieve international security this fundamental fact must be acknowledged. At a peace conference there should not be government delegates, but the peoples' representatives elected and sent by the peoples of the world to establish a proper world order in keeping with the modern world society.

Clearly this involves the acceptance of the federal principle in international government. The time is ripe for the division of sovereignty between the nations and the world. The step forward in the logical evolution of government must be taken, and the moment to take it is now. Yet what are the statesmen doing? Whilst the men and women of the armed forces of all the great nations of the world have fought and are fighting together as one great army to win the war, their statesmen are struggling to gain advantage for their respective nations at the expense of their allies, and in the process are losing the peace. Once again the older generation are mortgaging the future because they are chained to the past.

*Author's note:*

Here was a voice that deserved to be heard, the voice of a fighting officer. Was it heard? Was it acted upon? After the war, F/O Clements was elected a member of the Common Council of the City of London, on which he still serves.

*The Parliament of Man*

## IS PEACE DIVISIBLE BY FIFTY-FIVE?

Since the following article was published (five times, in England and Belgium), membership of the United Nations has increased from 55 by over 100, making the organization even more unwieldy.

### Is Peace Divisible by Fifty-five?
### 'Peace,' said Litvinoff, 'is indivisible.'

If this is correct, then the statesmen are blundering when they try to parcel it out among the fifty-five members of the so-called 'United' Nations. By its Charter, the United Nations Organization confers upon itself a paramount task: 'to maintain international peace,' and at the same time deprives itself of the power indispensable to the performance of that duty. It leaves the power in other hands, distributed — or rather, dissipated — into fifty-five separate and mutually self-cancelling contingents.

The General Assembly is permitted only to 'discuss' and 'make recommendations', either to the member Governments or to the misnamed 'Security' Council. The Security Council cannot make a decision, let alone take action, unless the Big Shots are all agreed and two stooges vote with them, in which case of course there is no need for any formal organization to keep the peace anyway. If they disagree, UNO is paralyzed[1].

This is not to decry the value of UNO as an international debating society. The world still needs, alas!, a table round which the interplay of power politics can — with luck — proceed without bloodshed, and across which the guns can be pointed without the triggers being pulled. But we must recognize the ever-present danger that the disputants will adjourn to the battlefield. In the absence of peaceful means of deciding disputes and enforcing the decision, war remains the only arbiter. Even when UNO can reach a decision it cannot enforce it except, in the last resort, by embarking on war. We are asked once again to put our trust in an international organization that can keep the peace only by waging war.

There is but one basic cause of war: anarchy. The sole cause of

---

[1] 1992 note: The only two Security 'amendments' since then have made matters even more difficult.

## Don't Mend Old Sacks with New Twine

international war is international anarchy. Anarchy is what is says:

'Absence of government.'

There is but one cure for anarchy:

The presence of government.

Ergo, the only cure for international war is international government; the only cure for world war is world government. One may ask: 'Do we have to wait until World War III before we can say with certitude that UNO is no government?' Fortunately, the answer is 'No'. It is beyond the powers of any one author or statesman to specify all the powers and qualities that a world government must possess, but it is possible to demonstrate, here and now, over and over again, that UNO is not a government and is therefore incapable of curing or even ameliorating existing international anarchy.

UNO is not a government because it does not possess governmental power. Such power will never be conferred upon it so long as the peoples of the world do not trust it to govern in the interests of the governed. They will never trust it so long as it continues to be a cartel of sovereign states, a consortium of nominees of fifty-five separate national governments. One might as well expect the peace of the U.S. union to be maintained if Congress consisted of nominees from the forty-eight separate states, and if federal laws could not pass into operation until they were ratified by forty-eight separate legislatures. The position would be worse if the law did not operate upon individuals, but only on and through the State Authorities.

I shall not here discuss whether or not UNO can be converted into a government, except to point out that any important amendment such as this would require unanimous Four-Power[2] assent. Some means must, however, be found, and found quickly, of establishing an international government, by which I mean an organization based upon the following principles:

---

[2] 1992 note: Since the amendments to the Charter made in 1965 (Arts.23 & 27) this would now need five-power agreement, besides several other complicated requirements. Indeed, there may not be a sufficient number of members of the United Nations that are *qualified to ratify a democratic federal constitution*, even if their representatives voted in favour of it! For this reason alone, it is unrealistic to expect the UN to reform itself adequately.

◆ Its laws must not require ratification.

◆ The Representatives to the International Parliament must be elected not by the State Governments but by the people (thus reducing the risk of national bloc voting).

◆ International law must operate directly upon the individual citizens, not through the intermediary of the separate national governments. (The only way to enforce laws upon States as such is by war, or acts of war.)

◆ The International Government must have full governmental power in matters that have been agreed to fall within the sphere of international affairs, but this sphere can be restricted to, e.g. defence, foreign policy, inter-state aviation, and sufficient taxation powers to enable the international government to finance its legitimate activities.

War has hitherto failed to exterminate the human race only because the inadequate weapons previously employed could not compete with the birth rate. Now, in the atom bomb alone, we have a tool that can do the job nicely.

Bertrand Russell expressed the views of the Atomic Scientists (and of many political thinkers) when he recently broadcast the following words on the B.B.C.:

> 'There must be one central government, ... strong enough to insist on the substitution of law for anarchy ... Either we must, within the space of a few years, consent to an entirely novel form of political and military organization or, if we fail in this, we must expect a world-wide disaster surpassing in its horror all that past misfortune enables us to imagine.'

The task of creation that faces this generation is the most momentous in the history of the world. The alternative is chaos.

* * *

## UNO SLAYS BERNADOTTE

Written before I was aware of the fact that though men attack wolves, wolves do not attack men, this protest at the murder of a fellow federalist found the approval of six British, European and American

## Don't Mend Old Sacks with New Twine

editors, two of whom translated it into German and Dutch, respectively:

### UNO slays Bernadotte

'And Abram stretched forth his hand, and took the knife to slay his son' (Genesis, Chap. 22, v.10).

If a man is sent inadequately equipped into the midst of two rival packs of wolves, it may seem logical to blame the wolves when he is torn to pieces, but it is childish to give them all the blame. The world has been shocked to learn that one or other of the warring factions in Palestine has assassinated a Swede, instead of one of their 'official' foes. We rightly condemn the dastard who wielded the fatal tommy gun, and the clique of petty power politicians whose orders he was obeying. But it is not enough to blame the wolves.

I was privileged to read, only last month, the latest instalment of Count Bernadotte's memoirs, with a view to their eventual translation into English. I was immediately impressed with the admirable character of the man, and his fine philosophy of life. On my way to Luxembourg in preparation for the annual congress of the World Movement for World Federal Government (WMWFG), I discussed with a prominent Belgian federalist how to get the Count into our movement. The Belgian pointed out that Bernadotte could read and that he was intelligent; if at this late hour he had still not signed up as a federalist, therefore, he was too slow for our purposes, and should not be approached cap in hand. In Luxembourg the following day I was informed that Count Folke Bernadotte, U.N. Mediator in Palestine, had joined the Council of Honour of the World Movement for World Federal Government. So far as I could gather, he had enrolled on his own initiative.

The implication was obvious: like Sir John Boyd Orr, former head of U.N.'s World Food Organization, now President of WMWFG, he had seen how futile is the misnamed 'Security' Council, and how unworkable is the U.N. Charter from which the Council derives its duties and by which it is deprived of the ability to carry them out.

The world allotted to Bernadotte a task without the power to perform it. When one is given a job to do without the proper implements, there are two alternatives: one is to say 'Give me the tools and I will do the job, but not otherwise.' The other is to try to 'make do' with what lies to hand. Count Bernadotte was too great a humanita-

## The Parliament of Man

rian to refuse the high duty placed upon him. But the world should not demand two martyrs when one will suffice. His successor, if any, will have more altruism than sense.

### Pernicious principle

There is war in Palestine, sometimes overt, sometimes covert, because there is no alternative means of settling disputes and enforcing the settlement. This requires a superior agency that can arrive at decisions (which UNO cannot) and enforce them without war (which UNO cannot). The only way to avoid deadlock is to adopt the majority vote in a voting procedure by which the votes cast truly reflect the political power behind them; the only way to enforce decisions without war is to enforce them directly upon the individual citizen, not upon states and governments as such.

(The only way to coerce communities or their governments is, in the ultimate resort, by war).

Bernadotte died because the 'United' Nations is based on the pernicious principle of keeping the peace by making war. He died because its 'Security' system is an evil sham, a death trap for peace-loving nations and for idealists who love their fellow men.

Count Folke Bernadotte died on the altar of a false god, because the blind leaders of the blind worship the perverted principle of a league of sovereign governments, and because their noisy self-congratulations drown the voices of those world citizens who support the only constructive alternative: international federal government.

To the millions of federalists throughout the world, and to their myriads of sympathizers and supporters, Folke Bernadotte's death is a call to action. He died a martyr to our Cause.

*1992 note:*

Palestine, desperately needing a *government* after the British left it to its fate, was instead made a Mandate of the United Nations. It needed bread and was given a stone, as was German South-West Africa.

It is not surprising that Israel, Palestine's successor, seems to treat the U.N. with the contempt it deserves, as − at best − a nuisance to be tolerated, and − at worst − as a nuisance to be ignored.

In fairness to Israel, it must be pointed out that other states treat with contempt U.N. decisions with which they do not themselves agree. Witness the few days of grace which President Bush granted the U.N. in order to give it time to resolve to permit its blockade of Iraq to be enforced.

Incidentally, although – due to a coincidence of very rare factors – the U.N. has recently been able to reach decisions, this does not necessarily mean that we shall not have to wait another forty-five years before such factors coincide once again.

In a region where, years ago, the British drew frontiers in the desert sand and taught the Arabs the doctrine of the sovereign state, and in a world where the 'peace-keeping' organization can do so only by initiating warlike acts, statesmen are faced with a choice between two evils: war or appeasement. Opinions differ as to which is worse.

\* \* \*

## MASS HYPNOTISM AS AN ALTERNATIVE?

At least one reader failed to see that this article – published both in England and abroad – was satirical. One editor, I know not whether from sadism or absentmindedness, printed a letter in which this reader agreed with me, except for some minor objections in defence of league principles. On reading his reply, I began to doubt whether it is wise to use satire to promote such a serious subject as federalism! Humour should never need to be explained, but as the matter is so important I have marked with asterisks the main items of irony or sarcasm in this section! The reader must supply his own asterisks for the rest of the book!

### Mass Hypnotism as an Alternative to Government

Political scientists have throughout the ages sought long and earnestly for an alternative to government as a remedy for the disease of anarchy. In our own day, when the most dangerous form of anarchy is international, the anarchy that exists between the several dozen separate national sovereign states of the world, the theorists would have us believe that the only cure is international government.\*

This view has been courageously\* challenged by Mr Trygve Lie, Secretary-General of the 'United' Nations. 'The United Nations way,' he says, 'is the only way to peace.'

## The Parliament of Man

Nothing could be more dogmatic that this, except perhaps for the famous phrase: 'I am the Lord thy God ... I am a jealous God.'

In the science of governing the world without government, much valuable* pioneering work was done by the creators of the League of Nations, a laudable* attempt to scrape away the symptoms of war without harming the precious* germ of national sovereignty which causes it. Some cruel critics tend to take the view that a 'peace-keeping' organization is a failure if it fails to keep the peace, but it is generally admitted that, with the exception of the war years*, the League of Nations was a brilliant success.*

The principle of co-operation among governments enshrined in the Covenant of the League of Nations and in the Statute of Westminster[1] was accordingly embodied in the Charter of the 'United' Nations. This week is 'United' Nations week, and our slogan, and the title of this week's sermons, is 'The Only Way'. The cinemas will be showing 'Kill or Cure' or 'I will Repay the Doctor'.

Except for a few minor details in which it was more dainty, more delicate, than the old Covenant, there was nothing new in the United Nations Charter. Meticulous care was taken in drafting it to deprive the new organization of the power to carry out its decisions, and every difficulty was placed in the way of reaching decisions. This of course was a necessary safeguard, since the voting power was allocated in such a manner that the choice would inevitably be between agreed decisions that will not be put into effect, or unilateral action before decisions can be reached. The Charter is a skilful blend of these two ingredients, plus a large admixture of deadlock, an unfailing antidote to government well-known to political scientists since the earliest times of Polish history[2].

But this was not all. Members of the old League of Nations Association had pertinently pointed out that it was not enough for the nations to promise to be good. The people should also promise to be

---

[1] The 'Charter' of the British Commonwealth.

[2] Voting in the Polish parliament had to be unanimous. *1992 Note:* Incidentally, the present system of proportional representation has resulted in a parliament that is almost equally badly paralysed, leading to the current witticism in the country to the effect that where two Poles are gathered together, not only are they poles apart, but they represent at least three political parties.

## Don't Mend Old Sacks with New Twine

good. The League would not have failed* if only the people in all the lands had fallen on their knees and prayed for peace, if all the statesmen had gently tended their incipient haloes and governed (sorry, co-operatively organized) the world like demi-gods instead of like men. Government would have withered from the earth, and the era of perfect anarchy and perfect peace would have arrived*. And so, the new 'United' Nations Association has added one more ingredient to the UNO peace panacea. It is mass hypnotism.

Hypnotism has, of course, long been employed by medicine-men to induce tranquillity. Machiavelli recommended its use by a Prince who wishes to allay the suspicions of his enemies before subjugating them; serpents exert its soothing influence upon their prey before devouring it. It was doubtless with these antecedents in mind that Miss Dorothy Thompson[3], U.S. political scientist (believing that American peace and prosperity has something to do with Federal Government) described the UN Charter as:

> 'Something worse than nothing. It is nothing behind a facade of illusory security. Its sole purpose is to lull people to sleep in the face of danger.'

Even its critics cannot deny the somniferous effects of the Charter itself. The cathartic value of U.N.A's mass-mesmerism is, of course, considerably enhanced by the incessant chant: 'The Only Way, the Only Way', from pulpit, press, parliament and perambulator. When it is realized that UNO is the only thing that stands between us and an international law-making parliament and a government to enforce world law upon individuals by process of law, not war, critics should admit that perseverence in *the only way* to avoid government is well worth* the risk of a third deluge of blood.* In the meantime, if the people — except of course the die-hard advocates of international federal government who are allergic to hypnotism — can be made to 'hope for peace, pray for peace, think peace, believe peace and dream peace' (Prof. R.I.P. van Winkel) one day perhaps they may sleep in peace.

* * *

[3] (Cassandra). Once interviewed Hitler. The first U.S. correspondent to be expelled by him.

## SEQUEL TO THE DIKBARTON HOAX

In much the same vein were the following two articles:

### Report to His Excellency I
### Sequel to Dikbarton Hoax

(Your Excellency will please excuse my spelling; for secretarial reasons I am obliged to write this report in English)

You will recall that the Charter of the Untied Nations, as drafted at Dumbarton Oaks, was given final form at the subsequent San Fiasco Conference. The Charter is a Treaty, or Pact, between or among the High Contracting Parties, and is intended to ensure the peace of the world.

Assuming that the peace of the world will consist of the separate picccs, however, provision was made in the Charter for Regional Pacts, designed to protect the various regions from wars which UNO is designed to prevent.

I can report progress in this direction. By means of the Atlantic Pact it is hoped to create a pacific Atlantic: by means of a Council of Europe it is hoped eventually to unite sixteen or more members of the 'United' Nations in a unity that will be rather less of a plurality than UNO has turned out to be.

This development, too, follows the line that the peace of the world will be made less insecure it we create one or more little talking-shops inside the big talking-shop. (I should add that the British Government has taken the precaution of depriving the Council of Europe of the power which UNO itself so obviously lacks – the power to act upon decisions. It must be admitted, however, that they are right in maintaining that a debating society cannot be converted into a government merely by conferring paper powers upon it. As Your Excellency has so often impressed upon me, a Peace-Keeping agency cannot perform its duties unless it can enforce its decisions without waging war, and it cannot do this unless and until it is enabled to enforce its decisions upon individual citizens.)

Behind the scenes of UNO itself, this trend toward little wheels within the big wheel found expression in the creation of the 'Interim Committee of the General Assembly' (popularly referred to as the 'Little Assembly') The Little Assembly appointed a sub-committee. I

## Don't Mend Old Sacks with New Twine

quote below from James Nevins Hyde's report published in *International Conciliation* (No. 444):

> A comprehensive account of the approach and conclusions of the sub-committee and the Interim Committee will be found in the Preliminary Report ('Implementation of Paragraph 2(c) of the General Assembly Resolution of 13.11.47') of the sub-committee, which the Interim Committee adopted; the final report of the sub-committee and the report of the Interim Committee to the General Assembly, is substantially the same as the sub-committee's final report. Some members have seen in the beginning of this work a continuation of the Geneva tradition of organized measures for collective security.

Your Excellency will no doubt wonder what effort, if any, was made to ascertain whether the Geneva tradition of attempted 'government of governments, by governments, and for governments' made any contribution to security or, indeed, whether so-called collective security is an adequate substitute for international government. The position is obscure, but the foregoing facts regarding the deliberations of the Little Assembly, gleaned from J. N. Hyde's report, may throw light upon this question:

> 'In some of the discussions a distinction between mediation and conciliation was brought out. The Sub-Committee felt that ... it would be useful to consider what distinction, if any, exists between mediation and good offices ... It was suggested that in the future the scope and practice of arbitration might be considered ...'.

While the Little Assembly is debating the difference between mediation, conciliation, arbitration and good offices, and ignoring the difference between a debating society and a government, Your Excellency would be well advised to buy armament shares.

Discussing the proposed duties of 'a qualified conciliator' (whatever that may mean) the Little Assembly heard an objection to a resolution stipulating that the parties to a dispute 'shall meet'. This was amended to read that they 'shall be invited to meet'. As Your Excellency may appreciate, the risk of war vanishes to nil when a Power realizes that she will not be instructed to meet her enemy across the table, but merely invited. I must confess I had some difficulty at first in seeing how this made a tittle of difference, but I bow to the superior wisdom of statesmen. Still, considering the great difficulties in which they always land themselves when trying to juggle with international 'law', it is surprising they do not try to devise a system in which it operates directly upon individual human beings, instead of on governments as such.

China and the USA submitted a proposal suggesting *inter alia* that: 'the Interim Committee might also usefully examine the General Convention to improve the means of preventing war concluded at Geneva in 1931.'

Unfortunately, however, there was no reference to the rather more modern suggestions for abolishing war by means of international federal government. The Lebanon energetically sponsored a plan for setting up a permanent Committee of Conciliation 'capable of inspiring confidence and inducing by its sheer prestige and high moral purpose the requisite spirit of conciliation between the nations.'

In Your Excellency's next despatch, will you kindly inform me whether your sheer prestige and high moral purpose have been sufficiently sheer and sufficiently high to raise enough taxes from our people to pay my salary for the past quarter? Or did you use some other power by which to finance the welfare of our State?

\* \* \*

### Report to His Excellency II
### (The Dim. Ass.)

In my previous despatch I reported upon the progress made by the statesmen with the now fashionable policy of creating ever diminishing units within the wider 'unity' of the 'United' Nations, in the somewhat optimistic attempt to bolster up that frail and tottering organization.

I am able to report a fresh development in the direction of 'smaller wheels within the big wheel – smaller talking-shops within the big talking-shop.' From my last report Your Excellency will have learned of the latest news of the so-called 'Little Assembly' and of its subcommittee. It has since been my good fortune to be present at the first meeting of an even smaller and more august body – the Diminutive Assembly – which claims (with what authority I cannot say) to have been entrusted with the task of arriving expeditiously at decisions (which UNO cannot do), and enforcing them without war (which UNO cannot do, either). As your Excellency would be quick

## Don't Mend Old Sacks with New Twine

to point out, such a task is beyond the mandate and strength of any so-called 'authority', unless it be a government responsible to an elected parliament and having the right to enfore its decisions directly upon individual citizens, no matter what their nationality. Nevertheless, the futile deliberations of the Diminutive Assembly (the Dim. Ass. for short) may serve as an instructive example when the time is ripe for the extension of representative and responsible government across national frontiers.

The session opened on a note of informality from Mr L. O. U. Costeller, of Ruritania, who protested that Britain was plotting to prevent Ruritania from reincorporating into her territory the splinter State of Toprighthandcorneria. Mr Costeller ruled out force as a means of protesting further, because the Pope had spoken out against the use of force in this and in other matters. Mr Costeller objected to outside interference in the affairs of Ruritania. Ruritania would govern herself her own way and would tolerate no attempts by anyone outside her own borders to influence her course of action. If Toprighthandcorneria were restored to Ruritania, Ruritania could stand against the world.

Mr B. A. D. Abbott, of Toprighthandcorneria, suggested that Mr Costeller was out of order, since UNO's job, as Mr Evatt had already pointed out, was not to make peace but to tell the nations how to keep it when they had got it.

Count Bellagrandi Fiasco agreed, and called the first item on the agenda: the maintenance of the Charter of Human Rights.

Mons. Protocol pointed out that, according to the Charter of Human Rights, every human being has the right to an International Organization capable of upholding and defending his rights. Doubts had arisen whether UNO was such an organization. How, for instance, could UNO restore to an individual rights that had been denied to him by his national government? We should not get anywhere until UNO had its own police, like G-men or Mounties, to supplement the separate state police.

Senator Dumbarton H. Oaks pointed out that G-men and Mounties knew where they were because they had specific federal laws to enforce and uphold, whereas UNO police would be a band of poor bewildered stooges with no clear terms of reference, there being no international legislature to make the laws they were to enforce.

They would never know where their next pay packet was coming from, or how soon it would be before yesterday's orders were countermanded. If UNO's treatment of the Palestine problem was any criterion, the UNO police would be just a batch of enlisted Bernadottes[1], thrown to the wolves of either side, and expected to carry out half-a-dozen conflicting and contradictory policies in as many months.

'Before you talk about law enforcement,' he said, 'you have to have some law to enforce. An international government must come before an international police force could be established.'

Madame Dilys d'Alliance disagreed with this view, contending that the public would lose faith in UNO unless we did something sensational in the way of creating a UNO police or Guard in nice smart uniforms. And anyway, the nations should be asked to promise to give every facility to the UNO Guard in the execution of its duties. 'The nations must sign away some portion of their sovereignty for the sake of world peace,' she declared.

Mr Serge Pantz considered that the nations could sign away their sovereignty until they were all blue in the face, but so long as they retained it de facto we were making no progress whatsoever. In his view, sovereignty could be merged only by merging electorates, i.e. by creating a common electorate for the election of a common legislature. The separate electorates could remain in being, for the election of national governmment for purely national affairs.

Senor Postponi ridiculed this idea as utopian. Lake Success[2] was rightly named, he averred. Diplomatic history was a long record of failure, and he was quite prepared to believe that UNO would succeed no better than the League of Nations. 'But if at first we don't succeed,' he said, 'we should try, try again.'

Mr Serge Pantz agreed that the statesmen should try again, but they ought to try something else next time, instead of a league of

---

[1] Count Bernadotte was a member of the Council of Honour of the World Movement for World Federal Government, but nevertheless rashly agreed to try to perform UNO's task in Palestine, without the tools. He was assassinated there in 1948.

[2] Site of one of the conferences leading up to UNO.

*Don't Mend Old Sacks with New Twine*

sovereign states, bound together by paper promises. The meeting was dissolving into disorder when Count Bellagrandi Fiasco announced the adjournment.

\* \* \*

## COUNSEL FOR EUROPE

Encouraged by the success of my 'Socratic Lullaby' I wrote the following — also based on an actual conversation — which was published abroad in English and German:

**Counsel for Europe**

**Christopher Hamilton:**
What does P.U.D.C.W.W. stand for, Daddy?
**HSB:** *Paignton Urban District Council Water Works, I suppose.*
**CH:** Can we go to Urban tomorrow, Daddy?
**HSB:** *Urban's not a place, old man. It means 'for the town'.*
**CH:** Then why don't they say so? What does the Council for the town do?
**HSB:** *It arranges about keeping the streets clean and tidy and properly lit, and car parking and where the new buildings are to go and for the police and lots of other things, and how to share the cost among the people who live here.*
**CH:** Does the King send the Town Council to Paignton, Daddy?
**HSB:** *Goodness me, no! We English are democrats. We make our laws ourselves. The Council are elected by the local people. That is one reason why they obey the bye-laws. They made them themselves.*
**CH:** But most of the people in Paignton are visitors. They didn't make the bye-laws, did they?
**HSB:** *They have their own local councils and bye-laws at home, which work quite well, so they are prepared to accept other local bye-laws when they go visiting. If they don't, the police deal with them.*
**CH:** Does the Paignton Town Council have its own Hot Air Works, too?
**HSB:** *Wherever did you get that idea from?*

## The Parliament of Man

**CH:** Well, you said the Council of Europe was mostly hot air!

**HSB:** *That was a metaphor. It means it is all talking and no doing. The Council of Europe has been given a wrong name, like the United Nations. It is not like a Town Council: it has less power than the Paignton Urban District Council because it isn't able to make laws.*

**CH:** Like you said the United Dairies had more power than the United Nations Security Council because it can deliver the goods and it has a Board of Directors that can make decisions and carry them out!

**HSB:** *Good for you, Christoff!*

**CH:** But why do the newspapers make such a fuss of the Council of Europe? They said it would be the beginning of a Parliament for the World.

**HSB:** *They make a fuss of it because they don't understand it, and because the so-called statesmen make a fuss of it, too.*

**CH:** Why do they?

**HSB:** *The politicians are trying to persuade the people that it is the last word in political science, whereas in this atomic age they have revived an idea that was not new even before the age of steam. It is just another League, a little UNO with a new name, and with Southern Ireland playing the nigger in the woodpile instead of Russia. The only good thing it has shown so far is that men will vote with foreigners of their own party-political views, against their own countrymen who hold opposing political views. But the Council of Europe is not a Council at all, but an Assembly.*

**CH:** What's the difference?

**HSB:** *Well, the Congress of Europe at the Hague wanted the first official get-together to be a temporary body – what is called a Constituent Assembly – to draft a Constitution for Europe, that is, to make the rules for having a government for Europe as a whole. This Constituent Assembly would break up after the Constitution had been approved by the various member nations. A real European Parliament would then have been elected, with power to make laws about European affairs as a whole, and to enforce them without making war.*

**CH:** But surely, Daddy, the police can make the people obey the law without making war.

100

HSB: You've got something there! In fact anything that cannot be enforced by what I call peaceful policeful action is not law at all. That is why it is so silly to talk of international 'law'. But you see, there are no European police because there is no European Parliament to make the laws for them to enforce. You can enforce law without making war only if you enforce it directly on each person, each citizen, not on the separate governments or nations.

CH: Does that mean that the Council of Europe is just pretence?

HSB: I'm afraid so, Christoff.

CH: Like giving a baby a dummy to keep it quiet whilst it starves to death?

HSB: Yes.

\* \* \*

## PARASOLS VERSUS PARACHUTES

Here is another article which survived only in a German version (*Die Welt von Morgen*, Düsseldorf). I have translated it back into what might have been the original English:

### Parasols versus Parachutes

Most people are unaware that UNO cannot serve as a peace-keeping instrument. Many believe that everything depends on the intention, and not on the instrument. But if you wish to leap from an aircraft in mid-air, you use a parachute. You dare not trust a parasol, telling yourself: 'I can rely on my goodwill and determination.'

In spite of this reassurance, you break your neck.

In world politics we need an instrument, an organization, that can really keep the peace. Matters have been taken far too lightly in the past.

The Netherlands Foreign Minister, Mr van Kleffens, has given it as his view that UNO can avert only those conflicts that would not lead to war anyway, and the famous American columnist Dorothy Thompson is of the opinion that UNO is even worse than nothing, because it is nothing hidden behind a facade of illusory security.

*The Parliament of Man*

## THE FEDERATION OF THE WORLD

The following appraisal of my pamphlet *The Federation of the World* appeared in *Peace News* on 24 March 1950, by a reviewer unknown to me. The entire pamphlet was later published in *Humanity*.

**A recent pamphlet**
*The Federation of the World*
**by Harold S. Bidmead**

When I was at school our drawing master would set us working and then come round to criticize our effort. Sometimes he would advise alterations, sometimes make them himself, and sometimes, in hopeless cases, growl: 'rub it all out, and start again.'

That, briefly, is Mr Bidmead's advice to those who are trying to make the United Nations look like the Parliament of Man.

With wit and humour, sarcasm, analogy and a little logic, his pamphlet launches a vigorous attack on the present constitution of U.N. It is, he declares, nonsense to say that UNO is a step in the right direction. There is such a thing as trying to leap an abyss in two leaps, and even a step in the right direction is futile if progress is obviously so slow that one cannot possibly arrive in time. The setting up of a league is, however, a step in the wrong direction, a step from world anarchy to *legalized* world anarchy.

The only hope, for which there is still time, is to consign to the limbo where it belongs the perverted principle of 'a league of sovereign governments' and to begin to form a world-wide international government.

T.R.D.

*1992 Note:*

Over 40 years of experience of the United Nations have, in my view, completely justified the criticisms I levelled against it from the outset. This, of course, relates only to the futility of its purported peacekeeping rôle. However, recent events, particularly in connection with Iraq's invasion of Kuwait, give rise to the idea that I would have been a more successful prophet if I had made the following proviso to my assertion that the United Nations was incapable of reaching effective decisions in matters of world security and of putting them into practice:

## Don't Mend Old Sacks with New Twine

'The Security Council will be able to decide on sanctions against an aggressor provided that: the aggressor is clearly threatening interests that are common to all other members (e.g. petrol for their motor cars etc.), and the communist world has become so weak that the veto is unlikely to be used for dogmatic reasons.'

At the time of writing it remains to be seen whether sanctions against Iraq, and the blockade to enforce them, will be effective, though there are reasonable prospects of success because, through a one-in-a-million chance, the aggressor is in this instance too bankrupt to be able to offer sufficient in bribes to possible blockade-busters.

Similarly, events have almost miraculously coincided to enable neighbouring states and other members of the United Nations to agree to send troops to protect Saudi Arabia. This still leaves the old problem, to which my earlier writings continually referred, as to who will be in charge of any international force set up under the UN auspices? Even President Bush, weeks after the trouble started, has been careful not to say that the USA would be the leader.

Some idea of the chaotic conditions to be expected was given in a report of a meeting of the Arab League prior to its decision to send a joint force to Saudi Arabia. Its spokesman could give no coherent account of the deliberations in this respect, but added: 'Of course, we must not forget that Zion is the real enemy.'

Even if the problem of unified command were solved satisfactorily on paper, every Arab or Moslem, in no matter what uniform, will be suspected as a possible partisan in the aggressor's 'holy war' to protect Mecca and Medina from the infidels. The United Nations force will have a fifth column, far more dangerous that the one of which General Franco boasted when the term was first used. We shall be fighting, simultaneously, both a Crusade and a war to keep our motor cars comfortably running.

It is significant that Saddam Hussein is not a religious man, and the State of Iraq is secular, but he is using religious arguments in his fight. This is just one more item of evidence that religious strife may be more the result of national statehood than the cause of it. Federation enables ethnic and religious borders to be drawn where strategic considerations previously forbade it. A federation could accommodate Moslems, Jews and Christians without strife, provided the boundaries and other conditions were just, though the world may have to wait for present generations, brought up to hate each other, to die out before that era can be ushered in.

Some 'idealists' will, of course, be fighting to punish the aggressor, though if (ideally) execution is not an appropriate punishment for murder, then neither is destructive war an ideal punishment for aggression.

Another significant element in the United Nations sanctions against Iraq was that the USA's immediate action to implement the U.N. resolution was criticized by some states on the grounds that the U.N. had voted sanctions but had not voted that they were to be enforced. The implication was that if the complainant states had voted in favour of sanctions, they had done so only because they did not expect sanctions to be implemented![1]

This tended to confirm our earlier predictions that even if the U.N. ever succeeded in reaching decisions, there would still be grave obstacles to their being obeyed.

---

[1] Since this was written, the USSR has voted against enforcing the blockade for which it originally voted. Later still, it amended this to permit force to be used only under the ægis of the U.N.

# CHAPTER 6

## THE COMMONWEALTH OF GOD
## (Civitas Dei)

As an introduction to my friend Lionel Curtis, C.H., I make no apology for reprinting the following review of his pamphlets which was published, *inter alia*, in *Free Europe* and the *Fortnightly Review of International Affairs* in August 1943.

Concerning Lord Lothian's reference to Lionel's 'determination to remain in obscurity', I would comment that just before publication of his book *World War, Its Cause and Cure*, Curtis expressed regret at his former modesty. Taking me solemnly by the arm, he rather flatteringly said to me:

'If you are ever offered a knighthood or any other distinction, Harold, do not turn it down! You will find that people will afterwards listen more assiduously to what you have to say. I have made that mistake in my life, and I now regret it.'

In 1949, Lionel Curtis was made a Companion of Honour, one of the favoured 100 — belated but well merited recognition. Thus he thereafter took precedence above the Knights Commanders even of the Orders of the Thistle and St. Patrick, of the Bath, of Merit, of the Star of India, of St. Michael and St. George, of the Indian Empire, of the Royal Victorian and of the British Empire.

When he passed over, all the trumpets will have sounded for him on the other side.

## FAITH, DECISION, ACTION

The disarmament of Germany and post-war settlement are discussed *ad nauseam* in the Press, in Parliament and on platforms – but seldom the one question that governs all others – the question how we are to equip ourselves with the strength necessary to do all the things we are pledged to do. Few of the would-be planners of the New World seem to understand the basic principles of Power. For example, to chant the soothing formula 'The Big Four Together will maintain world peace', without considering its implication, is as rational as to declaim: 'O Churchill, Roosevelt, Chiang Kai-shek and Stalin, live for ever!' and to expect that they will. Neither is it any use constructing a sixty-horse-power League when the League type of harness ensures that each horse pulls in a different direction.

To discuss problems such as these the B.B.C. brought a new voice to the microphone one evening last February, and to my ears it seemed that the British lion was at last on its feet again, mentally as well as physically. Mr Lionel Curtis, Fellow of All Souls College, Oxford, whose voice it was, did not presume to preach to any nation but his own. But he did urge upon his fellow voters in the United Kingdom 'the fact that in this century the British Commonwealth, as now constituted, has failed to prevent two major wars. The League of Nations formed on the same model has failed to prevent this second war ... We should tell the Dominions that we are prepared to consider with them the creation of a government which commands wider resources than those of Great Britain and Northern Ireland for the common defence. But any government which commands the resources of countries beyond the British Isles must, on the principles for which we are fighting, draw its authority from the peoples of those countries, no less than from the peoples of the British Isles. All this applies no less to our Allies, especially to Belgium, Holland and Norway ... The real key to peace is to plan not for the weakness of our enemies, but for the strength of those who seek peace as we do.'

The speaker was well qualified to give advice. In 1901 he was appointed Town Clerk of Johannesburg by Lord Milner. After the South African war he was entrusted with the task of organizing Local Government throughout the Transvaal. Some years later he was associated with Philip Kerr, who afterwards became Lord Lothian, in organizing the movement that led to the Union of South Africa. When, in 1917, the British Government adopted the policy of establishing responsible government in India, Mr Curtis suggested the system known as Dyarchy. This was adopted by Lord Chelmsford and Mr Montagu and became the basis of the first step towards responsible government in India embodied in the measure passed by Parliament in 1920. In 1921 Mr Curtis was secretary of the Conference that negotiated the Irish Treaty and till 1924 was adviser to the British Government in Irish affairs. In 1938 he accompanied Lord Lothian and Mr Ernest Bevin to the unofficial Conference on British Commonwealth Relations, held at Lapstone, near Sydney. After the Conference, Honorary degrees were conferred on Lord Lothian and Mr Curtis by Melbourne University. After Lord Lothian's death, Mr Curtis edited his *American Speeches*.

Lionel Curtis has an uncanny gift of firing others with enthusiasm for his ideas; this he combines with a relentless determination to employ his talents to the utmost benefit of mankind, coupled – as Lord Lothian once put it – 'with an equally relentless determination to remain in obscurity'.

It has been said of him that his greatest contribution to political thinking was his conception that the scientific method must be applied to the study of international affairs. In founding Chatham House (the Royal Institute of International Affairs) he did for international affairs what was done for science when the Royal Society was founded. He has since made an even greater contribution to the public good of the world – the results of his own researches into the causation of war and the principles of enduring peace. The three volumes of his *Civitas Dei* – in his own words 'a book too long for all but a few to read' – had appeared between 1934 and 1937. His first popular pamphlet, *Decision*, applying his findings to the questions of the hour, was published in 1941, followed by *Action* in 1942 and *Faith and Works*[1] this summer (all published by Oxford University Press).

Each has something new to say, and deserves to be read for its own sake. Each has the same main theme running through it:

> The safety of free systems is always to look to their own strength and not to measures for weakening their enemies . . . In 1914 the British Commonwealth had failed to prevent the outbreak of world war. In 1919 a League was constructed on the model of the British Commonwealth, into which that Commonwealth was incorporated. By 1939 the two together had

---

[1] Faith, if it hath not works, is dead. (Epistle James, 2.17)

completely failed to prevent the outbreak of an even more terrible war. (*Decision*).

At the close of the last war public opinion was possessed by the one idea, the League of Nations, by the belief that the peace of the world could be based on compacts between sovereign states. In this war public opinion is again possessed by one idea, that the peace of the world can be based on compacts between the sovereign states of the British and American Commonwealths. The principle is the same, and its second application will lead on to calamities great as the first, and perhaps in one generation. (*Action*).

'Influence is not government' (George Washington). I have often used these memorable words in answering those blind leaders of the blind who have taught the world that international problems can be solved by co-operation only, and have helped thereby to lay it in ruins ... Should a system which has failed to prevent two major wars be commended, as it has been commended, to our Allies as one which can be trusted to prevent future wars?' (*Faith and Works*).

*Decision* contains a notable study of the difference between despotic and democratic systems, and an analysis of the principles of supranational government discovered by Washington and his associates in 1787:

> The central body was powerless as a government so long as its authority was derived from a number of sovereign states. It could make effective decisions only if it derived its authority directly from the citizens themselves, and was thus able to enforce those decisions directly on every citizen. Its laws must not have to run the gauntlet of all the separate legislatures before they become valid.

It also includes a chapter on the implications of the British offer of union to France. The main argument is that a joint defence system should be initiated immediately after the war by the United Kingdom and such of the Dominions as feel that they are ready forthwith to comply with the obligations it implies. One set of ministers and legislators would thus handle defence and matters inseparable therefrom; while in each component State another set of ministers and legislators would be free to handle their own domestic and social affairs. The system could in time be broadened to include European democracies, e.g. Belgium, Netherlands, Denmark, Norway. If once the Western Democracies had united with the British Commonwealth for their common defence, it should become possible to extend the same system, with the same obligations and responsibilities, to Britain's allies in Eastern Europe – the USSR, Poland,

## The Commonwealth of God

Czechoslovakia, Jugoslavia and Greece. If the USA were to join such a system, the era of world wars would be finally over.

*Action* deals with objections that had been raised concerning its predecessor. It shows what machinery the United Nations require to implement the Atlantic Charter. There are some who confuse the issue of international government by implying that the question is intimately bound up with the fate of Germany, or that the establishment of an international government depends on our being lenient to the Germans. These misguided people overlook the fact that no matter how we treat the Germans, whether history will judge us to have been over-lenient or over-harsh, or to have given them their just deserts, the United Nations should at least take the precaution – in advance – of forming themselves into a permanent Defence Union, if only to be sufficiently strong to face up to the consequences if and when our sins of omission and commission should catch up with us. Curtis takes the sensible view:

> 'I regard as chimerical any proposal to include the Germans in an international commonwealth which has not already included the American as well as the British Commonwealth, and that will not be within one generation after this war.'

*Faith and Works* is the best pamphlet of the three. It received a gratifying welcome in the Press. Sir William Beveridge, in a half-page review in the Observer said:

> There must be both national Governments and an international Government. This double theme is developed by Mr Curtis with a combination of eloquence, practicality and historical illustration which make, between them, an argument of compelling force.

Appended to the pamphlet is a declaration signed by some forty people, drawn from all walks of life, many of them of great eminence and erudition, proclaiming:

> We find ourselves convinced that ... we cannot begin to discharge our commitments under the Atlantic Charter unless we create a government which commands resources wider than those of Great Britain and Northern Ireland. It is clear that such a government must derive its authority from the peoples who provide those wider resources, as well as from the peoples of the United Kingdom.[2]

---

[2] See the note at the end of this chapter for a list of signatories.

# The Parliament of Man

These pamphlets should be read by all who feel tempted to put their trust once more in a revived League of Nations, by those who defend or attack national sovereignty without understanding it, and, in fact, by all who are interested in the peace of the world in general and of the small nations in particular.

\* \* \*

## TRADE IN A FEDERATION

The following of my many reviews of *Faith and Works* was translated into French and Spanish and appeared, *inter alia*, in New Zealand, South Africa, France, Luxemburg and the U.S.A.

### In a World Federation, How Would Trade Fare?

If the declared aims of the United Nations are to be achieved, a Battle for Freedom from Want must follow this war. But the nations cannot fight that battle if they are at the same time engaged in economic warfare amongst themselves. Attempts to abate trade war by means of agreements between States that retain the power to break their pledges inevitably fail. It is time we explored the alternatives.

In his latest book *Faith and Works*[1], Mr Lionel Curtis shows how closely related are the twin problems of Freedom from Want and Freedom from Fear of War. He sets out to show how we must organize the United Nations, and the British Democracies in particular, if the world is to achieve prosperity after the war. It is not enough to make reasonable profits on a good turnover if they are nearly all swallowed up in taxation to pay for defence preparations or to fill a foreign exchange equalization pool.

Our first step, says Mr Curtis, should be to set up a popularly elected parliament and government for the British Commonwealth as a whole, to deal with international affairs, leaving all other powers with the separate governments where they now rest. Other democracies should be invited to join such a system at the outset or subsequently; it would thus be a nucleus of eventual world government.

This book, perhaps the most authoritative of all such proposals, would give the central government power over only defence, foreign

---

[1] Oxford University Press; with Foreword by Sir William Beveridge and a declaration of support signed by forty prominent men, including Sir Henry Price, Lord Craigmyle and Lord Meston.

policy, colonies, civil aviation, and effective means of financing such activities (since an 'authority' that relies on voluntary contributions, whether based on paper promises or not, cannot be regarded as a government). The author would thus leave all internal and social affairs, including the incidence of taxation between one tax-payer and another, to the national governments as before.

The only type of inter-State or foreign trade that such a government would control would thus be trade in armaments and accessories. But there are other, more far-reaching proposals by which the federal government would be given powers to regulate all inter-State trade and trade with countries outside the federation (cf. 'Peace by Federation' by Sir William Beveridge in *World Order Papers 1940*, published by the Royal Institute of International Affairs). In Mr Curtis' view a federation could keep the peace without possessing such powers. On the other hand, all federalists are agreed that a central authority having power over economic matters (schemes erroneously termed 'economic federation'), but lacking full powers over the instruments of military and political warfare would not be a federation at all, and would tend to break up sooner or later into warring fragments.

It is surely not over-optimistic to hope that the lessons of experience will this time lead at least the democratic nations to retain their present system of pooled defence, and perpetuate it under a common parliament which will ensure that, for all time to come, their differences will be settled by bloodless litigation in accordance with an agreed constitution. Such a system might well be so strong that none would dare to challenge it, so just that none would wish to attack it, and so successful that all would clamour to join it.

One only has to consider the implications of Lease-Lend, the Hot Springs Conference, the pooling of merchant shipping, and the innumerable Joint Economic Boards, to realize that in view of the undesirability and sheer impractiblity of unravelling these inter-Allied arrangements – involving the equation of money with time and blood – those nations that pool their arms in a permanent United Nations system might also decide to entrust the federal government with power to supervise these matters as well, namely: inter-State and foreign trade relations, and inter-State and foreign currency policies.

This does not necessarily mean free trade throughout the federation, nor does it necessarily mean there would be a federal monetary unit (e.g. Unitas or Bancor) or that exchange rates would be immutably fixed between the federating states. Such matters would be

## The Parliament of Man

decided by the Federal Parliament in the best interests of the federation as a whole.

It must be borne in mind, however, that an international financial and trade system based on the Keynes or Morgenthau or similar plans is unstable so long as 'it rests upon international treaties to which States voluntarily adhere. A State would be free to join or not to join the Clearing Union, and − having joined − free to resign at will.' (Barbara Wootton. M.A.Cantab. − 'The Keynes Plan,' *Federal Union News*, June 1943.) Keynes himself admits this, for he describes his plan as an instrument of international government, implying that an international government will be needed if the instrument is to be properly wielded.

My conclusions, therefore, are as follows:

International anarchy can be cured only by international government. Such a government must derive its powers directly from the citizens, through a popularly elected parliament, and its laws must act directly on the citizens, not through the medium of the separate parliaments. Such a government can therefore be composed only of democratic peoples.

Where we cannot get international government we shall have to be satisfied for the time being with an improved league system, plus any peaceful influence the federation can exert in its foreign relations.

The international government might be empowered to regulate inter-State and foreign trade in the same way as the national governments normally regulate domestic and foreign trade. It is impossible to foresee which trades, if any, would benefit more than others from such a system. It can be said, however, that only within a federation can international collaboration be adequate to tackle many of our economic evils, e.g. unemployment and pauper standards of living. The cost of maintaining armed forces within the federation would be negligible compared with the combined cost of arming each State separately against every other state, and the economies would be available for raising standards of living all round.

\* \* \*

## A COMMONWEALTH OF PEOPLES

Over a dozen periodicals, including the *Imperial Review, Empire Record, World Community, Twentieth Century, Blackfriars, Plan,*

# The Commonwealth of God

*St.James Leader* (Canada), *Speculative Mason, Independent,* and *Arbitrator* published the following version of my reviews of *Decision and Action*, under the heading:

## A Commonwealth of Peoples

Provided we do not blind ourselves to its present defects, nor leave its latent potentialities unexplored, the British Commonwealth method of regulating international affairs is regarded in some circles as a model suitable for wider application.

However, as Lionel Curtis pointed out in *Decision and Action*:

> In 1914 the British Commonwealth had failed to prevent the outbreak of world war. In 1919 a League was constructed on the model of the British Commonwealth into which that commonwealth was incorporated. By 1939 the two together had completely failed to prevent the outbreak of an even more terrible world war.

Curtis classified political systems under two heads: organic (states such as Great Britain, federations such as USA) and inorganic (*con*federations, leagues, alliances). The British Commonwealth he regarded as a mixture of both, its effective functioning — such as it is — being primarily due to some degree of hegemony exercised by the Mother Country. Curtis argued that inorganic systems were unstable and that — as regards international coalitions for war purposes — 'history, when it comes to be written, always shows how the inorganic bond of alliance hastened defeat or delayed victory'.

'Organic' does not just mean 'organized', nor does it merely imply a system having constitutional power to expand its boundaries or admit new members. The distinction is that which George Washington made between 'influence' and 'government' when persuading the American States to scrap their ten-year-old League of Friendship in favour of the federal union that has developed and endured to this day. His collaborator Alexander Hamilton, writing in 1787 for the *Independent Journal* on 'the characteristic difference between a league and a government' urged:

> We must extend the authority of the Union to the persons of the citizens — the only proper objects of government ... In an association where the general authority is confined to the collective bodies of the communities that compose it, every breach of the laws must involve a state of war; and military execution must become the only instrument of civil obedience. Such a state of things can certainly not deserve the name of government, nor would any prudent man choose to commit his happiness to it.

## The Parliament of Man

Unless a league is to die on its feet it must have government power. But unless this power is to degenerate into an instrument of despotism it must be derived from the consent of the governed. This implies a common elected parliament to deal with affairs which in the constitution were agreed to be of common concern to all the partners, and a common government answerable to its citizens through the Union parliament.

No democratic nation should experience any insuperable difficulty in accepting these proposals, and the only theoretical arguments that could be opposed to them are arguments against the democratic principle itself. Affairs common to all might be defined as defence and foreign policy, and administration of all international conventions. A written constitution would be necessary, since the powers of an international authority must be precise and cannot be left undefined or unrestricted.

The system such as is here advocated would be the dynamic without which no looser world-wide association of states could hope to succeed.

The pressure of world events towards international unity is inexorable. Let us harness these forces for the common good and steer them the way we wish them to go, rather than remain supine and allow ourselves to be driven hither and thither by every wind that blows, sheltering from every fresh storm under some ramshackle improvisation. That nations must wherever practicable enter into organic constitutional union for the specific purpose of safeguarding their liberties is a lesson which the failure of leagues, alliances and other symptoms of collective insecurity has proved up to the hilt. It is equally clear that, once having taken this step, every nation could with an honourable conscience claim the right of complete independence in affairs that are its own private concern. Only thus can we ensure that the world of the future will be built on a pattern rather more inspiring than that of a multi-cellular sponge, with nothing to choose between one cell and another. Looked at in this light, the solution herein proposed may be the only means of securing at the same time the safety and independence of nations.

We who are inherently capable of establishing a genuine international government among our own peoples owe it to ourselves, and to those who may look to us for guidance and leadership, to take a

*The Commonwealth of God*

first step towards a democratic Commonwealth of Peoples in the cause of world peace.

As General Smuts once prophesied of the new world order:
'We hope to build a Union which no Hitler of the future, and not even hell itself, shall venture to challenge again.'

* * *

## THE BRITISH COMMONWEALTH AS A NUCLEUS OF WORLD GOVERNMENT

One day in 1947 I received an urgent telephone call from Lionel Curtis, Fellow of Old Souls College. Could I come down to Oxford that week-end for an important conference with him regarding his forthcoming book *World War, its Cause and Cure*. Ever since *Faith and Works*, where I had been honoured to be included in an appendix listing those who had assisted in its preparation, Lionel had used me as a sort of sparring partner for this subsequent book.

In any case, I was glad of any excuse to meet once again with this most stimulating federalist colleague. In his youth, Curtis had been one of Lord Lothian's team of young men which attained much achievement, and Lionel was now a great believer in teamwork (though he not surprisingly treated his 'cabinet' on the American rather than on the British pattern).

Arriving in Oxford on the Friday, as agreed I was met with the news that Lionel would be busy that evening, but had arranged accommodation for me in his secretary's flat (she was away). He hoped I could find something to occupy me in Oxford until the following day.

On meeting him the next morning I was pleased to be able to tell him, in reply to his question, that I had spent a most enjoyable evening at a public dance at the Town Hall. He was deeply intrigued, surprised — and I seemed to detect an air almost of shock.

'But what on earth did you do for a partner?' he asked, clearly mystified.

'Oh,' I said, 'I danced all evening with the prettiest girl in the room.' (This, to my mind, was true!)

Very seriously, Lionel Curtis addressed me as follows:

'Surely, Harold, you felt it your duty, as a Christian gentleman, to dance with the homeliest girls?'
Not sharing his gravity, I replied:
'No, Sir, I thought it was my Christian duty to leave the homeliest girls for the homeliest men.' (I was then single again.)

Lionel ordered for us a magnificent luncheon, accompanied by sweet cider in silver tankards, which was served in his study on piles of books, and we then got down to the one item on the agenda. Whether he had solved his other problems in the time that had elapsed since his telephonic summons I do not know, but all that now remained was for him to say:

'A very important matter is still to be decided. The publishers have asked me what colour is to be the cover of *World War, its Cause and Cure*?'
I replied, without a moment's hesitation:
'Olive green, of course.'
(If, as I devoutly hope, the reader will read this book, he will see that the cover is indeed *olive* green).

Curtis accepted this immediately, with apparent satisfaction, commenting that such a swift answer related more aptly to his pamphlet *Decision*.

A was naturally a trifle crestfallen at the thought that my journey to Oxford had not been occasioned by more world-shaking considerations, but it seemed clear that Lionel wished to show some recognition of my help, e.g. the score or so of reviews of his pamphlets I had had published so far.

A year later, at the Congress of Europe at the Hague, I reminded Curtis of this incident when the organizers cunningly divided the participants into a Political Committee (the doers) and the Cultural Committee (the talkers). This clever manoeuvre resulted in almost complete unanimity in the Political Committee, and even the Cultural Committee managed to decide that the European symbolic colour should be green. (It is not olive green, but the colour now seen on European motorway signs.)

This was the occasion when Curtis confided in my ear, whilst in the tram taking us to the Amsterdam public meeting, that 'the Dutch seemed just the sort of people one would like to federate with.'

I seem to recall that it was that same afternoon in Oxford that

## The Commonwealth of God

Curtis introduced me to Quintin Hogg, who was strolling in the garden outside the study window. Hogg[1] treated us to a lecture on the reason why, as a politician, he could always say, fearlessly, exactly what he thought, since no matter what the electorate did to him he would still finish up in Parliament – in the House of Lords by reason of the law of succession.

This we took as evidence tending to confirm the argument for an Upper Chamber of the Federal Parliament, so that at least some voices could be raised that were not inhibited by the next general election.

I was the guest of All Souls for dinner that evening, with Sir George Trevelyan, the author of *A History of England*, etc., on my one hand and Lionel Curtis on the other, along with several other gentlemen whose names now escape me.

I recall yet another incident, which took place on a previous occasion, in the garden of Lionel's home, which I remember most clearly for its delicious apples. Although opposed in principle to divorce, Curtis supported me in my decision to divorce my first wife. He took that occasion to confide in me that, having rather late in life married his secretary, he was overjoyed that he had done so, now realizing that marriage can be one of life's greatest blessings.

I have thought fit to include the above anecdotes, as illustrations of the fact that even great men are human.

When the time came to review *World War, its Cause and Cure*, the periodicals accepting my review included *International Affairs* in New Delhi, India, as follows:

### World War, its Cause and Cure, Lionel Curtis, Oxford U.Press
#### The British Commonwealth as a Nucleus of World Government

In the battle for peace, the main enemies are apathy, ignorance and prejudice. Those who are neither apathetic, ignorant nor prejudiced are mostly rogues, and if the battles against the first three are won, the rogues can be mopped up afterwards.

---

[1] Afterwards Lord Hailsham; he later temporarily relinquished the title to become Lord Chancellor of England.

## The Parliament of Man

If our strategy is sound we can afford to make tactical mistakes and still win through to victory, but if our strategy is unsound no amount of tactical brilliance will redeem us from disaster[2].

The strategic objective of all peace builders should be to establish a nucleus international government that will live and grow. We have to create a new nation; a nation of nations, not a league of nations.

Even if every citizen in a certain geographical or idealogical area could be persuaded to endorse a Charter of Rights and a Federal Constitution, this would not necessarily ensure the success of the Union. The League failed because the States Members would not work the Covenant. True, a continuous series of near-miracles is required if a covenant between sovereign states (e.g. UNO) is to function.

It is far less difficult to make a popular constitution work, but it is none the less true that it is not enough to bring an international government into being; it must also be made to operate. We must also recognize that the constitution will not be established at all unless the prospective constituent peoples believe it can be made to succeed, and for this they will have to feel a high degree of mutual trust.

Will the people of Europe trust each other to operate an international constitution, when many of them have not yet learned to wield a national one, or to unite their warring factions within their respective frontiers? Would, for instance, a maritime nation surrender sovereignty over its navy to an international authority derived from an electorate of which a majority have never even seen the sea? Will a nation that is at present responsible for the defence of a quarter of mankind scattered over the face of the earth, surrender its arms to a cosmopolitan body on which its own sister nations are not represented? Can the people of this island afford to cast British foreign policy – such as it is! – upon the troubled waters of clashing antipathies and hatreds – into the linguistic whirlpools of Europe?

A majority of our fellow citizens might answer these questions in the negative; others would perhaps be prepared to put them to the test of practical experiment.

[2] Dictum of Admiral Mahon, quoted by Curtis. Desert Storm was a classic proof of the truth of this dictum. Note that in essence this is a question of definition, showing the vital difference between strategy and tactics.

## The Commonwealth of God

The practical course would appear to be to build world unity on the unity that already exists. If the member nations of the British Commonwealth were to discuss among themselves the establishment of a Commonwealth Parliament for Commonwealth defence, the proposal already mooted on several occasions over the radio and in *The Times* and other newspapers, could be revived, namely: that our friends in Western Europe should be invited to join in at the outset, since their defence problems are inextricably involved with our own.

(Incidentally, their voting power would serve to redress the balance between the United Kingdom and the various Dominions. In a community where all are minorities, minority rights are better respected.)

Such an initial federation would be a promising nucleus, for it would have 'induction points' all over the world for the recruitment of new members. It would have friendly 'bridge-heads' on the Continent of Europe. Canada and Australia would be links in its liaison with the USA. Once the United States joined in, the whole of the rest of Europe could be expected to come in without fear of German preponderance, and with every prospect of extending a genuine welcome to Russia[3] if she was yet prepared to participate.

It must be remembered that the admission of any new member to any nucleus federation would set up new stresses and strains, which must be taken up and stabilized before the process is repeated. This may be one reason why so few of the existing national federations have expanded in this manner.

Eminent statesmen have proposed that the 'geographical unit' of Europe should also be regarded as the political unit most likely to constitute the nucleus of a world federation. But its Eastern frontier would partition the USSR; this alone demonstrates the absurdity of looking upon Europe as a natural political entity. And how could a European nucleus grow? By 'absorbing' the USSR, the Middle East and North Africa? Would such expansion make membership look more attractive to other nations still on the waiting list?

One can sympathize with proposals for a nucleus to consist of the British Commonwealth and the USA, or for a democratic federation open to any country, anywhere in the world, despite considerations

---

[3] 1992 Note: I meant the USSR. This remark could now be construed to mean the state of Russia, now that the USSR no longer exists.

of geography and defence strategy, but it seems reasonable to suggest that the first step in each of these schemes should be to try to thrash out a common British Commonwealth policy on the question. Otherwise, if the Government of Great Britain and Northern Ireland takes the initiative it will be apt to give the impression that we are prepared to sacrifice the Dominions for Continental or American ties.

A common argument in favour of European federation is that 'all the other wars have started there.' Even if, for the sake of argument, we accept this premise, we need not accept the implication that the next war, if any, will start in Europe. Besides, if we always applied the remedy where the pain was, the Faculty of Medicine would be in sorry disgrace today.

Once created, the federation must live and grow. But its actual creation also has a bearing on our problem. A horse that is led to the water is more likely to drink than one that has to be driven. The federation that is least difficult to create will be most likely to flourish.

Let us explore the lines of least resistance; otherwise the task will prove to be immeasurably beyond our strength.

If this country were to be divided over the issue of *international* government as India is divided over the religious question, we should have failed indeed. But the idea of a federation of the British Commonwealth and the democracies of Western Europe enjoys wide support. The series of pamphlets written by Lionel Curtis, Fellow of All Souls, Oxford, which culminated in his book *World War, its Cause and Cure* has been welcomed — in at least six languages — by a large and representative section of the press, ranging from Commerce, Agriculture and Shipping, to the various political and religious creeds, from the organs of the Protestants, Catholics, Freemasons, Christian Scientists and Atheists, to those of the Empire and Crown Colonial associations, and in the London, provincial, suburban and foreign press. In no instance is the need for better Commonwealth unity disputed.

It would perhaps be a fair criticism of the Curtis school of thought to say that some enthusiasts give the impression that the British Empire has a greater responsibility to uphold world peace (and a greater responsibility for the two failures) than have the other Powers. Such zeal may be excessive, but it errs on the right side. If we

## The Commonwealth of God

all considered it our duty to strive to accomplish more good than our neighbours, the world would be a better place than it is.

And the fact remains that the British Commonwealth is pledged to help maintain world peace, but is inadequately organized for the purpose of pulling its proper weight. The 130 million people in the USA speak with one voice to the world, as do the 170 millions in the USSR. The 80 millions in the self-governing territories of the British Commonwealth speak with six dissonant voices, or sometimes with a U.K. voice and several dutiful echoes. Due to our lack of organic unity we have been inadequately equipped to aid in the prevention of two wars which our apparent disunity had invited.

Mr Churchill and Field Marshal Smuts, instead of preaching to Euope, should help us put our own house in order, the better to fit ourselves to urge reforms on our European friends. Britain's most signal contribution to world order would be to embrace the principle of federal union that already unites the States of America and binds together the Republics of Soviet Russia.

Let us consign to the limbo where it belongs the perverted principle of 'a league of sovereign governments' which twice[4] in this century has deluged the world in blood.

Let us instead build a union that is so strong that none dare attack it, so just that none will wish to harm it, and so successful that all will clamour to join.

* * *

## THE NEUTRALITY OF EIRE

So far as I can see, *The Imperial Review* of 30 September 1944 was the only periodical I approached that was sufficiently motivated to print the following article, but it may still be of topical interest to those concerned with problems of neutrality in general:

### The Neutrality of Eire

The neutrals are at war with both sides. Citizens of the United Nations, fighting with the conviction that they have Right on their

---

[4] Written before the Korean war, which — at least technically — affected all the members of the U.N. and thus the world.

side, naturally regard their neutral neighbours with feelings not unmixed with rancour. Few would view the attitude of de Valera with greater disapproval than does the writer.

But it is difficult to repress a sardonic smile at the expense of those purblind politicians and self-styled statesmen who in the past have argued that the system called the British Commonwealth of Nations, as epitomized in the Statute of Westminster, was the acme of perfection, because it conferred upon each member nation a licence to take, at any crucial moment, a course divergent from that followed by its colleagues. The apologists for the Statute of Westminster are among those who most clamantly affirm that Eire has now forfeited her right to be regarded as a member of the Commonwealth, whether she may wish to exercise that right or not.

### A Flaw

The charlatans cannot have it both ways. Eire's neutrality reveals the fatal flaw in the Statute of Westminster, a flaw which has been hidden from most of us because the blind men who led us contrived to put us in blinkers.

But it will be argued that a system that compelled a minority to fight unwillingly by the side of the majority would be worse than the present set-up, where at least we know where we stand. The force of this objection disappears when the problem is examined from all its aspects. For one thing, even Irish apologists for Eire's neutrality argue that her citizens already make very substantial private contributions to the United Nations' war effort. This is no doubt true. If Eire's citizens were in the war as the result of foreign policy of which they had approved, and in the formulation of which they had contributed their due share, could we really argue that her percentage of objectors, 'conscientious' or otherwise, would be any higher than our own?

Such was the crazy pattern of international relations that in the early stages of the war the small nations had but two alternatives: to oppose Germany and suffer the fate of Jugoslavia, or to await their turn and hope that the juggernaut would break down before their time came. It is no reflection on our gallant allies to say that Holland, for example, might still be neutral if she had not been invaded, that it is conceivable that the USA might have stayed out of the war so long that we would have been defeated, had it not been for the God-sent

## The Commonwealth of God

miracle of Pearl Harbour — Japan's idiotic mistake in punching a spectator on the nose instead of giving her belligerent enemy the 'knock-out'. South Africa escaped the stigma of neutrality by the votes of only thirteen[1] of her M.P's. Ironically enough, the defeated neutrality resolution included a clause to the effect that she would continue to expect protection by the British fleet. Had it been passed, His Majesty King George would, in England, have been at war with Germany, whilst continuing friendly relations with her from his South African throne.

Bearing these considerations in mind, we may still reproach Eire for her neutrality, but have we really lived down our own past — Munich, for instance?

### No Law of Nations

It may be objected that Eire would no longer run the risk of suffering Jugoslavia's martyrdom. But it is more difficult to plunge into war when danger is decreasing than when it is looming large. It was the realization of imminent peril that spurred Britain to do in September 1939 what she had shrunk from doing two months earlier.

No nation should be neutral before the law. But there is no law of nations : so-called international law is but a figment of imagination in the minds of optimistic diplomatic ostriches. It is formulated by no legislature, enjoys the approval of no international electorate, and cannot be enforced except on the precarious basis of mutual collective back-scratching or reciprocal retaliation. Let us call it anything else but 'law'.

It should be obvious that there is something vitally lacking in our Commonwealth. In truth, it is only the project of a Commonwealth, still to be realized in practice. Apart from its ties of blood, language and a shared Crown, it is a league of nations, with all the faults and undemocratic anomalies of a league system. In a true commonwealth, all citizens are free and equal before the law. But we have no law for the Commonwealth as a whole, no law-making body. It is admittedly desirable and necessary that the six nations should have their six separate parliaments, making separate national law for each, but in Commonwealth affairs there should be one common legislature making laws that are of common concern to all — e.g. defence,

---

[1] I wrote thirteen, but on reflection I realize that this should read seven, since their votes would have cancelled out the other six.

## The Parliament of Man

foreign policy, civil aviation and the financing of these activities.

In a commonwealth the law-making body is elected directly by the citizens, and its laws act directly on individuals, not through their separate State parliaments. The only way to enforce decisions on States is by war, or threat of war. Policemen cannot do their work in bombers, a fact often forgotten by planners of an international 'police' force.

Mr Herbert Morrison, appalled like most of us at the terrific and steadily-growing congestion that faces Parliament, has suggested that in the interest of efficiency we must increasingly adopt the authoritarian methods of our enemies, whereby the Executive makes the laws. But surely, the solution of the problem is for us to be more democratic, not less. A popularly elected international parliament should relieve national parliaments of the inhibiting problems of defence and foreign policy, enabling them to apply their full energies to the pressing exigencies of health, education, housing, social security and so forth. As Sir William Beveridge has said:

'To win wars is not enough. We must prevent them. We can do so by placing international security in the hands of an international Government, by setting the Government of each nation free for its national tasks, free to build for all its citizens, in accord with their national ways of life, an ordered opportunity for service and freedom from fear and want.'

### Uniting Ireland

There is every reason why Eire would wish to become a full and loyal member of such a Commonwealth, in which neither Eire nor Ulster could dominate the other, nor be dominated by Britain ; it would perhaps be the only way to unite Ireland. That Eire is a republic is irrelevant. States like Belgium, Norway, Holland and other neighbours who may look to us for security could also be included, and far from professing allegiance to the King of all Britain, they have their own kings and could continue to retain them. Neither would Republics be out of place in such a system.

To those who agitate for Eire's exclusion from the British Commonwealth I would say:

'Let us first remove the beam that is in our own eye, otherwise Eire may not be our only neutral next time. No good purpose can be served by advocating the permanent alienation of our errant western neighbour. If on the other hand we invite her after the war to become a full member in a truly United Commonwealth of Peoples, we may create a framework without which no looser world-wide association of states could hope to preserve world peace.'

* * *

**DOMESTIC AND FOREIGN POLICY**

The following article, inspired by Lionel Curtis' works, also enjoyed world coverage:

### Domestic and Foreign Policy – Drawing the Line

One of the factors making for instability in international systems based on co-operation of sovereign States – systems such as the British Commonwealth of Nations, the old League of Nations and the Pan-American Alliance – is the disconcerting effect that a change of government, constitutional or otherwise, in any one partner can cause in the system as a whole. As a corollary, a new government for any nation can often destroy overnight the foundations of national security which the foreign policy and defence programme of its predecessors had established. In short, lack of continuity in national foreign policies and instability in collective 'security' (so-called) are symptoms displayed by international systems based on collaboration among free and independent nations.

It is easy to fall into the error of thinking that if we can eliminate these syptoms we shall have cured the disease that causes them. If foreign policy and defence can be separated from home affairs, this would contribute greatly to the security of the nation and to the peace of the world in general.

Doubtless with these considerations in mind, Lord Chatfield asked the Government in the House of Lords some time ago whether they would consider the practicability of obtaining agreement that national defence policy should in future be a non-party matter. He proposed that there should be a National Defence Council. If it could be made imperial, so much the better. The Council should be composed somewhat as follows: The Prime Minister as Chairman, the leaders of the principal political parties, the Foreign Secretary and the Defence Ministers, and he would like to add certain non-political members. If the Dominions take part, there should be 'adequate Dominion representation.'

The Earl of Perth pointed out in the debate that national defence and foreign policy were quite inseparable.

While this two-day debate was in progress the Government was strongly criticized in the Commons for treating a vote on education (home affairs) as a reflection on their prosecution of the war (foreign policy).

The same problem has, in essence, come to a head in other democracies, notably in USA.

Let us see, therefore, whether the proposal so generally welcomed by the House of Lords really attacks the germ of the disease or whether it is a foredoomed attempt to scrape away the symptoms.

Firstly, any stability gained by setting up machinery depending on all-party agreement would be nullified by:

◆ The difficulty of obtaining and retaining all-party agreement on matters on which there exists ample scope for legitimate disagreement.

◆ The fact that foreign policy and defence would be entrusted to a body either devoid of power to manage them with vigour and success, or – if it had the power – with no mandate to exercise it.

Unless some degree of governmental power were to be vested in the Defence Committee, ultimate responsibility for the adoption or rejection of its recommendations would rest with the Government of the day. Of what use is all-party agreement on defence and foreign policy if it can be vetoed by the party in power, or if – as Lord Chatfield suggested – the party with a majority in Parliament retains the power of the purse? And what happens if, say, the United Kingdom agrees to the recommendations of the Imperial Defence Council and the Canadian parliament repudiates it?

If foreign policy and defence had been taken out of the arena of party politics, how could the Cabinet of the day ever argue that it had a madate to veto the recommendations of the Defence Committee? *Per contra*, whence would it derive its authority to accept the recommendations of the Committee, which – like its individual members – itself had no popular mandate? And whence would Members

## The Commonwealth of God

of Parliament derive their right to vote or withhold money to finance such recommendations?

At general election meetings, are questions such as the following to be ignored?:

'If you were elected to Parliament, and then you, or a member of your Party, went to the Cabinet or onto the Foreign Policy and Defence Committee, would you support a proposal to form an alliance with X, or to admit Y and Z into the Commonwealth of Nations?'

Other questions in this category are those dealing with, e.g. conscription, nationalization of the arms industry, and so forth.

Opinions, particularly in the House of Lords, may differ on the advisability of allowing the common voter even to think on such problems, but the country would not stand for their being put beyond popular control. Foreign policy cannot be effective without popular support, for in the last resort the strength of any foreign policy is measured by the manpower behind it. So long as defence and foreign policy are election issues they will remain party issues. (That does not necessarily mean that the cleavages of opinion on these matters will be along the same lines as differences on domestic issues.) The predominant party must be decisive, i.e. must become the executive of its policy — it must be, for defence and foreign affairs, the Government of the day.

There should be one government for domestic matters and another government for foreign policy and defence, with one important proviso:

The latter must spring from a separate Parliament, whose electorate must be wider than the electorate of Britain and Northern Ireland. It should be at least as large as the combined national electorates of all the self-governing members of the British Commonwealth. Better still, it should be even wider and should embrace, for example, the democracies of Western Europe who may look to us for security. Ideally, it should comprise all those peoples that are inherently capable of forming a genuine international government to uphold peace. As Sir William Beveridge has said:

'The force on which international justice rests must itself be international. It cannot be composed of men owing their whole personal allegiance to one particular nation. They must owe

## The Parliament of Man

allegiance to a Government which is itself directly responsible to the citizens of many nations. There must, in other words, be both national Governments and an international Government.' (Introduction to *Faith and Works*, by Lionel Curtis.)

* * *

*Note:*

A list of the signatories to the pamphlet *Faith and Works* mentioned in the footnote on page 109 is as follows:

| | |
|---|---|
| ADAM, Tom | MacGREGOR, Prof. D. H. |
| ASTOR, The Viscount | MALCOLM, Sir D. O. |
| BAKER, Sir Herbert | MANSBRIDGE, Dr Albert |
| BENTLEY, F.H. | MARRIS, Sir William |
| BENTWICH, Prof. Norman | MESTON, The Lord |
| BIDMEAD, H. S. | MOORE, Cyril |
| BOWLEY, Professor A.L. | NELSON, C. |
| CRAIGMYLE, The Lord | OAKESHOTT, W.F. |
| DAVIES, The Lord | POWER, Sir John |
| EWING, A. M'L. | PRICE, Sir Henry |
| FAWCETT, Professor C. B. | RANSOME, Patrick |
| HOLT, Robert | RICHMOND, Adml. Sir H. W. |
| JOHNSON, Dr. John | ROBERTS, R. Hugh |
| JONES, Sir Roderick | ROBERTSON, Sir C. Grant |
| KEETON, Professor G. W. | ROBIESON, W. D. |
| KENYON, Sir Frederic G. | SMITH, Nowell |
| KER, Edwin | STEWART, Sir P. Malcolm |
| LEATHER, Captain Hartley | UNGOED-THOMAS, A. L. |
| LIVINGSTONE, Sir Richard | WARD, Eric |
| | YOUNG, Pat |

# CHAPTER 7

# PRACTICAL STEPS TO WORLD UNITY

The practical steps that could be taken towards a better world have not greatly changed since the following article was published, inter alia, in New Zealand, entitled:

**PRACTICAL STEPS TO WORLD UNITY**

Among supporters of the 'United Nations' there is no need to urge the desirability of *international* unity. Among democrats it is also unnecessary to argue the indispensability of *national* freedom, the right of nations to protect themselves from undesired foreign interference in those purely national affairs that are the concern of none but themselves. The problem is how to combine international unity with national freedom without endangering either. To sacrifice one is to lose both.

The failure of the League of Nations and its copy-cat successor the 'United' Nations demonstrated how too much (technical) freedom, or sovereignty, for the states members meant that there was no real organic unity; this lack of stability rendered the sovereignty of the members mainly illusory, for the 'freedom' of each was nothing more than a futile scramble, every nation competing against every other nation to do what few of them really wished to do, namely: prepare for war. It is equally obvious that excessive insistence on international unity – in matters where unity is not essential – means an unnecessary limitation of national freedom. The problem of international government is therefore how to find the judicious compromise.

## The Parliament of Man

All who believe in the possibility and desirability of achieving such a compromise are federalists, for federal union means common government for common affairs and national self-government for national affairs. National independence cannot be preserved in isolation. Since those matters that were previously the separate 'foreign affairs' of the different nations were in reality the common concern of them all, they should henceforth be dealt with in common. The supreme merit of a federal union is that where the freedom and welfare of its citizens are best served by their being united, it unites them, and where their freedom and welfare are best served by their remaining separate it leaves them the liberty to develop their own lives in their own way. Federalists are not fanatical cosmopolitans advocating the absorption of all nations into a super-state. The federal type of union ensures the survival of those cherished national characteristics that make for variety and diversity in the world, whilst suppressing the evil types of nationalism that breed hatred and war.

I shall not see it in my lifetime, but if only we could start along the right road, our children or grandchildren might even see a grand federation strong and safe enough to contain Jews and Arabs, Moslems and Christians, Northern and Southern Ireland, lions and lambs, Armenians and Turks, Greeks and Romans. Why not? Our little world contains them already.

International law will be effective only if and when it legislates for and acts directly upon individuals instead of on nation states only. This is actually achieved by federation, because it is a union of peoples, not of governments. By this means, Lincoln's famous principle is applied in an international context; in international no less than in national affairs we at last achieve government of the people by the people for the people. Federation is the only means by which the crying need for international peace-keeping machinery can be reconciled with the vital democratic principle that power must ultimately reside in the people.

In a federation the citizen has two servants: his national government and the federal government. If we fail to federate, international affairs will once again lie at the mercy of blind, incalculable forces which the un-coordinated efforts of statesmen will be unable to control. By federating we acquire the constitutional right and ability to guide our own destinies in true democratic fashion, by free vote in a freely-elected parliament. Only by such means can we ensure that

## Practical Steps to World Unity

the issue of war and peace will be in the hands of the ordinary men and women of all countries, who will choose peace. International federal government will remove those grievances that often tempt peace-lovers to choose paths leading to war and self-destruction.

The federal parliament would have the constitutional right to make laws only on specified matters of common concern to all federal citizens, including the power to finance itself. It would thus have sole authority over external affairs and defence. It might also be given substantial (shared) powers over such matters as currency, tariffs, migration and colonial administration. All other powers would remain where they now are, with the national parliaments and their electorates. The constitution would not allow the federal government to meddle in national affairs, not the states to interfere in federal affairs. In borderline cases a Federal Supreme Court would decide.

Note that, contrary to, e.g. the Hague Court, the Supreme Court would not only 'decide' cases. It would 'settle' the case, in the sense that it would have not only the right, but also the power and ability, to enforce its *decisions*, without violence, without recourse to gunboats.

Territories that were previously colonies or dependencies of states which federated would be in an improved position. Those which did not immediately obtain their freedom would be nearer to it, for in the administration of all colonial territories the aim would be to promote the utmost well-being of the inhabitants and to provide as soon as possible for democratic self-government.

As regards standards of living, it is probable that the living standards of the developing countries could be raised to highly satisfactory levels and at accelerating speeds, without having to lower the standards of the developed countries. Immense and immeasurable funds would be released by federation, if only through the economies in armaments and administration, and through general rationalization.

Federation is not a quack cure-all for every political, social and economic evil. Within a federal system, however, these evils could be more efficaciously tackled than ever before. Only within a federation can international collaboration be adequate to address such economic ills as unemployment and pauper standards of living. The cost of maintaining armed forces in the federation would be negligible compared with the combined cost of arming each state sufficiently to outface all possible combinations against it. The economies would be liberated to raise standards of living all round.

A skeleton cannot be said to be a very complete man, but it is a very incomplete man who has no skeleton. Similarly, it would be a very ramshackle New World that had no federal backbone. On the other hand, economic 'co-operation' alone, if it left the participants in possession of the instruments of political, military and economic warfare would not be 'federation' and would be doomed to break up sooner or later into conflicting fragments.

We cannot expect at the outset to create a federation embracing the whole world. But it is to be hoped that those nations not sufficiently advanced politically to be able to accept the conditions of a democratic federal constitution would be linked to each other and to the federation by an improved league (confederal) system, or some such other next-best-thing to union, to be admitted to membership of the federation as soon as they were able and willing to join. Thus in due course the federal commonwealth would embrace the whole world. Its citizens would in time come to think of themselves not primarily as Englishmen, Germans, Americans and so forth, but first and foremost as men and women all equally members of the great human family.

*Note:*
The essence of this article appeared, with my blessing, in a front-line newspaper in Belgium over the signature of my young federalist friend Leonard Zeidman. This was but one of many articles 'syndicated' in this manner.

I next met him by chance, on a post-war visit to Paris, on the eve of his wedding to a girl whom he had 'liberated'. His wedding reception at a world renowned Paris hotel was the first and last occasion on which I have partaken of *escargots*.

\* \* \*

## WAR, THE RECURRING DECIMATOR

Still much inspired by Streit's *Union Now*, I offered the following illustration of the practical steps which could be, and still could be,

## Practical Steps to World Unity

taken towards an ideal world. It appeared, *inter alia*, in the *Imperial Review* and elsewhere, including New Zealand. (The pun is only for mathematicians.)

### War, the Recurring Decimator

It has been said that what men learn from history is that men learn nothing from history. In one sense this is all to the good, for direct personal experience is the spice of life. But when this refusal to learn results in recurrent wars and thereby threatens to extinguish all civilization and even mankind itself, it is permissible to remark that life has become too spicy by far.

Many optimists feel that the threat of world war has now receded to such an extent that arguments for its abolition are both unnecessary and irrelevant. Even if this were so, the world is still beset by other problems which only supranational government could tackle efficaciously.

If, after World War I, men had looked back into a century and a half of history, World War II might never have come about. In 1777 the thirteen American States had formed themselves into a 'League of Friendship' under a Covenant which, on parchment, was stronger and better constituted than were the 1919 or 1945 editions. It was in fact a confederation – a league with the pitfalls more elaborately disguised.

Consequently, by 1786 America was faced with much the same crisis as overtook the world in 1938. Her solution of the problem should have taught us how to solve ours. Let us compare the two situations.

Two centuries ago it took five months to travel from the most remote parts of the American confederation to Washington. The entire world today is minute in size compared with the small territory then covered by the founders of modern America[1]. The rebel states had together fought an eight-year war of independence against a common enemy, German-born George III of England, but with varying degrees of belligerency, verging in several instances on vir-

---

[1] 1992: In the world of fibre-optics, which transmit messages at lightning speed, and will enable tomorrow's computers to perform tasks in half an hour that today take a month, Washington D.C. is as close to Downing Street, London, as Boston, Massachusetts, was to the sea when the famous tea party was held.

tual neutrality; some had fought starving, unshod and in rags, whilst the arsenals and warehouses of their more prosperous allies bulged with rotting stores, their streets thronged with young men of military age.

Within three years of the Versailles Treaty of 1783, the States had already become slaves to their newly-won 'independence'. Each regarded the citizens of the others as foreigners and potential enemies. As John Fiske pointed out:

'Under the universal depressions and want of confidence well-nigh all trade had stopped. ... Trade disputes threatened war between New York, New Hampshire, Vermont, Connecticut and Pennsylvania ... The States issued worthless money, ... misery was rife and armed mobs broke up the law courts ....'

In *Union Now*, to which book I am indebted for the above quotation, Clarence Streit remarks:

'When these troubles culminated early in 1787 with the attempt of Shay's rebels to capture the League arsenal in Massachusetts, so strong was state sovereignty and so feeble the League that Massachusetts would not allow League troops to enter its territory even to guard the League's own arsenal.'

At the Philadelphia Convention summoned by George Washington in May, 1787, not one of the few delegates who troubled to attend had a mandate to create anything; they were there merely to patch up the League of Friendship. But Washington saw there was no future in the darning of an old sack with good new twine. Rejecting the lukewarm, half-way schemes that were being put about under the still popular pretext that the man-in-the-street would not stand for anything more courageous, he urged support for a novel system of government now known as federation.

The result was a constitution that survived even a disastrous civil war. (A modern federation would begin with the advantage of not needing to compromise with slavery and would, it is hoped, be so just and successful that none would wish to leave it.)

The main impediment to ratification of the federal constitution proved to be the State of New York. Accordingly, Alexander Hamilton, James Madison and John Jay embarked on a newspaper campaign to educate the people. By 1789 ratification was achieved. It

## Practical Steps to World Unity

is instructive to study some typical examples of their arguments, which have a lesson for us today.

Condemning compromise plans to put force behind the league, Hamilton argued that the States ought not to adopt a League Covenant of the type —

'which could only be kept in motion by the instrumentality of a large army continually on foot to execute the ordinary requisitions or decrees of the government. And yet this is the plain alternative involved by those who wish to deny it the power of extending its operations to individuals. Such a scheme ... would instantly degenerate into a military despotism.'

As for —

'the project of conferring supplementary powers upon Congress, this would involve that either the machine, from the intrinsic feebleness of its structure, will moulder into pieces, in spite of our ill-judged efforts to prop it up; or, by successive augmentations of its force and energy, as necessity might prompt, we shall finally accumulate in a single body all the most important prerogatives of sovereignty, and thus entail upon our posterity ... that very tyranny which the adversaries of the new Constitution either are, or affect to be, solicitous to avert.'

Writing in the *Independent Journal* on 'the characteristic difference between a league and a government', Hamilton urged:

'We must extend the authority of the Union to the persons of the citizens, the only proper objects of government. ... In an association where the general authority is confined to the collective bodies of the communities that compose it, every breach of the laws must involve a state of war; and military execution must become the only instrument of civil obedience. Such a state of things can certainly not deserve the name of government, nor would any prudent man choose to commit his happiness to it.'

He conceded, with classic irony:

'There is nothing absurd or impracticable in the idea of a league or alliance between independent nations for certain defined purposes precisely stated in a treaty regulating all the details of time, place, circumstance and quantity, leaving nothing to future discretion; and depending for its execution on the good faith of the parties. Compacts of this kind exist among all civilized nations, subject to the usual vicissitudes of peace and war, of observance and non-observance, as the interests or passions of the contracting powers dictate ... Little dependence is to be placed on treaties which have no other sanction than the obligations of good faith, and which oppose general considerations of peace and justice to the impulse of any immediate interest or passion.'

It is my opinion that the public-spirited and noble-minded men whom we had to thank for the 1919 experiment in world government may have achieved the best that was at that time attainable[2]. They and their devoted disciples who strove so gallantly to make the League a success by no means deserve the opprobrium that has been heaped upon them. There are some of their number, however, who steadfastly refuse to learn the lessons the failure of the League taught us, and obstinately turn a blind eye to every danger signal. Many such attended the San Francisco conference which resulted in the United Nations. For them no censure is too severe, and I make no apology for using against their pernicious doctrine arguments employed against the die-hard supporters of the League of Friendship.

The following could almost have been written as comments on the United Nations:

'It is sometimes asked, with an air of seeming triumph, what inducement could the States have, if disunited, to make war[3] upon each other? It would be a full answer to this question to say — precisely the same inducements as have, at different times, deluged in blood all the nations in the world ...' (Hamilton).

'Leave America divided into thirteen or, if you please into three or four independent governments ... If one was attacked, would the others fly to its succour, and spend their blood and money in its defence? Would there be no danger of their being flattered into neutrality by specious promises, or seduced by too great a fondness for peace to decline hazarding their tranquillity and present safety for the sake of neighbours of whom perhaps they have been jealous, and whose importance they are content to see diminished.' (Jay).

[2] A U.S. Senator tried to persuade his country to join by arguing (rightly) that, by ratifying, the USA would commit itself to nothing.

[3] Now that military war may be becoming out of date, read 'economic war'. (The immediate source of quotations from Hamilton, Madison and Jay is *The Federalist*. My thanks are due to Messrs. Dent and Prof.W.J. Ashley.)

## Practical Steps to World Unity

'The most wild of all projects ... is that of rending us in pieces in order to preserve our liberties and promote our happiness.' (Madison).

'A band of bretheren, united to each other by the strongest ties, should never be split into a number of unsocial, jealous and alien sovereignties ... When a people or a family so divide, it never fails to be against themselves.' (Jay).

\* \* \*

## ARE THE ALLIES FEDERATING?

The following are comments on current events at the time, as published in *World Community*, New Jersey, and in UK papers, which have some bearing on recent history. Note the reference to an international police force.

### Are the Allies Federating?

The uninitiated, who only think they know what 'federation' means, are apt to talk about the so-called 'United' Nations as if they were federated. In actual fact they are no more united than were the allies in the last war, or Britain and France up to the separate peace.

I cannot be accused of spreading more alarm and despondency than already exists on the subject of the 'Unity' of the United Nations if I say that so far the ramshackle collaboration between them resembles nothing so much as an incompleted arch; it lacks the keystone of federal institutions which alone could give it stability.

It would be easy to make out a case to show that the allies are progressing towards a federal union, but it could just as readily be argued that there is no intention to have any federal keystone at all, that they will once more place their trust in the paper security of unenforceable compacts between States which retain the power (i.e. the ability) to break them at their own caprice. Already, plans are rife for an international police force to be controlled by an authority having none of the vital characteristics of a Government. Power behind the League is all very well so long as there is democratic control of the power behind the League. Otherwise the international force will degenerate into a gang of irresponsible SS-Men.

## The Parliament of Man

Being an optimist, I prefer to believe that the present-day statesmen have learned their lesson — namely, that a political peace treaty will be inadequate, that an economic peace treaty will be lop-sided, that in fact no treaty, pact, protocol or entente of any kind can guarantee peace. What is required is that in the sphere of international affairs (defence and foreign policies) the nations must where possible enter into complete political fusion. If they will do this (union is feasible among democracies) they can with honourable consciences retain their complete independence in affairs that are their own private national concern. That is what federation means.

But how far do the facts fit in with the hope that the statesmen appreciate the vital necessity and value of federation? General Smuts certainly does. In a speech to both Houses of Parliament he said:

' ... "The United Nations". This is a new conception ... much in advance of the old concept of the League of Nations. We do not want a mere League, but something more definite and organic, even if to begin with more limited and less ambitious than the League. "The United Nations" is itself a fruitful conception.'

### The Polish-Czech Agreements

The first of our Allies in the war were the first to turn towards federation. The Polish-Czech agreements of 11 November 1940 and 23 January 1942 recognize in principle a close political, military and economic union between the two peoples, not limited to these two countries alone. It would be open to others to join, including particularly Greece and Yugoslavia.

Reading between the lines of the Græco-Yugoslav Union Agreement of 15 January 1942, one feels that the intention is that this, too, should develop into full federation. To quote from *The Times* of the following day:

> The eleven articles of the compact, if they are carried into practice in the spirit in which they have been conceived, will make the two states one in their international relations ... Yesterday's treaty may indeed be a model for others of its kind.

The two countries regard themselves as but a potential part of a wider federation. The King of Yugoslavia, replying to the King of the Hellenes when the compact was signed, said:

> 'According to our conception, this agreement, even after the realization of the Balkan Union, will not attain its full significance

## Practical Steps to World Unity

until the rest of Europe is organized in such a way as to achieve a really new international order. ... We have reason to hope that beside the Balkan Union a Central European Union will be created on the basis of a Czechoslovak-Polish agreement ... These two Unions would create, together with a single common supreme organ, a great organization which would give serious guarantees for the peace and prosperity of Europe.'

In a message to *Federal Union News* of August 1942, the Ankara correspondent of *The Times* asserted that:

'The treaties signed a few months ago between Poland and Czechoslovakia and between Yugoslavia and Greece are considered here as encouraging symptoms for the extension of the federal system to other parts of Europe.'

And again,

'The best means of reconciling the two apparently conflicting principles of national independence and of partial curtailment of national sovereignty might be a federal system extended to the whole of Europe and eventually to other continents.'

He added that such ideas find much favour in Turkey.

### Norway's War Aims

Norway's war aims have also been published. To quote her Foreign Minister, Mr Trygve Lie:

'As an Atlantic people we want above all a strong organized collaboration between the two great Atlantic Powers — the British Empire and the United States.'

Eventually, he considers, this collaboration should develop into either a new League of Nations or a federal body with executive powers[1].

Mr Lie puts forward the constructive suggestion that 'it should not be impossible, even now, to prepare effective union between Great Britain and the Allied countries in certain regional tasks.'

---

[1] A League with executive power would be a new kind of despotism; a League without power would be as futile as it was before. The international authority must be democratically controlled. No authority short of a federal government will suffice.

# The Parliament of Man

## The British Commonwealth of Nations

It is often declared:

'There is federation enough in the British Commonwealth of Nations.'

It cannot be too urgently or too solemnly stressed that the relationship among the members of the Commonwealth is not federal. This fact contributed to this war as it did to the last. This time Hitler and Ribbentrop took a chance on our disintegrating at the crucial moment. As Lionel Curtis, the distinguished author of *Civitas Dei* points out in his recent pamphlet *Decision*:

> In 1914 the British Commonwealth had failed to prevent the outbreak of world war. In 1919 a League was constructed on the model of the British Commonwealth, into which that Commonwealth was incorporated. By 1939 the two together had completely failed to prevent the outbreak of an even more terrible world war ... The British Commonwealth had continued to function since 1919 by virtue of a British hegemony ... Will any realist with his eye on the map argue that Great Britain and a fragment of Ireland can, in this century or ever again, give the sense of security which her navy gave to the free communities from 1815 to the close of that century?

Lionel Curtis concludes that the solution is for the Commonwealth to federate.

The economic and defence systems of the USA and the British Commonwealth have been 'mixed up' in such a way as to point in the direction of a single English-speaking defence system, with a single air force, joint navies and a single monetary and interstate transport system.

In the meantime, however, it is obvious that until the various joint boards are subject to a common parliament with authority from the two peoples, and with power to make policy, the structure is not federal, and is more in the nature of an insecure improvisation. But the direction in which we are going was indicated by the headline with which one of the biggest London newspapers greeted Churchill's address to the US Congress:

'Churchill says "Federate".'

This reflected the Prime Minister's advocacy of federation in the Sunday press just before the war.

In less dramatic ways, many of our allies whom I have not specially dealt with are equally federally-minded.

## Practical Steps to World Unity

If British statesmen will only give the lead, a federal union of the USA and the British Commonwealth could be established, figuratively speaking, at a few strokes of a few pens[2], and the first instalment of the process would be an earnest of the whole. The European part of the union would then have to be built up piecemeal, a long and arduous process which can hardly hope to succeed unless it has behind it the stimulus and example of an Anglo-American federation constituted on the open-door principle. Through Federal Union we can give practical effect to the fact which we all realize at heart: how dependent everybody is on everybody else, everywhere in the world.

One of the famous suffragette sisters, Sylvia Pankhurst, was running a weekly paper − *The New Times and Ethiopia News* − for Emperor Haile Selassie. I relieved her as (part-time, honorary) editor one fortnight to enable her to take a holiday. I ran the following series of articles during her absence and for a few weeks after her return. It was also 'syndicated' in a Yorkshire weekly paper.

Again reverting to mathematics, it occurred to me that if:

c = the difficulty in squaring the circle, and
g = the difficulty in squaring the globe, then
$$g = c^2$$
In plain language, putting the world to rights is more difficult than the old problem of squaring the circle.

Fortunately, the problem is not insuperable, federation being the solution.

I called my series: *Squaring the Globe*

---

[2] 1992: This rather rash phrase does not correctly convey my views at the time. I believed that some sort of avalanche effect, a chain-reaction, could be set in motion if some trusted leader were to fire popular imagination. A constituent assembly could be convened 'at the stroke of a pen'. There was never any idea in my head that union could be sprung upon the people without their consent.

# The Parliament of Man

## Squaring the Globe I
## Danger of Deadlock

The 'wider and permanent system of security' promised in the Atlantic Charter is manifestly intended to rest on four main pillars – USSR, USA, Britain and China. If they can remain in concord, or reach decisions by a three-to-one vote[1], world affairs should work fairly smoothly. It is perhaps mischievous to ask: 'What if a state of deadlock comes into existence?' But whatever else happened, the world would in such case divide into two camps.

Statesmen are feverishly casting about them for some sort of 're-insurance' against such a contingency. Lord Halifax, General Smuts and Mr Curtin (Premier of Australia) rightly see that the British Commonwealth must secure unity among its own members if it is to make its fullest contribution to world unity. Mr Mackenzie King (Prime Minister of Canada) differs from this view. (He maintained in his speech to the Ottawa House of Commons on 31 January that the idea of a common British Commonwealth policy on defence and foreign affairs 'runs counter to the establishment of effective world security.') The regional agreement between Australia and New Zealand on foreign policy is symptomatic of this uneasiness, but it is inevitable that such unfortunate instances will be repeated if the counsels of Mr Mackenzie King prevail. It is quite natural that Americans have accused our Pacific brethren of 'jumping the pistol.'

Perhaps this pact, signed in January, is already a dead letter, for Mr Frazer (Prime Minister of New Zealand) said, on 19 July, that it was not feasible to divide the world into areas, leaving each to look after its own security. On the setting up of a new league of nations, he agreed that the Big Four should hold permanent seats on the Council, and all participating nations, large and small, be represented in the Assembly. It must be armed with the powers and machinery to give effect to its decisions.

Of Commonwealth unity, Mr Frazer said that the New Zealand Government was well satisfied with the system of prior consultation, but was agreeable to any practicable suggestions making for an even better system, and for still closer co-operation, if possible.

Mr Curtin, speaking to the Australian Federal Parliament two days earlier, said that regarding his suggestions for improved machinery

---

[1] Must have been written before the veto was decided upon.

## Practical Steps to World Unity

for co-operation within the Commonwealth, he had not sought, at the London Conference of Prime Ministers, to convert Mackenzie King to his point of view, nor could Australia accept Mr King's opinion that the present system of co-operation worked with complete success. He went on:

> 'Our readiness to associate in world organization does not lessen the realism of our membership of the British Commonwealth.'

He believed that any organization for the preservation of peace must include all the Great Powers. The corrective of domination by the Great Powers must be an assembly of nations moulding policy on a democratic basis. The world organization should be buttressed by regional arrangements, and should have combined naval, military and air staff.

A study of the full reported texts of these and other speeches of Commonwealth Prime Ministers made since their meeting in London clearly shows that, as far as Commonwealth unity is concerned, the chief, if not the whole, value of the conference was that it showed how foolish it is to count on agreement between governments, even when they claim to be bound together by sacred and indissoluble ties. To entrust the enactment and maintenance of international law to a consortium of sovereign states is as crazy as to expect Great Britain to maintain law and order at home if every Act of Parliament had to be ratified by the County Councils.

Mr Curtin's ideal of an assembly of nations moulding policy on a democratic basis, and wielding effective military power, can be achieved only by the introduction, however gradually, of some system of responsible and representative government into international affairs. Such was the main theme of Lord Davies' teaching.

If the proposed new league of co-operating governments is regarded as a step towards ultimate world government, all well and good. We must acquiesce in it because it is perhaps the only type of organization that can embrace the whole world in its present backward state of development. But statesmen who look upon such a system as the ultimate political ideal are condemning this planet to a constant succession of world wars.

It would be unfortunate, to put it mildly, if unwitting preparations for a fresh deluge of blood were to be made before this war had been brought to a 'victorious' conclusion.

# The Parliament of Man

Those who have been conversant with the proceedings of popular assemblies; who have seen how difficult it often is, where there is no exterior pressure of circumstances, to bring them to harmonious resolutions on important points, will readily conceive how impossible it must be to induce a number of such assemblies, deliberating at a distance from each other at different times and under different impressions, long to co-operate in the same views and pursuits.

Alexander Hamilton, *Independent Journal* New York, A.D. 1787

## Squaring the Globe II
### Bretton Woods — or Just forty-four Trees?

The failure of the League of Nations to accomplish the main task for which it was established is often attributed to the criminal folly of statesmen. True, it might appear to be a symptom of insanity that they attempted so vast a task with so flimsy powers and such ramshackle machinery, but it is both unjust and ungenerous to condemn as criminals those League pioneers who tried to walk where even angels might have feared to tread.

The patient toil that led up to the signing of the final draft of the United Nations' Monetary Agreement at Bretton Woods last week resulted in the delegates of forty-four nations agreeing not to agree until their Government had agreed to do so. In a cautious attempt to deny rumours from the U.S. that Australia's heart was not in the affair, Mr Curtin has issued a long statement to the effect that the Australian Government has 'neither accepted nor rejected the results of the conference.'

It is cold comfort to reflect that this attitude differs little from that of all the other participants.

### 'Primary' Obligation

Mr Morgenthau (U.S) said, to quote the *The Times* of 24 July:

> ... he was certain that no delegation had for a moment lost sight of particular national interests, and added that the American delegation had been 'at all times conscious of its primary obligation, the protection of American interests.'

Internationalism à la mode!

## Practical Steps to World Unity

Voting power in the proposed Monetary Pool will be based on a combination of two undemocratic principles: 250 votes per State, irrespective of population, plus one additional vote for each part of its equivalent of US $100,000 in the fund. Of course, it is good practical politics to weight voting in proportion to power (in this case, wealth) since decisions thus made have a better chance of being translated into action. But is the weighting in this instance sufficiently drastic to achieve that end?

In the event of the agreement being signed on behalf of Governments having at least 65 per cent of the total quotas (but in no event before 1 May next) the Monetary Fund will come into existence. Its object is to provide short-term credit to States members, so that they will have no pretext for indulging in financial juggling harmful to international trade. In addition, there will be a World Bank to meet long-term needs in the post-war world.

**Membership voluntary**

The scheme is notable for an ingenious system of sanctions, whereby member States pay fines on a rising scale for exceeding their quotas. It seems, however, badly equipped to meet the need for change in a changing world. Alterations in the par value of a member's currency can be made only on the proposal of the member, and a member can even claim exemption from a uniform proportionate change in the par value of all member currencies that might be decided upon by all its colleagues. A member State can also withdraw from the scheme at its own whim.

Lord Keynes has described the plan, when it was still in its initial stages, as an instrument of international government, implying that an international government will be needed if the instrument is to be properly wielded. This hits the nail on the head. If we could be assured that international security will be maintained by an international authority that is an authority, and not a mere debating society, we could safely leave the financial experts, oil kings, dieticians and airline operators to muddle through their respective affairs on the basis of agreements, pacts and treaties between sovereign governments. But in the absence of a reliable system of international security, these separate functional approaches towards world government are like the stones in an arch lacking a keystone — liable to collapse at a crucial moment and crush us beneath its ruins.

## The Parliament of Man

After the last war we made the mistake of concentrating too much upon the political aspect of reconstruction. This time we may make the dangerous mistake of neglecting political for economic factors. But international economic 'co-operation' alone, if it left the participants in possession of the instruments of political, military – and therefore also economic – warfare, would be doomed to break up sooner or later into warring fragments.

The International Postal Union, the I.L.O., the Bank of International Settlements, the Hague Court of International Justice, the First, Second, Third, Fourth and Fifth Internationales, the various religious, political and cultural bodies with world-wide ramifications, these are some of the veins and tissues that help to make the world one living body. But, without a backbone, Man could not walk uprightly upon the earth.

Squaring the Globe III was also published in *Plan*.

### Squaring the Globe III
### A Museum Peace

The hope that the present war will finish before another one starts is merely an extreme example of the widespread public pessimism engendered by the atavistic tendencies of statesmen. In this connection, two passages stand out in Mr Churchill's speech in Parliament of 2 August:

> 'I am glad that the war is becoming less of an idealogical war between rival systems, and more and more the means by which high ideals and solid benefits may be achieved by the broad masses of people in many lands and ultimately in all.' (Cheers)

True, Mr Churchill made a distinction between 'idealism' and 'ideology', but there is more in his remark than a mere play on words. Dictatorships are often, if not usually, genuine attempts to confer 'solid benefits' on the 'broad masses of the people.' The evil of Nazism is not so much the fact that it degenerated (as authoritarianism inevitably degenerates) into government of the people, by the Gestapo, for the Führer. It is a denial of the belief in the peoples'

## Practical Steps to World Unity

ability to learn to govern themselves. Though most democrats would admit that democracy cannot be conferred upon the whole world round a conference table, that the vast majority of the world's population requires protection, education and encouragement in the art of self-government, there is a vast gulf of ideology between those who tolerate the despotism of Spain, Portugal[1] and Turkey, and those who are resolved that Lincoln's ideal of government of the people, by the people and for the people shall not perish from the earth. (All governments are ostensibly 'for the people.')

Dealing with the future organization of the world, the Prime Minister said:

'In spite of all urges that we should take the lead in laying down the law, I personally would prefer to hear the opinions of other powerful nations before committing our country to too many details. Can we not be content with the broad declarations on which we are all agreed, that there is to be a world council to preserve peace which will, in the first instance, be formed and guided by the major Powers who have gained the war, and that thereafter other Powers, and eventually all Powers, will be offered their part in this world organization?'

If peace merely had to be preserved as in a museum, the constitution of the Council of Curators would not be of vital importance. In the real world of tomorrow, however, any organization to keep the peace will have to possess powers far greater than those conferred by the mere signing of a piece of parchment.

Some may perhaps take encouragement from the way in which the sanguine term, 'United Nations', has captured popular imagination, being almost regarded as a magic formula with mystic powers. The Big Four have been elevated to a position second only to the Holy Trinity. But there is danger in unthinking optimism.

Though it may be taken as an earnest of good intentions, 'United' is a misleading description for a congeries of States which retain forty-four separate Foreign Offices, War Ministries and Propaganda Bureaux, and therefore the power to make separate conflicting decisions on matters of common concern, behind the backs of their

---

[1] Among my contacts was a refugee from Portugal and another from Goa, who both described the Salazar regime in much bloodier terms than did his loyal ally Britain.

## The Parliament of Man

colleagues. Encouraged by the fact that two of the Big Four have refrained from growing Polish Governments on their soil, Mr Churchill, to judge from his speech quoted above, seems resigned to a post-war system of attempted government of States, by States and for States.

### Democracy across frontiers

We are told by experts that, although the League of Nations failed last time, the principles of the Covenant are eternal. It is indisputable that men will never cease striving to achieve what the League tried to provide, but the League principle of voluntary co-operation among sovereign states is powerless to prevent the extermination of the human race. I use the word 'sovereign' advisedly. I am well aware of the common belief that a State is no longer sovereign if it has verbally renounced its sovereign 'right' to act as judge and jury in its own case, even whilst retaining the power to break its pledge. It is rightly pointed out that the League lacked the force to make its decisions law (when it succeeded in making a decision). But this was not the reason why it failed. Of what avail would it be to put 'force' behind a League when the very nature of a League organization means that the force would consist of competitive and self-cancelling contingents supplied by States that retain the power to withdraw from the common pool without warning?

Democracy must leap the frontiers, as and where it can. We must unite people, not governments; the former is an ideal, the latter an impossibility.

\* \* \*

### Squaring the Globe IV
### First Aid – then Cure

The measures requisite to convert the world from war to peace conditions will be so much in the nature of First Aid that it would be churlish to cavil if the statesmen appear to be improvising makeshifts for the purpose. Recognizing this, *The Times* endeavoured, in a leading article on 8 August, to disarm the criticism of impatient idealists who demand that the world shall become a Utopia the moment the last shot has been fired. True, the world body politic will

## Practical Steps to World Unity

have to undergo artificial respiration for an interim period, but even the most sophisticated convalescent has a hankering after the genuine article as far as breathing is concerned.

It is still legitimate to criticize contemporary statesmanship when it becomes manifest that the big politicians are blindly confusing first aid with remedial treatment, and are about to prescribe 'the mixture as before' in the form of functional agreements, pacts, treaties and protocols among States which retain the power to break them at their individual whim.

### A United Ministry of Shipping?

On 9 August the British Foreign Office announced that maritime members of the United Nations had come to a further agreement regarding the continued pooling of shipping resources, the arrangement not to extend beyond six months after the end of hostilities in both hemispheres. Ten percent of the time we have spent in destruction will, of course, be quite inadequate for the task of reconstruction; happily the agreement does not rule out a more permanent type of collaboration in shipping matters after the interim period. Let us hope that the Shipping Pool will develop into the future United Nations Ministry of International Transport. Will the cart come before the horse – the Ministry before the Government?

### No friction over oil

The same week saw the signing in Washington of an Oil Agreement between the USA and Britain, terminable at three months' notice by either Governmment, and intended as the preliminary to a multilateral agreement with Russia and other oil-bearing regions. This was hailed by the sober London *Times* in these words:

> 'It is highly satisfactory to record the removal of any danger of misunderstanding between the two countries (USA and GB) on the distribution of the world's oil resources.'

The Agreement proposes to set up an International Petroleum Commission. Recommendations of the Commission, if approved by both Governments, will be issued with a view to their adoption by American and British oil companies. If such ramshackle advisory machinery could remove 'all danger of misunderstanding' the world would have entered the Millennium centuries ago.

## The Parliament of Man

'We may sign Kellogg Pacts, and Kelloggesque Pacts until there is a shortage of parchment and gold pens, and we shall have done nothing real for the peace of the world.'

H. G. Wells

It is nevertheless encouraging to note that our two governments, as at present constituted, are agreed at the present moment on the subject of oil, and may with luck continue in agreement for at least three months. It is fortunate for our national life that relations among the County Councils and among the States in America are on a more stable basis than this.

### International feudalism

In the international sphere, however, the world is still in a condition of feudalism. We cannot *govern* our own affairs, merely *wangle* them, on the basis of mutual back-scratching or reciprocal retaliations. Power rather than justice determines our fate. In feudal times, national affairs were run by means of pacts between the feudal overlords, with a King or Pope exercising over them as much sovereignty as he could gather into his hands. Instead of one sovereign (an international electorate) the world today is to have four (USA, USSR, Britain and China). In this respect Earth is no further advanced than England was at the time of the Heptarchy, except that the international robber barons will have to work through national Foreign Offices.

### League not ideal

Destructive criticism needs as its corollary constructive proposals. We have to live in the world as we find it, not as we would wish it to be. But we must try to move it in the right direction. The Four-Power Conference has been postponed until 21 August, but even this extra week for preparation can hardly give us anything better than a world league of co-operating governments. I therefore suggest that the results of the Conference should not be hailed with salvoes of guns, fanfares of trumpets and journalistic hyperbole. Instead, the statesmen should make a sober announcement that their new creation is not the absolute political ideal, but merely the best practicable alternative to complete international anarchy; that they intend to steer the world towards the goal of world government in world affairs, plus national self-government in national affairs.

*Practical Steps to World Unity*

It might be poetic justice that what began as a 'phoney' war should end with a 'phoney' peace. But in such case the peace might last no longer than the war.

\* \* \*

### Squaring the Globe V
### Edward I plus George Washington

This series of articles presents the view of the growing body of opinion that favours federation with an international government for international affairs.

The Four Power Conference on world security is on diplomatic level; before its conclusions can be ratified there will be ample time to secure improvements in any arrangement which, in this imperfect world, is bound to fall short of the ideal.

The first editorial in the current issue of *The Economist* (12 August) dealing with the future of Germany, has as its keynote the following passage:

> Of the settlement that is being proposed today, this unhappy prophesy must, with all solemnity, be made: Not only will it fail to preserve the peace. *Inevitable war is being built into its very foundations.*

This series of articles has consistently uttered warnings lest our infant sons should have to fight and writhe and bleed out their young lives on some future battlefield because we, their parents, neglected to provide effective means of settling international disputes. Judicial decisions are not 'effective' if they cannot be enforced. On the other hand, force without justice is tyranny. How to provide both, therefore, is the statesman's homework.

### Diplomats are not legislators

Here a few guiding principles may not come amiss. Diplomats should be progressively divested of the functions of legislators, functions which they have assumed without any popular mandate. The principles of representative and responsible government must gradually be extended into the international sphere. This involves a recognition of the fact that national legislatures, whether unilaterally or in concert, have no right to make laws for citizens other than their own constituents. To make laws bearing on an international community we need an elected international legislature, embracing as much of the world as is at present practicable.

It has been proved empirically that popular self-government over any wide area depends on two major discoveries in political science:

◆ The principle of representative government discovered by Edward I of England: the members of a legislature must be empowered by their electors to make laws that do not require ratification by the constituencies.

◆ The principles of inter-State government discovered by George Washington and his associates :

a) Representatives must be elected not by the State governments but by the citizens (thus avoiding national bloc-voting).

b) The laws must act directly on the citizens, not through the intermediary of the constituent governments. (The only way to enforce laws upon States as such is by war, or threat of war.)

c) The supra-State Government must have full governmental power in its own sphere, but *this sphere can be restricted to a limited number of specified fields*, e.g. defence and external affairs.

### A Union of Peoples

If these principles are ignored, there can be no real hope of enforcing any peace terms − Carthaginian or other − upon Germany for any length of time, unless they are so mild as to encourage her to prepare for a third world war. On the other hand, in the extreme case of these principles winning the widest practicable acceptance and application, the result would be a Union of Peoples so great in extent and power that we need fear the resentment of the vanquished no more than the arrogance of our co-victors. Victors who no longer dread their defeated enemy can dare to be as stern or as magnanimous as occasion may demand.

The peace-loving nations will not find security merely by seeking to make their potential enemies weak; the most likely result of such a policy would be to intensify their enmity and increase their number. We must seek security in our own strength. If the 'United' Nations do the wrong thing to Germany after the war, and throw away such unity as they have so far achieved, a third German war may indeed be inevitable. If, on the contrary, the victors do the right thing by

## Practical Steps to World Unity

Germany, political perverts there and in other countries will refuse to recognize it as such; the German problem would remain.

Instead of wasting time speculating on what to do with the remnants of Germany after the war, we should decide what the 'United' Nations are going to do with themselves, and we should start doing it now. No matter whether history will judge us to have been over-lenient or unduly harsh, or to have given the Germans their just deserts, the 'United' Nations should at least take the precaution – in advance[1] – of forming themselves into a permanent Defence Union, if only to be sufficiently strong to face up to the consequences if and when our sins of omission and commission catch up with us.

The Russian draft plan to be placed on the agenda includes provision for an international air force. This is encouraging, but the success or failure of any international force will depend on the constitution of the controlling authority.

\* \* \*

In the following article, by my cryptic remark regarding the Gadarene swine I seem to remember that I was implying that the first few animals were at least pioneers!

E.R.Stettinius, Jr., the U.S. Foreign Secretary, was one of the US signatories to the U.N.Charter, 26 June 1945.

### Squaring the Globe VI
### Will War End Before Peace Begins?

The elephant has been in labour and produced a mouse. Mr Stettinius the chief midwife, described it as a peace-keeping organism consisting of an Assembly of all peace-loving States and a Council formed of a smaller number, including the 'princial States' and a number of other States elected periodically. There would be an International Court of Justice for justiciable disputes, and other instruments for the peaceful settlement of other international problems (including therefore those falling into the category for which Lord Davies wished to provide a Court of Equity). Its Genevan parentage is not in doubt.

---

[1] As a propagandist, I did not flinch from using pleonasms!

## The Parliament of Man

Mr Stettinius invited questions from the Press, but these produced little or nothing in the way of replies. It transpired, however, that a 'peace-loving' nation is to be defined as one that is willing to accept the arbitration of disputes. Since all post-war nations have everything to gain and nothing to lose by protesting their devotion to the principle of conciliation, every nation will be a 'peace-loving' state until it has resorted to war in defiance of an arbitration award.

### A Fire Extinguisher

Mr Roosevelt seems to realize this, for in his subsequent review of the results of the Conference, he stated that the Big Three wanted to end future wars by 'stepping on their necks before they grow up'. The rest of his speech showed that he, at any rate, does not wish to mislead the people by pretending that the new League — or indeed any league — could prevent war. Provided the international machinery functions, however, it can be used to extinguish conflagrations[1] before they become world-wide. Mr Roosevelt's attitude is laudable, and gives hope for the future. A statesman is a politician who, among other things, is prepared to tell the people the truth as he sees it, no matter how unpalatable it may be, and even if he knows that they will reward him by turning him out into the wilderness to waste his warnings on the desert air. The big politicians who perform on the public stage with one eye on 'the Gods' and the other in the wings where the next election is impending, distort their own vision and pervert their faculty of self-criticism. As leaders they rank with the second half-dozen of the Gadarene swine.

### A political monstrosity

The present American President has not fallen into Wilson's error. Will he be the one who will show the world how to create an international peace-keeping organism which, though at first it may be no bigger than an acorn, may be expected to grow into an oak that will one day shelter the earth?

Mr Stettinius referred to the Constitutional Convention of 1787. If he will study the arguments then used, since justified by 150 years of American history, he will see that, just as a mouse can never grow

---

[1] The tragic and disastrous Korean War is an example of United Nations firefighting: devastate the victim of aggression!

into an elephant, so a league can never grow into a government (though it may, of course, pave the way for one).

> Adversaries of federal measures cherish with blind devotion the political monster of an *imperium in imperio*. This renders a full display of the principal defects of confederation necessary, in order to show that the evils we experience do not proceed from minute or partial imperfections, but from fundamental errors in the structure of the building[2], which cannot be amended otherwise than by an alteration of the first principles and main pillars of the fabric.
>
> Alexander Hamilton, *Independent Journal*, New York, 1787

Even in these so-called enlightened times, however, the nature of sovereignty is misunderstood, as much by its detractors as by its supporters, even by many of those who rightly aver that politicians who offer both national sovereignty and peace are professing to cure the disease of war without harming the germ that causes it. Many years ago the *Manchester Guardian* coined an historic phrase when it said that the League of Nations would prevent all wars save those that were likely to occur. *The Times* has just minted another –

> '... the two incompatibilities of the Moscow Declaration: "the sovereign equality of all peace-loving States" and "the maintenance of international peace and security".'

But one would have thought that the eminent professor who writes *The Times* leaders dealing with the conditions of Peace would have realized that nations are still sovereign even if they have 'concerted in advance' on measures to keep the peace, so long as they retain the power to withdraw from the concert as soon as the conductor appears.

Can anybody produce any argument, evidence or historical proof that sovereignty can be surrendered in any other way (apart from subjection under a despotism) than by uniting the peoples into a common electorate for their common affairs? This could be done for the world some day, though no-one now living may see it, and it could be done for the democratic peoples forthwith.

\* \* \*

---

[2] The League of Friendship.

## The Parliament of Man

The following article was written while the Dumbarton Oaks Conference was still in progress. *How Green is my Valley?* was a best-seller at the time. I should also explain that the United Nations was the name for the allies; I was not alluding to the U.N. The mention of New York as an Italian city referred to the fact that Italy entered the war on one side and came out of it on the other.

### Squaring the Globe VII
### How Green are our Allies?

Mr Bidmead expresses an independent view on the future international organization of world society, which evokes wide interest today

To the extent that the Quebec Conference deals with post-war problems it seems to be an attempt to shore up what *Punch* has called the Dumbarton Hoax, herald of an era in which we shall be unable to see the dead wood for the treaties. Readers should not be disappointed if I turn to smaller, but less insignificant happenings.

Ever since the early days of intercourse between nations there has been 'functional co-operation' among them in the fields of commerce, science, religion and politics. Due to the so-called 'shrinkage' of the world as time went on the nations were jostled ever more closely together. Ever closer became their 'functional co-operation' and ever more destructive became their wars. It is not suggested that the one was the cause, the other the effect, but that the former is no real deterrent of the latter.

### A functional function

The Conference of Imperial Labour leaders in Whitehall the other day has been hailed as a fashionable piece of 'functional cooperation' and greeted as another nail in the coffin of war. Unfortunately, however, the Press seems to be blind to the fact that the only way in which political parties in the British Commonwealth, and beyond it, can effectively work together is within a common Parliament yet to be established, to deal with those affairs that are common to us all.

Sir Walter Citrine suggested that the British Commonwealth system of co-operation should serve as a model for less happy breeds of men, but in the USA forty-eight self-governing communities, sovereign in their domestic affairs, live peacefully together in a state of unity that pays good dividends in the way of prosperity and mutual

## Practical Steps to World Unity

defence. In the USA there are no neutral States; the largest Irish city in the world[1] fights with the United Nations because its inhabitants shared democratically in formulating the foreign policy that brought Uncle Sam into the war. The largest Italian city[1] in the world entered the war on our side. In contrast, Whitehall made[2] Eire's bed, and is surprised she will not lie on it.

If Britannia's foreign policy had derived from a Commonwealth Parliament representing all her citizens, we should have been spared the sorry spectacle of South Africa escaping the stigma of neutrality by the votes of only seven of her MPs. (Ironically enough, the defeated neutrality resolution included a clause to the effect that she would continue to expect protection from the U.K. fleet. Had it been passed, King George would, in England, have been at war with Germany, whilst continuing friendly relations with her from his South African throne.) Instead, there would have been no call for the South African Parliament, any more than the Legislature of any American State, to vote on the issue. But if some busybody had organized a referendum it would no doubt have been as much in support of the war effort as any other members of the United Nations.

### Third time

In this century, the British Commonwealth, as now constituted, has failed to prevent two major wars. The League of Nations, formed on the same model (co-operation among governments) has failed to prevent this second war. Yet British statesmen are asking their (presumably intelligent) Allies to put their trust a third time on the same kind of set-up as a guardian of future peace. How, they may ask, can the British Commonwealth system be extended to non-British nations having no bonds of kinship or allegiance to a common Crown, and probably no common language? British taxpayers might pertinently ask, too, whether it would mean that the responsibility for the defence of the entire system would remain, as at present, the first charge on the meagre resources of Great Britain and Northern Ireland. Would it mean that the other members of the new Commonwealth of Nations had to fall in with a Whitehall foreign policy? Could Sir Walter satisfy them on these points?

---

[1] New York.

[2] Eire was a so-called 'neutral', sheltering Nazi U-boats.

## The Parliament of Man

The recent exchange of correspondence between Mr Churchill and Lord Cecil, League of Nations pioneer, makes depressing reading. One can understand the Prime Minister's desire to comfort his old friend in his declining years. But when the future of children still in their cradles is at stake one should not mince words.

The principle of co-operation among governments has twice in this century deluged the world in blood. Britain's most signal contribution to world order would be to abandon that principle as the basis of her own commonwealth, and as the basis of her relationship with other like-minded nations. The principles of representative and responsible government must be extended into the international sphere.

# CHAPTER 8

# FEDERALISTS ON THE PEACE PATH

The Federal Union resolution to the effect that federalist organizations throughout the world ought to unite came to fruition in August 1947, when the first Congress of the World Movement for World Federal Government was held. This was the year the Cominform, too, was established.

My report on the conference, besides being published in several British papers, was translated into French by a French-language paper in New Hampshire, U.S.A., *l'Avenir National*[1].

Report from Montreux, 23 August 1947:

### Federalists of the World Have United

'I wish you all success. Two years ago I said:
 "The idea of World Government must be carefully nursed in order that the right atmosphere may be created. It is not something that can be imposed from the top, but must be the result of growth."
Such growth your movement is designed to foster.'

This message from Mr Ernest Bevin, British Foreign Secretary, was among those read out at the opening of the first Congress of the World Movement for World Federal Government in this beautiful city last Sunday.

---

[1] The paper must have made some investigations into my identity; a footnote stated that Harold Bidmead was a heraldic designer for royalty and *la noblesse*, making the necessary research to devise armorial bearings, and was also an illuminator of parchments and vellum. This was correct except for one detail. It related to my father Harold W. Bidmead.

*159*

## The Parliament of Man

Since then, more than 400 delegates and observers from twenty-eight federalist organizations in twenty-four countries have worked all through the sweltering days and far into the nights to hammer out a policy and to create a world organization to implement it. More than a hundred delegates and observers are sleeping on straw in the municipal gymnasium. Others more happily placed from the point of view of wealth or currency allotments are lodged at world-famous hotels. The deliberations have proceeded with a fine disregard of such factors, and of nationality, language, colour or creed.

The debates have not been without their dramatic moments and crises. One sensed that some new force was painfully finding its way into the world. A 'Declaration of Montreux' was ultimately agreed *nem con*. It runs, in essence:

> 'The United Nations Organization, as at present constituted, is powerless to stop the drift to war. The choice lies, not between free enterprise and planned economy, nor between capitalism and communism, but between federalism and power politics.
>
> Mankind can free itself for ever from war only through the establishment of a world federation, based on:
>
> ◆ Universal membership – open to all people and nations.
>
> ◆ Transfer to the world federal government of such legislative, executive and judicial powers as relate to world affairs.
>
> ◆ Enforcement of world law directly on the individual.
>
> ◆ Creation of supra-national armed forces capable of guaranteeing the security of the world federation. Disarmament of member nations to their internal policing requirements.
>
> ◆ Control by world federal government of atomic development and the like.
>
> ◆ Power to raise adequate revenues directly and independently of state taxes.'

The Declaration also approved a plan submitted by the British Parliamentary Committee for the Crusade for World Government, which is backed by 100 British M.Ps.

Henry Usborne, M.P., the Hon. General Secretary of the Committee, stated:

> 'We shall unite the world not by conquest but by consent; not by

## Federalists on Peace Path

argument of force but by force of argument.'

The scheme aims at organizing unofficial ballots throughout the world to elect a World Constituent Assembly which would draft a constitution of World Government. The Constitution would be subject to ratification by the peoples; when 50% of the nations, or nations comprising 50% of the world's population, have ratified it, the World Government would be established. World Government cannot wait, says the scheme, until all ratify. To do so would perpetuate a veto.

The Rev. Gordon Lang, M.P., Chairman of the Parliamentary Committee estimated that the Constituent Assembly could be elected by 1950 – three years hence.

'Amazing things have been done in the cause of slaughter in three months', he reminded the Congress, 'and as much can be done for peace.'

Victor Collins, M.P., supporting Mr Lang, stated:

'Without World Government we are under sentence of death; not a very long sentence, either.'

Of the German 'problem', the consensus of opinion seemed to be that the only way to 're-educate' Germany and at the same time relieve the 'victors' of the cost of occupying and sustaining her would be to bring her into a federation so wide that she would be a minority – as would other nations – with only a minority share (if any) in the armaments possessed by all.

Opening a public discussion on the Russian aspect of the problems, Mr Henry Usborne argued:

'We have no right to expect another nation to answer the question of World Government until we have succeeded in making our own nation answer it.

Only after America, Britain and France and many others besides have actually agreed to surrender their armed forces to a supra-national federal authority – only when this has actually been done may be hope or can we expect to know the attitude the Russians will then adopt.'

Mr M. Shawcross, M.P., supporting both Mr Henry Usborne and Professor Girard, stated that he would expect Russian support for the plan to be, eventually, better than from other nations. The Russians were familiar with the theories of federation on which their own constitution was based. The Russians were a multitude of peoples, religions and languages, all combined under a central government[2].

Furthermore, it had always been a basic principle of socialist philosophy that the essential unity of mankind must be established or there will never be real peace or prosperity.

Professor Hans Thirring of the University of Vienna, and a member of the Austrian Peace Society, stated that a German translation of the book *Anatomy of Peace* by Emery Reves, was enjoying a wide circulation in Austria and that Communist opinion there was that — with provisos — Russia would be prepared to accept a world federation solution but felt that the westerners would not offer them adequate safeguards in the constitution.

Professor Girard of France considered that if a federation were to be established under a non-idealogical constitution, based not on outmoded concepts of international law but on a directly elected legislature, the benefits to the participants would be so great and so obvious that Russia would not wish to exclude herself.

*Editor's footnote:*
Jack Grove, who also attended this Congress, writes:
> Not the least encouraging sign here is the large number of young people who are present — many of them as delegates representing some twenty-eight organizations from all parts of the world. The world tomorrow is their world, and they seem determined that the 'old men' shall not again — and for the last time — lead them down the suicidal path that leads to war.'

\* \* \*

[2] *1992 note:* The USSR has now collapsed because of the failure of communism, not of federalism. It could, however, also be argued that the way in which Stalinism rode roughshod over the federal constitution bears a large share of the blame. In which case, of course, the communist populace is also to be blamed for failing to defend their constitution, failing to realize that the price of freedom is eternal vigilance.

Mr Harris Wofford,(now US Senator for Tennessee) of U.S.A. Student Federalists, reached the same conclusion in his scholarly analysis of Russian Communism, which might be summarized by the slogan:

'Voters of the World, Unite!'

## Federalists on Peace Path

The next Congress I attended was that organized by Winston Churchill and his son-in-law, Mr Duncan Sandys for the following May, in The Hague. As I was not a professional journalist, my application to cover the proceedings was at first declined. However, I toured Fleet Street and its environs, and eventually collected requests from nearly a dozen periodicals to cover the Congress on their behalf. The fees I eventually collected, though modest, plus one for lecturing as a substitute for Mr R.W.G.Mackay, the author of *Federal Europe* and chairman of the British delegation, defrayed the entire expenses of my trip, including my return air fare. (Mackay was socialist M.P., but the Labour Party Secretary circulated his Members urging them not to attend! His letter was ignored by the majority.)

Though this was not officially a federalist conference, the federalists soon demonstrated their preponderance; I therefore make no excuse for including my report in the series.

The Hague Congress was, of course, the inception of the EC.

## FEDERAL EUROPE IS CONCEIVED

My report on the Hague Congress as it appeared in *World Affairs* (London Institute of World Affairs), October 1948. (Europe must be united by design, not by accident.)

### A Design for the Occident

'We need not have disputes about who originated this idea of United Europe. There are many valid modern patents. But we may all yield our pretentions to King Henry of Navarre, King of France, who, with his great Minister Sully, between the years 1600 and 1607, laboured to set up a permanent committee representing the fifteen – now we are sixteen – leading Christian States of Europe ... This he called "The Grand Design". We are the servants of the Grand Design.'

Winston Churchill, opening The Congress of Europe, The Hague,<br>7 May 1948

With these half-jocular words, spoken in the centuries-old Hall of Knights before an audience consisting of their Royal Highnesses Princess Juliana and Prince Bernhard, many members of the Nether-

## The Parliament of Man

lands Government, judges from the International Court of Justice, 800 delegates from twenty-six countries, 250 journalists and members of the public, Mr Churchill tactfully allayed what smouldering jealousies there may have been among the various sponsors and initiators of the Congress of Europe. His speech raised speculations in many minds whether the delegates, in the main, had travelled so far merely to remodel an archaic plan for a league of fifteen or sixteen sovereign States directed at an Eastern Power, or whether a more constructive proposal would be engendered by their deliberations.

### Motives

Questioning my fellow-travellers on the way, I had discovered that they had — as most of them expressed it — 'open minds' on the means to be adopted to attain the objectives set by the Convenors: the Joint International Committee of the Movements for European Unity, which envisaged *inter alia*, 'the establishment of a complete Federation with an elected European Parliament'. The majority of those who answered the summons to The Hague were not avowed federalists. There was even scepticism as to the utility of the undertaking; doubts were freely uttered whether our exertions would prove to be worth while. A comment in *The Times* on the eve of the Congress, to the effect that it might do more harm than good, seemed to have sown perplexity in irresolute minds.

Sir John Anderson[1], with whom in the company of Lady Anderson I shared a seat in the coach from Schipol Airport to The Hague, confessed that he intended to hear the views of other delegates before he revealed his own. He considered, however, that the language question would be the main stumbling block in devising a genuine European parliament. He was not impressed with the suggestion that the solution might be a 'walkie-talkie' translation system such as those used at the Nürnberg trials.

One of the twenty-six Socialist M.P.s in the British delegation assured me that his motive in attending was at first mere contrariness. 'Much as I wanted to come,' he explained to me, 'I had decided that I could not spare the time. I am eternally grateful to Morgan Phillips for his letter urging us not to attend. But for him I should have missed an exhilarating experience and an historic occasion.'

[1] Cabinet Minister. Gave his name to a type of domestic air raid shelter, see also Chapter 9.

## Federalists on Peace Path

Some flocked to The Hague as do pilgrims to Mecca, firm in the faith that good would come of it, yet with little knowledge upon which to base any confident prophecy. Indeed, perhaps it was instinct rather than intentions that brought the Congress together. When instinct brings birds together they are traditionally 'all of a feather'. It was a pleasant surprise to find that in this instance their plumage was by no means so violent in hue as the alarmists had predicted. True, some of the distinguished personages there could perhaps be classed as intellectual reactionaries in the sense that their mental vision was focused on the glories of Europe's past, but in this they may be no worse than the blasé young men who look upon the present and see 'no future in it'. But the Congress of Europe was certainly not a hotbed of irrational anti-Communist, anti-Russian hysteria. The delegates were in the main more interested in the positive aspects of freedom, and were concerned to give Russian foreign policy full credit for having made the unification of Europe an objective of practical politics.

### The Real Issue

To the dismay of those who had come to The Hague intending to take a great step forward in the evolution of a new, peaceful world society, caution was the keynote of the opening speeches. *The Times* reported the next morning that both Mr Churchill and Monsieur Ramadier had repudiated 'any federalist revolution', and commented that 'only the course of debate at The Hague will reveal how far these opening speeches will satisfy those delegates who desire to set up a new and untried scheme of international government on the ground over which established governments, chosen by the people, are already working together.' Nothing could have expressed more succinctly the issues for which the Congress of Europe was to be the battleground: federation versus *con*federation; government versus debating society; genuine union or league; peace or national sovereignty. Few could have foreseen the swift and spectacular victory of those who desired to try an 'untried scheme' if only because leagues and confederal structures had failed everywhere and every time they had been tried.

In the opinion of many present, it was a matter of urgent practical politics to thrash out and decide a controversy that has hitherto been generally regarded as academic; whether 'governments chosen by the people' are really the right agencies to choose the members of an

## The Parliament of Man

international 'authority', or whether international authority should be wielded only by representatives elected directly by the peoples themselves. Mr Kristensen, a Danish delegate, agreed with a Swedish colleague that 'union must not be a union of governments alone, but a union of peoples, parliaments, trade unions, professional organizations and the like'. Count Coudenhove-Kalergi, speaking in the name of the European Parliamentary Union, asserted that the peoples and the Parliaments of Europe were readier than their governments to accept federation. Monsieur Maccas, Greece, and Miss Tenderloo (Netherlands) spoke in support of equal representation for States, whereas her compatriot Max Geesteranus supported Monsieur P. O. Lapie (France), who demanded: 'As for equality, it must be established as between men, not as between States'. Monsieur Lamalla (Belgium) preferred a compromise, with State equality in an Upper House and popular representation in the Lower. He cited the dual system of Switzerland. Monsieur Ramadier had pleaded in the first plenary session that 'Europe cannot be created by a sort of federalist revolution which would weaken the governments without increasing their collective strength'. Then, paradoxically and almost in the same breath came his peroration:

'Proclamons farouchement; l'Europe ou la mort!'.

And a cynic commented[2]:

'Rather hot mustard on a somewhat tasteless sandwich!'

The same evening, on our way to dine at the Kurhaus at Scheveningen, I asked Monsieur Ramadier whether his conception of European law was that it should operate upon individuals, or upon States as such. He replied unhesitatingly:

'Sur les états, naturellement'.

Somebody intervened to argue that this was, in effect, advocating the use of war to keep the peace. Monsieur Ramadier agreed that the Nürnberg verdicts had set the precedent − if precedent were needed − for the application of international law to individuals. He conceded that the progressive realization of this principle as a preventive measure should be an ideal, but − he added − it was a long-term aim.

### Triumph of Federalism

The two men who most decisively influenced the change of tempo

[2] I claim credit for this remark!

## Federalists on Peace Path

from 'cautious' to 'urgent' were Dr Hendrik Brugmans (Netherlands) and Mr R. W. G. Mackay, M.P. chairman of the British delegation; and author of *Federal Europe*. The former leaped into action immediately after Ramadier's first speech. In words which the audience applauded every bit as vigorously as they had greeted the presence of Mr Churchill, the dynamic Dutchman alleged that Europe was being undermined by lack of faith on the part of Europeans themselves. But surely, he asked, they had not lost their taste for rebellion. The paramount task of our time, he considered, was to federate Europe.

'We are not at all, not in the slightest,' he reiterated, 'not in the least bit interested in diplomatic structures like the old League of Nations or a European UNO ... To talk of a United Europe without conceiving a European government and a European parliament is entirely unrealistic'.

Count Dr Nicoló Randini, former Italian Ambassador to Great Britain, who followed him, declared on behalf of the Italian delegation:

'Our aim is the federal union of Western Europe; ... a customs and economic union supported by the federal power, which would lead gradually to the unfettered circulation of citizens, raw materials and capital across all the internal frontiers of Europe.'

A proposal which originally required the creation of a European Deliberative Assembly was amended by deletion of the word 'Deliberative', Mr Mackay contending that what was wanted was a body that could act, not merely discuss; Europe needed a European government, with effective powers, not another council of Foreign Ministers. So spectacular was the manner in which radical ideas captured the imagination of the Congress that a wag with a flair for parable put into circulation the story[3] of a dejected little man discovered by a friend on the back fringe of a tumultuous mob during the French Revolution, who was asked:

'Why tag along with this *canaille*?'

'I have to,' he replied ruefully, 'I'm their leader.'

A long but pertinent memorandum distributed by the French federalists made a deep impression, and Mr Kenneth Lindsay, M.P. (Ind.) paid tribute in plenary session to the 'burning conviction that ani-

---

[3] I claim kudos for this, too!

mated the federalists in the Assembly'. Speeches made in committee by Monsieur Alexandre Marc, member of the secretariat of the European Union of Federalists, were greeted with long and enthusiastic applause, because he took his stand unequivocally upon federalist principles.

### Leagues under a cloud

Only slight lip service was paid to UNO. An attempt made by Major Manningham-Buller, M.P. (Cons.) to delete a reference to UNO's inadequacy to provide law and order was defeated in committee by eighty-two votes to seventy-two. Some were inclined to assume that to give a league the *right* to govern peacefully is tantamount to giving it the *power* to do so. But Air Vice-Marshal Bennett, chairman of the United Nations Association, seemed to be well aware of the fundamental changes that are necessary in man's thinking before he turns from the confederal to the federal idea. During luncheon one day at the Hotel Central, The Hague, he was enthusiastically brandishing a full-page article that had appeared in the *New York Times* by the chairman of Standard Oil Company of America, a plea for international government on a world-wide scale.

'There is a whole column here,' he told us, 'which I should like to incorporate word for word in official UNA policy.'

The passage in question described how, in the author's opinion, UNO could be transformed into a world government. Incidentally, the opinion was expressed by one of the Congress members at the table that the very existence of the United Nations was a barrier against world government, and that the desire to convert it, rather than abolish it, was a hindrance to progress towards something better and adequate.

The essential difference between confederation and federation was also stressed by Monsieur Paul Reynaud, who pointed out in the Political Committee's session that afternoon that if the parliaments were to elect the members of the proposed European Assembly, this would be tantamount to the members electing themselves. He became the leader of a vigorous drive to have an elected European Assembly based on 'one citizen, one vote', rather than on the confederal (league) principle of State equality. Monsieur Reynaud was emphatic that this should be established within six months.

## Federalists on Peace Path

### A Constituent Assembly

The Committee regretfully decided that, even if a Constituent Assembly could be appointed without any delay whatever, it would require some months to agree upon a draft constitution. Bearing in mind that this document would then have to be ratified before the European Parliament could be elected, it was unrealistic to expect results as soon as Monsieur Reynaud considered to be essential. The outcome was that the Political Resolution, as passed in its final form by a plenary session some hours ahead of schedule, demanded:

'... the convening, as a matter of real urgency, of a European Assembly chosen by the Parliaments of the participating nations, from among their members *and others*, ... to advise upon immediate political measures designed progressively to bring about the necessary economic and political union of Europe; to examine the juridical and constitutional implications arising out of such a union or federation ... and to prepare the necessary plans.'

The resolution provided that the Assembly should report within three months on its labours, and that it should make proposals for the establishment of a court of justice with *adequate sanctions*, before which any *citizen* of the united countries would have redress for any violation of his rights as formulated in the proposed Charter of Rights. The Congress further asserted its '... conviction that the sole solution of the economic and political problems of Germany is its integration in a federated Europe'. A communiqué issued by a largely attended meeting of the Socialists of all countries represented at the Congress of Europe, under the chairmanship of Mr R. W. G. Mackay, announced that 'the meeting was completely unanimous that at The Hague substantial progress had been made towards a democratic federation of Europe.'

A certain amount of publicity has since been given to the forthright views expressed by some members of the British delegation upon the 'Reynaud' plan mentioned above, but it was reported that its author eventually declared himself satisfied with the outcome. Some of those who listened to the cut and thrust of the debate on this topic could not understand why a proposal of this nature should be opposed by Mr Mackay, for instance, whose writings on a federal Europe had marked him out as a federalist in a hurry for practical action. Professor David Mitrany, delegate for an American peace organization, and tireless advocate of the functional approach to international organization which men – alas! – follow only too readily, even without pedagogic exhortation, later expressed himself mystified by the attitude of Monsieur Reynaud's critics; he has even gone so far as to insinuate that their warning that Monsieur Reynaud should try to 'hasten more slowly' really cloaked a deep-laid plot to extricate the British Empire from European entanglements!

### Delegates or Representatives?

Unfriendly critics have deplored the use of the word 'delegates' to describe the participants. Perhaps it was just as well that they were not delegates, in the sense that the organizations they represented did not instruct them how to vote. Delegates voted according to their own consciences; they were also representatives in the sense that their credentials were checked beforehand, and it may safely be presumed that few organizations such as were there represented would lend their names to irresponsible persons. The Congress of Europe was Europe in miniature, a cross-section of the cultural and intellectual strata, perhaps, but a cross-section nevertheless of those sections of society that tend to activate the rest. One would have concluded that the assembly was distinguished more for its representative character than for any predicted propensity to agree among themselves.

### Among those present

There were twenty ex-Prime Ministers and twenty-eight ex-Foreign Ministers. The Austrian delegation consisted of six members of the National Council, the Secretary-General of the Economic Council, the Rector of the University of Innsbrück, three industrialists and a merchant; the sixty-eight Belgians included Monsieur Paul van Zeeland, a Minister of State, five deputies and three senators; there were thirty-two Danes, including four ex-Ministers; Eire had eight delegates, including two senators; the French delegation of 185 included Count Coudenhove-Kalergi, Monsieur Edouard Daladier, Monsieur Francois Poncet, Monsieur Paul Ramadier, Monsieur P. H. Teitgen, Marquis André d'Ormesson (French Ambassador to the Netherlands), the rosette of the Legion of Honour being everywhere in evidence; the Sarre delegates consisted of the President of the Council of Ministers, the Secretary of State, two Ministers and a lawyer;

## Federalists on Peace Path

there were fifty-one from Germany; the twelve dozen British comprised sixty-one Members of Parliament (of whom twenty-three Conservatives, twenty-six Socialists), and included Sir Adrian Boult, Peter Fleming, Hore-Belisha[4], King-Hall (chairman of the Press Committee), Richard Law, John Masefield, Earl Russell and Sir Arthur Salter, to name but a few at random; the eighteen Greeks included four deputies; Iceland was represented by a former Social Minister; fifty-seven – well assorted – came from Italy; Prince Constantin of Liechtenstein, President of the Liechtenstein Movement for a Federal Union of Europe, attended with two of his colleagues; Luxembourg, which has an absolute majority of federalists in its Parliament, sent eight delegates; the Netherlands counted among its fifty-nine delegates the Presidents of Royal Dutch Shell, Philips Lamps, K.L.M., and Unilever, and many popular radicals such as Jef Last, Dr G. J. van Heuven Goedhart (editor of the socialist daily *Het Parool*, and Professor Berkelbach van den Sprenkel, Professor of Theology, who spoke at the mass meeting in Amsterdam in favour of one army for Europe; of the twelve Norwegians, six were members of the Lower House and one was the President of the Upper House; seven of the nineteen Swedes were Members of Parliament; 'little' Switzerland was magnificently represented in numbers and quality (with thirty-nine); Mr S. A. Yalman represented Turkey. The thirty-five observers from Eastern Europe included Mr Hj. J. Procope, former Finnish Minister of Foreign Affairs, Mr R. Pilsudski (Poland) and Monsieur Grégoire Gafencu, ex-Minister of Foreign Affairs for Rumania. Señor Salvador de Madariaga, ex-Minister for Spain, made an unexpectedly tactless speech at the closing plenary session implying that he would like to ride rough-shod over federalist principles and create a Europe, all of whose fair cities, London, Rome, Paris, Warsaw, Belgrade and Stockholm, would be owned in common by a cosmopolitan community of neo-Europeans! Perhaps this was merely an example of the misleading effect of magniloquence!

### Verdicts

Few who heard Senator Pieter Kerstens (Netherlands) introducing us to each other when he opened the first plenary session, would have expected unanimity to proceed from such a heterogeneous gathering:

---

[4] Ex Cabinet Minister; gave his name to Belisha pedestrian crossing.

'Little more than a year ago,' he reminded us, 'it was largely thought Utopian to bring together socialists, liberals and conservatives, religious believers and freethinkers, big employers, bankers, financiers, economists and trade union leaders, parliamentarians and scholars, military people and artists, under one common denominator, that is to say to bring all those divergent individuals together on a programme of common interest. Today this Utopian ideal has become a fact. Once more the idealists have proved to be more practical than the self-styled realists.'

And yet, the Rt. Hon. Duncan Sandys was able to proclaim in his valedictory speech:

'The objectives we had in mind when we decided to organize this Congress were threefold: first to demonstrate the widespread support which exists for the cause of European unity; secondly, to secure an exchange of views and arrive at agreed recommendations for action; and, thirdly, to provide a new and powerful impetus to the campaign. Having regard to all the political uncertainties and controversies with which we were confronted, we realized that there was a risk of failure or fiasco. But in great enterprises great risks have to be taken. If, as at one time appeared possible, important elements in the life of Europe had altogether abstained from participation, the Congress might have been robbed of its influence and authority. By your presence, many of you at considerable personal sacrifice, you have made this the most representative assembly of independent citizens that has ever met to deliberate upon the fate of Europe.'

In an oblique reference to a gloomy (unfulfilled) prediction that had appeared in the press, Mr Sandys went on:

'Had our debates revealed deep rifts or irreconcilable divergencies upon policy, the holding of this Congress would have weakened and not strengthened our cause. There have, of course, been differences of opinion in certain matters as there always will be wherever free men meet together to discuss their affairs. But I think you will agree that our debates have resulted in a most remarkable measure of agreement.'

### Staff work

Bringing together these worthy citizens of Europe was but part of a feat of organization, the performance of which exceeded all expec-

## Federalists on Peace Path

tations. With one-tenth of the staff that a government-sponsored conference would have enjoyed, and without the organizational advantages that a permanent parliament has over a transient gathering, the Secretariat worked day and night to provide the Congress with complete texts, in French and English — and sometimes other languages — of all resolutions, amendments, minutes and important speeches. No detail was neglected by our charming hosts. The high-vaulted chamber of the Riddersaal, blazing with heraldry in rich bright colours, was hung with glowing tapestries and a 'Banner of Europe', the device which flew over all The Hague; the pavilion of the Dierentuin, where the Political Committee met, was bedecked with elegant pedigree tulips. Their Royal Highnesses Princess Juliana and Prince Bernhard received us at a sumptuous State reception at Kasteel oud Wassenaar, an old chateau in sylvan surroundings; dinner was served each evening to the entire company in the Restaurant of the Kurhaus, Scheveningen, that seaside resort whose name was a shibboleth during the war. Other repasts were taken at one or other of The Hague's leading restaurants, so that we enjoyed all that the excellent Dutch cuisine has to offer.

### 'The Aim and the Design'

A special train conveyed us to Amsterdam, where the populace became almost Latin in the fervour with which they greeted Mr Churchill, symbol of liberation, and then listened stolidly but appreciatively whilst he and his colleagues explained that European union would not come about by mere accident, by just waiting for it, and expounded what Mr Churchill called

' ... the aim and the design of a united Europe, whose moral conceptions will win the respect and gratitude of mankind and whose physical strength will be such that none will dare molest her tranquil sway.'

\* \* \*

*1992:*

Surely the time is now ripe for a similar gathering designed to unite the world!

## CITIZENS OF THE WORLD UNITE

Shortly after the Hague came the second Congress of the World Movement for World Federal Government, which I attended and reported on. My article both reported what world citizens had done and invited others to do so, being entitled:

### Citizens of the World Unite

Nearly two hundred official delegates and many more observers, from a score of countries throughout the world, gathered together at the Cercle Municipal, Luxembourg, under the patronage of the Grand Duchess Charlotte and Prince Felix, for the second annual congress of the World Movement for World Federal Government.

The movement was formed this time last year in Montreux, Switzerland, to unite twenty-four federalist organizations in various parts of the world, with a mandate to work for a world federal government with legislative, executive and judicial powers to enforce world law directly on the individual. The number of its member organizations has now grown to over seventy-three. Delegates were able to study the first issue of a full-size four-page monthly, Le Monde Fédéré, published by the WMWFG in French and English.

Addressing the opening session, Mr Emery Reves, author of the world best seller *The Anatomy of Peace*, called upon the West European nations to initiate the evolution towards World Federation. He said that many people in Western Europe realized that their national institutions were no longer powerful enough to protect them against the miseries of wars, and felt the necessity to create a higher legal order for their own protection and prosperity.

### Year's Growth

A French Abbott, Grouès Pierre, a delegate of the Comité Francais pour les Etats-Unis du Monde, told a press conference that the movement had grown considerably since its inaugural meeting a year ago. Monsieur Jean Larmeroux, retiring President of the WMWFG, reported that in France two hundred French M.P.s had joined the movement; there was a very strong federalist group in the British House of Commons; in Luxembourg the federalist M.P.s comprised about three-quarters of the total votes of the House; Italy's group of

## Federalists on Peace Path

two hundred and forty M.P.s was growing daily, and similar successes were reported from the Netherlands, Scandinavia and elsewhere.

Speaking of the movement's attitude towards Western Union, Monsieur Alexandre Marc (France) recalled that the Montreux Declaration was in favour of regional understandings and that the door was open to federal groupings. Europe was not the only important area, and all federations on a regional basis would have to be welcomed provided they were steps towards universality.

### In Russia

Replying to a question as to what encouragement the ideal of federal government received from the USSR and the Eastern European countries, Abbé Grouès Pierre reported on his recent visit to the USSR, Czechoslovakia and Jugoslavia, where he had found that federalism was regarded as the only practical theory of world government, whether it came about as the result of the triumph of Marxism or by any other means. In practice, however, the movement was looked upon with suspicion in those countries, federalists being regarded as the tools of capitalists who were exploiting them with the intention of capturing the markets of the world!

In an interview, Mr Ahmet Emin Yalman, editor of the well-known Turkish daily *Yatan* said that in Turkey the movement was young but rapidly growing, counting amongst its members some prominent personalities in the Government and the National Assembly.

The Congress divided into about a dozen Special Committees, which reported to the Plenary Sessions later in the week. The report of the Sub-Committee on East-West Relations stated that the World Federalist movement had no designs against the just interests of any nation. It continued:

> 'Since peoples or nations not inclined towards World Government will be influenced by practical evidence of the intentions of other peoples or nations to establish World Government, it is urged that steps be taken to press on with the holding of any World Constituent Assembly open to all states at any stage.'

The Congress approved in principle a policy statement declaring that:

> '... peace based upon justice is the first right and first freedom of mankind. ... The conflict of ideologies today accentuates but does

not necessarily create the present world-wide insecurity. ... Such insecurity and danger are the products of general anarchy among nations.'

The declaration goes on to state that peace depends on the existence of enforceable law, which requires government — government on the world level.

The Luxembourg Declaration calls for a world federal government, 'endowed with properly delegated power, and responsible not to nations but to peoples. ... The World Constitution and world law enacted thereunder shall be binding not only upon governments,*but directly upon individuals.*'

*  *  *

*Note:*
About this time the World Federalist Press Association (Association de la Presse Fédéraliste Mondiale) was formed, and I was a founder member. I soon discovered that the membership card, like many other Press Cards, permitted entry into many places where the bearer really had no business to be!

See Illustration, p 56.


**I MEET A FUTURE PRESIDENT OF INDIA AND HALF-WIN A NOBEL PEACE PRIZE**

It was in the summer of 1949, while covering the third WMWFG Congress that I met a future President of India, who was already a keen federalist at that time.

Reuters in London had appointed me their representative for the purpose. I had a full-time job, but I had already imbued my managing director, Sven Frisell, with the federalist 'bug', and he gave me a week's leave of absence.

As a sideline, one of my first tasks for Tidningarnas Telegrambyrå (TT), Reuter's Stockholm agency, was to cover the arrival of India's second Ambassador to the USSR, the late Sir Sarvepalli Radhakrishnan (later to be Vice President, then President, of India), who was breaking his first journey to Moscow in Stockholm. Many press

## Federalists on Peace Path

One of the meetings of the Federalist Press Association was held in Geneva on 4 January 1951. This photograph was taken at the meeting.

Key to the photograph starting at the 7 o'clock position and going clockwise around the table:
1. Italian Federalist.
2. Italian Federalist.
3. Probably Guy Marchand, the Treasurer.
4. Yugoslav federalist.
5. Henri Koch, (koch'en Heng), Luxembourg federalist, one-time secretary of Federal Union, U.K.
6. Harold S. Bidmead.
7. Secretary: G. B. de Vos, journalist on *Vivre*.
8. Vice-President: Jean F. Collin, Editor of *Vivre*, Belgium.
9. President: Madame Sella, Editor-in-Chief, *Notizie Federaliste Mondiali*, Italy.
10. French federalist.
11. Dutch Federalist.
12. ?

## The Parliament of Man

hounds turned up at the Grand Hotel to meet him. All were denied audience, as His Excellency was tired and needed to rest.

I showed my World Federalist Press Card, complete with photograph, and sent a message through to him to the effect that I was an active federalist (I knew he was one). I received word back that he would give me an interview on one condition.

'What is that?' I asked.

'That you will grant him an interview.' was the reply.

We chatted over cups of Indian tea, attentively listened to by his entire entourage, and later that day I was happy to telex Reuters an exclusive report which included his Excellency's warm message of encouragement to the Congress. I cannot now find the text, but as it is technically Reuter's copyright I would hesitate to repeat it here.

This scoop made me feel like a real reporter!

### Teeth like pearls

I took yet another break from reporting the Congress when I went shopping at Stockholm's 'Selfridges' – Nordiska Kompaniet. On entering the store I was met by a bevy of beautiful girls bearing badges to the effect that they were volunteer interpreters for foreign shoppers. Approaching the most pulchritudinous, and taking care to employ none of my vernacular Swedish, I asked her in halting English whether she could help me in this difficult city. We started on a tour of the departments, broken by a hasty luncheon ('a working girl must stay busy') and I purchased several articles which I subsequently gave away. Once I had revealed my command of her native language (she herself had several) a dinner date was arranged. For this my divinity arrived consummately attired, and wearing a string of pearls which were as genuine as her smile.

I later told her her teeth were like pearls (and believe me, Pearl's teeth are perfect!) After dinner I chartered a taxi to show us the sights of Stockholm, after which my companion directed the driver into one of the royal parks and to stop outside a magnificent set of gilt wrought iron portals. He protested in his Stockholm 'cockney' that it was unseemly to park outside this kind of private residence. Metaphorically drawing herself up to her full height, my goddess announced 'I live here.'

Indeed, during the conversation I had learned that her father had

## *Federalists on Peace Path*

much to do with ensuring that the Nobel bequest was sufficiently well invested to yield all the munificent prize monies distributed every year. The hint was dropped, jocularly of course, that if I played my cards right tonight my new acquaintance might suggest to the Norwegians a suitable recipient of the Peace Prize. It was time a federalist won it!

By a coincidence,(?) it was announced two months later that the 1949 Nobel Peace Prize had been awarded to Lord Boyd Orr of Brechon, the President of the World Movement for World Federal Government, whose Congress I was in process of reporting. Needless to say, ever afterwards I have felt that I won the prize myself, by proxy! Perhaps I should have played my trump card?

We corresponded avidly after that, though a vital meeting was thwarted by a thief relieving her of all her money and travel documents — the crook who may have changed my life!

\* \* \*

My report read as follows:

### Stockholm World Government Congress
### Boyd Orr Re-elected President

'The people of all countries hate the thought of war. They want a world in which people of all nations with common interests can meet in peace and friendship. ... The strong desire for world peace is shown by the number of international organizations working for world government.

In this world crisis every person of common sense and goodwill should respond to the call to join one or other of these international organizations ... The people of the world can have the Four Freedoms if they are willing to join together and work for them.'

LORD JOHN BOYD ORR, President of the World Movement for World Federal Government, made this appeal at the opening of the Movement's Third Annual Congress, in Stockholm, on 29 August. The World Movement for World Federal Government was created, he said, so that the people of all countries could, with one voice, call on the governments to stop the political conflict that is tearing the world apart, and begin to co-operate with each other on international measures for the benefit of all countries.

## The Parliament of Man

The re-election of Lord Boyd Orr as President was unopposed.

The Congress, which met in the House of Commons of the Swedish Parliament (Riksdag) Building, was attended by 350 delegates and observers as well as representatives from twenty international organizations specially invited.

Among the commissions into which the Congress divided was one on Atomic Energy. The commission's Report, presented by Dr Kowarski, assistant to Prof. Joliot-Curie, and adopted without amendment, states that:

'... the control of atomic energy cannot usefully be discussed as an isolated problem since the problem concerned is one of the basic factors of national power. Effective atomic energy control is impossible except under a supra-national authority; the Committee would therefore like the concept of this authority widened, and advocates national and organic[1] approach to the establishment of world government.'

Reports were adopted on the Peoples' World Convention, to be called in 1950; World Citizenship; the transformation of UNO into a world federation; Parliamentary Action; and Regional Federation.

At the closing session of the Congress the delegates stood while a message of goodwill and encouragement from the Mayor of Hiroshima was read out by Morikatsu Inagaki (Chairman of Executive of Japanese Union for World Federal Government).

Those elected to the new International Council included Elisabeth Borgese, USA (daughter of Thomas Mann); Odd Nansen, Norway; Alexandre Marc, France; Raymond Swing, USA; Joe Heydecker, Germany; and Henry Usborne, Great Britain.

On the day the Congress opened, the Oslo City Council held a reception for the delegates in the Golden Room of Stockholm's beautiful Town Hall. There was also a public meeting attended by 1,000 people in the Blue Hall at which Abbé Pierre, President of the Executive of the Movement, spoke.

He warned the audience that at this moment in history when world unity seemed so near, science by a prodigious effort had put into the hands of man the power to bring about the destruction of the very universe.

[1] This is federalist jargon, alluding to the difference between a league (inorganic) and a government (organic).

*Federalists on Peace Path*

'Here is the problem before mankind: Will it be possible for him to realize the last step to unity without recourse to war? It is a matter of a complete change of conscience, both intellectual and moral; a matter of the survival of humanity, or of its self-destruction.

We cannot know now the full import of the extraordinary situation where all mankind is united and freed; what is sure is that there is great need for all of us to work for it, for this is the law of life and the will of God.

Will men act in time to limit the sovereignty of states? It is our job to establish the force that can do this.'

\* \* \*

## GOOD NEWS FROM GHENT[1]

The following year's WMWFG Congress was held in Ghent. The English version of my report (it was translated into German by a Belgo-Luxembourg paper) read:

### A further step towards World Government

Representatives from Argentine (1), Australia (2), Austria (1), Belgium (32), Britain (15), Ceylon (1), Chile (1), Denmark (1), France (6), Germany (3), Holland (10), Iceland (1), Italy (5), Israel (1), Luxembourg (2), Sweden (1), Switzerland (1), Turkey (1), USA (9) and India (1) recently met in Ghent, Belgium, to plan the Peoples' World Constituent Assembly to draft a constitution of world government.

In the minds of many of them the venue is already fixed – Geneva; the date, 30 December 1950.

Others consider that 'Geneva', the headquarters of the old League of Nations, may mislead the public into imagining that an international federation would be another league; they insist on the vital distinction between a debating society like the United Nations, and a government.

A tiny few are suggesting postponing the Constituent Assembly, not because the time is not ripe, but to let the world catch up with

---

[1] 'Yet there is time:' – *How they brought the good news from Ghent to Aix* – Robert Browning, 1842 – 1889.

## The Parliament of Man

events. But most are aware of the danger that if mankind does not soon abolish war, war will abolish mankind.

In Stockholm last summer the World Movement for World Federal Government appointed a Steering Committee to prepare for the World Constituent Assembly. The Ghent Conference was a symptom of rank-and-file impatience at official delays. However, the blessing of the Chairman of the Steering Committee, Mr Henry Usborne, MP, was read at the plenary session.

Fyke Farmer, initiator of a Tennessee law authorizing elections of delegates to the World Constituent Assembly, announced the introduction of a similar bill in Kentucky. Monsieur Diedisheim (France) reported on a similar draft bill in France. Monsieur Drese, Belgian MP, reported on the one in Belgium, mentioning the pilot elections at Nivelles (71% voted, 96% in favour).

Comparing federalism to aviation, Elisabeth Mann Borgesc said that the Ghent conference meant that world government was at last 'airborne'. Another delegate thought it would start a chain reaction of peace which in the next few months would gather sufficient power to exorcise war.

*Note:*
A twenty-four-page report in English, French, Italian and German was published the following month as a joint effort of the periodicals *Parlement* (Belgium), *Across Frontiers* (UK) and *Weltstaat* (Germany).

# CHAPTER 9

# PAX OR PACTS ?

*1992 note:*
Critics of federalism, then and now (forty years later) may well object that my opposition to the United Nations and indeed to all pacts and treaties, was mere 'baying for the moon', since we obviously could not have achieved a world-embracing federation at that time, nor could we have federated the parties to the North Atlantic Treaty without further ado. Something, such as a pact, was therefore better than nothing. However, if that 'something' was a deception, lulling the public into a false sense of security, 'nothing' would have been preferable.

The real purpose of my criticism, though perhaps badly expressed, was to encourage the statesmen to work towards federal union, to declare clearly and unequivocally that such treaties were intended as first steps towards a better goal, that they were signed *faute de mieux* and that it was recognized that treaties were, as the late Lionel Curtis used to say:

'... like reeds, not strong enough to lean upon, yet firm enough to pierce one's side with their broken ends.'

Another very cogent objection to my attitude might be: 'NATO has kept peace in the Atlantic ever since it was set up.' A similar argument could be applied to a safety net, woven of spiders' silk, that had never been used. Could one argue that it had saved the life of every tightrope walker who had walked above it? It could equally well be argued that the Warsaw Pact prevented World War III, or that the United Nations Charter should take the credit, or the atom bomb. Such instruments can prevent only those wars that are unlikely to break out.

## The Parliament of Man

The undemocratic and unjust voting procedures in the United Nations enable an aggrieved nation to protest that any decision is 'illegal'. Iraq is using this argument, though its plea is weakened by its allegation that, although it would never dream of attacking an Arab brother, it invaded Kuwait because that little country was preparing an offensive!! Israel does not even bother to argue. Consequently, even when United Nations decisions are invoked justifiably (as President Bush and others are now doing in the Kuwait dispute) the arguments have a hollow ring, and justly provoke claims of 'double standards'.

Even today, besides the 'little' wars being waged, or simmering, in most parts of the world, we are continually faced, in the international sphere, with warlike acts that are harmful and dangerous to the entire human race. Their numbers and frequency could be greatly reduced, not to say eliminated, if the principles of federalism were more widely applied. In this sense, the federalistic sermons that were preached half a century ago, even two centuries ago, are still topical today. Though some of their contexts are now outmoded, the main message is as true today as it was then, and perhaps even more urgent.

The following article was published in both English and German:

### Pax or Pacts?

On page 4 of the Paris Edition of the *New York Herald Tribune* for 1 March 1949 there is an article by Walter Lippmann advocating the maintenance of peace by the balance of power. What he appears to mean is the *over*balance of power in favour of the USA.

Rubbing shoulders with this article is one by Sumner Welles, former Under Secretary of State for Foreign Affairs, in which he urges the US Congress to adopt a resolution in support of the North Atlantic Pact. Mr Welles is worried. To him, too, it appears that peace can be assured only through the threat of war, and his article turns on 'the Constitutional provision which prevents this government from pledging a future Congress to wage war.' He is concerned to make it crystal clear that the USA will go to war to keep the peace.

Defending his country against the complaint of the *Manchester Guardian* that 'the United States should not have forced the pact if it were not able to deliver the goods,' Mr Sumner Welles points out that all the European governments were fully aware of the Constitutional

## Pax or Pacts?

limitations imposed upon the American Executive. He goes on to say:

> 'They know that a regional pact concluded under Article 51 of the United Nations Charter – which provides for consultation in the event of attack, which establishes the principle of one for all and all for one, but which reserves to each state the right to determine when aggression has taken place and the nature of the assistance it will render in the common defence – represents as far reaching a commitment as Washington can constitutionally make.'

Mr Welles thereby underlines that no pact under the U.N. Charter can be any stronger than the Charter itself, which is itself nothing more nor less than a multilateral treaty.

One would have thought that, faced with this 'discovery', a statesman of Mr Welles' stature would have propounded a viable solution, inevitably involving an amendment to the US Constitution. Instead he suggests a palliative.

He asks the present Congress to declare by joint resolution that it recognizes the need for a North Atlantic Defence pact and that, should the United States subsequently determine that one of the parties to such a pact had been the victim of aggression, the United States should then, as a measure of self-defence, render all possible assistance, including military support, in the common cause.

Mr Welles has no space even to mention the possibility that such a resolution might violate the U.N. Charter. Alternatively, if it does not violate the Charter, why must the victim of aggression be a signatory to the pact? And if the pact is under Article 51 of the Charter, what happens if the Security Council instructs the United States Government to defend itself by less violent means? Would it not be less hypocritical if statesmen were to face the fact that UNO is dead, that it was in fact stillborn?

One of the arguments Mr Welles employs to condition Congress in favour of his proposed joint resolution is that the American people must have learned that they cannot have their cake and eat it. But every pact in recorded history has been an attempt to have one's cake and eat it, to obtain benefits whilst retaining the right and the ability to decide when, how and whether to pay the price[1]. The article

---

[1] O.P.E.C. is a recent example (HSB, 1992).

concludes with a sweeping admission of this when he condemns former American foreign policy 'which sought to achieve security through such cheap and illusory safeguards as the Kellogg pact.'

It would be interesting to procure a price schedule and study the respective degrees of cheapness of the Kellogg Pact, the Pact of Locarno, the Covenant of the League of Nations, the United Nations Charter, and the Atlantic Pact, and to hear Mr Welles' reasons for the differences in price. One might conclude that the least expensive and most economical form of security is one that abolishes the principle of so-called 'balance' of power and substitutes the principle of representative and responsible government in the international sphere.

Democracy, as the late Lord Davies used to say, must leap the frontiers.

I heard an echo of this doctrine the other day when talking to Abbé Groués Pierre, French resistance leader and Vice-President of the World Movement for World Federal Government:

'The difference between civilization and barbarism', he told me, 'is precisely the difference between a pact and a law. The task of peace-keepers is to accelerate the evolution towards a world society in which international law becomes binding on individuals.'

Statesmen and political writers should awaken to the fact that the world has grown up since they went to school. Hiroshima was but one of the events that made nonsense of the international system in which Pacts to Preserve Peace can be enforced only upon governments and communities, and therefore only by measures unrecognizable from war.

\* \* \*

## PAX ATLANTICA?

I made another attack on pacts versus Pax in the following article published in *Parlement* in April 1949.

My comment that the U.S. had little practice in playing power politics no longer applies, though the practice the USA has had since this was written has not been enough to avoid unpopularity and – in

## Pax or Pacts?

some parts of the world — hostility. But it was interesting to hear President Mubarak of Egypt, the other day, urging that a major power such as the USA owes a duty to the world.

### The Pax Atlantica ?

Even as recently as 1911, Lord Bryce wrote that the foreign policies of the USA were, like the snakes in Ireland, notable by their absence. Though two wars have since ensued, leaving America somewhat older and perhaps a trifle wiser, an historian might still repeat that stricture. The remark no doubt implied that a foreign policy must be written off if it is not backed by the ability and determination to carry it through.

The isolationist policy that President Monroe first announced in concrete form in December 1823 actually harked back to President Washington's warning against 'entangling alliances' with European powers at the time of the conversion of the thirteen ex-colonies from a League of Friendship into the federal union that has existed to this day. But it is a far cry from 1789 to the present time, when a bomber can fly round the world non-stop, and when one of America's leading atomic scientists[1] has declared that a mere score of super atomic bombs would suffice to destroy every vestige of life in the USA. Since Monroe's time the world has shrunk alarmingly, so that it is today much smaller, in terms of speed and cost of transport and communications, than was the entire American continent a hundred years ago. The power-political frontiers of the USA now extend into the hearts of Europe and Asia, far beyond the North Pole and even into the stratosphere.

America's progress towards recognition of this fact was almost negligible until quite recent times, when the tempo was considerably accelerated under pressure of events. The defeat of President Wilson in the matter of membership of the League of Nations which he had done so much to create can be traced back to the Monroe doctrine and its effect upon American opinion. After World War I, isolation versus co-operation was for twenty years the great debate in American foreign policy. There was strong pressure of public opinion towards US intervention in the Russo-Finnish war.

---

[1] Prof. Harold C. Urey, Director of War Research on US Atomic Bomb Project 1940-1945. See Chapter 10.

Those isolationists who still remained after Pearl Harbour were converted by the atomic bomb. But they were not converted into world citizens.

A clever columnist invented the phrase that the US was 'trying to decide whether to secede from the world or to remain part of it.' There never was any question of the US seceding from the world, since she has never been part of it. One does not become part of a world community by means of 'entangling alliances'.

Nevertheless, World War II enormously stimulated the discussion of foreign affairs by the ordinary US citizen, and converted public opinion from a negligible factor into a force which the White House and the State Department now know they have to reckon with.

President Roosevelt was an influential educator in this direction, steering his country from neutrality to 'Cash and Carry', then to 'Aid Short of War' and then to military assistance in all its preponderating power. 'Lend-Lease' came in 1940. During the so-called 'phoney war' the story went round that the President was neutral; he did not mind whether the French or the British beat the Nazis.

The US Senate voted almost unanimously in favour of US membership of UNO. Expert evidence given before the Senate Committee on Foreign Affairs before the vote was taken was designed to prove that in committing herself to the Charter of the United Nations the USA committed itself to nothing. It is legitimate to speculate whether something better than a mere league, a world constitution that had to fight its way through the Senate by a small margin of votes, would have been less likely to fail now. The instigators of the United Nations Charter would have done well to recall the words of George Washington when he and his colleagues were persuading the thirteen American States to abandon their League of Friendship and adopt the present federal constitution:

'Perhaps another dreadful conflict is to be sustained ... If, to please the people, we offer what we ourselves disapprove, how can we afterward defend our work? Let us raise a standard to which the wise and honest can repair; the event is in the hand of God.'

This is not to imply that all the fault for the perverted principles enshrined in the Charter can be laid at the door of the United States. If the statesmen had remembered Washington's advice, later to be so magnificently justified in practice, Mr Ernest Bevin would not have

## Pax or Pacts?

felt compelled to say, in the British House of Commons on 23 November 1946:

> 'I am asked to re-study San Francisco. I have not only re-studied it, but when it was being developed I was gravely concerned whether we were really finding the right solution . . . We are driven relentlessly along this road: the necessity for a new study for the purpose of creating a world assembly, elected directly from the people of the world as a whole — a world assembly with a limited objective; the objective of peace.'

The United Nations, being a mere league — an assembly of sovereign states instead of a sovereign assembly of nationalities, inevitably revealed itself as a forum for power politics. This was, of course, a shock to the USA, which — despite assiduous reading of Walter Lippman — has had little practice in playing power politics.

This has led to extremists advocating a 'preventive' war (as if war could prevent itself!) and those at the other end of the scale advocating world government.

The Monroe Doctrine had left it to be understood that the USA would take steps to defend her vital interests no matter where they may lie, though of course in those days her ramifications were not so far-reaching as they are today. When, for example, in 1867 America purchased Alaska (bringing her to within 200 miles of Asia) and then, during the war with Spain, acquired Hawaii and the Philippines, few Americans saw any inconsistency with the Monroe Doctrine, regarding these moves as versions of the advice to 'go West, young man.' On the other hand, Monroe's undertaking (on considerations of reciprocity) not to interfere in European affairs somewhat inhibited American interventions in China, ending in the defeat of her partisanship of Chiang. Nevertheless, American support of Chinese integrity and independence has been fairly consistent, at least in theory, since the end of the Spanish war. The defeat in China may have been due to mislabelling as 'communists' middle-class Chinese who opposed Chiang's autocratic, incompetent and graft-ridden administration. It is predictable that American policy in China will soon readjust itself and eventually lend economic and political support to the new Chinese government in its inevitable 'Titoism' in order to assist it to divest itself of Russian domination.

The Monroe doctrine did not profess interference with the 'existing colonies or dependencies of any European power.' In 1870, President Grant brought this more up to date by asserting that 'hereafter no territory of this Continent shall be regarded as subject to transfer to an European power.' This illustrated the trend towards the modern interpretation: that no part of the American continent should be under European control. This psychosis has been a source of friction with, e.g. Britain, Netherlands and France over their Guiana territories.

The main plank of the Monroe platform: 'America for the Americans' — briefly dubbed 'Pan-Americanism' — did not until recent times result in the US binding itself by treaty to protect the other American republics. Without the existence of the British fleet it would have been impracticable in 1826 to forbid European armies to cross the oceans to suppress the newly-proclaimed independence of the Spanish ex-colonies in Mexico, Peru and Chile, which Canning recognized, calling in the new world 'to redress the balance of the old.'

This was the power behind American foreign policy in Monroe's day, the era of the Pax Britannica. Is there adequate power behind the Pact Atlantica?

The Atlantic Pact is the latest manifestation of present-day American policy, dubbed the 'Truman doctrine'. Attempts are of course made to show that it is a logical continuation of Monroe's implied threat to defend US interests no matter where they may lie, but it really marks a new break with classic isolationism, underlined by continued American occupation of Europe and Japan and the use of Marshall aid as an instrument of diplomacy.

A strong dose of American isolationism still remains, however; whereas statesmen in Europe are concerned to unite their countries in an organic federation, American diplomacy apparently expects them to place their faith in yet one more Pact to Preserve Peace. But this time Europe wants to be protected, not merely 'liberated'. One more Victory like the last one and Europe is sunk!

The crux of American Foreign Policy has thus come to be regarded as the Constitutional limitations on the Executive's power to implement its policy by — in the last resort — declaring war. The statesmen of Continental Europe are not misled by the wishful thinking of

## Pax or Pacts?

pressmen who promise that 'instant assistance' is the essence of the Atlantic Pact.

The very idea of a pact of this nature is based on the debatable assumption that peace can be preserved by threatening war. Acceptance of the idea of a pact involves the accceptance of this assumption. The question then becomes: 'How real is the threat?' If it is illusory, the pact is like a reed, weak enough to break when you lean on it, but strong enough to pierce your side with the broken end[2].

Consideration of American foreign policy necessarily involves a study of the means of carrying it out. The attitude of other powers, e.g. Germany and Japan before the last war, of the South and Central American States, and also of Britain (in commercial 'wars' over films, tobacco, cotton and food) have been aimed at testing the weaknesses of American foreign and commercial policies. European statesmen are now apprehensive as to America's ability to 'deliver the goods' (this time the phrase is the *Manchester Guardian's*) promised by the pact, i.e. her ability to afford the security which it professes to offer.

The President shares the treaty-making power with Congress (mainly the Senate). He cannot declare war without the consent of Congress. Congress can refuse to carry out a treaty (and thereby damage US prestige) or can use its power of the purse to render it useless. This it has done on past occasions, though it is only fair to say that such repudiations have made the USA's reputation for keeping or breaking treaties no worse, if no better, than the reputations of other countries with different constitutions, for treaties seem to be devices for obtaining benefits for oneself whilst retaining the right to decide whether, when and how, to 'deliver the goods' in exchange.

The prime question remains: Whether, and how, America will use her great power in the world. Will she use it like a blundering, inexperienced giant whose intelligence has not grown as rapidly as its body? Which philosophy will prevail? Little Truman's idea that the price of peace is military might, or Walter Lippmann's doctrine that the price is the balance of power (by which he means the overbalance of power in favour of the nation to which you happen to

---

[2] I 'stole' this simile from my friend and colleague Lionel Curtis, who had given me leave to use his words, in our joint propaganda efforts, as my own.

## The Parliament of Man

belong) or will America gradually come to realize that the price of peace is justice? In Mr Churchill's words: 'Justice is vain without her sword'. Commenting on this remark some years ago in the *Observer*, Lord (then Sir William) Beveridge wrote:

> Force adequate to maintain justice and peace cannot be supplied by any one nation. The force on which international justice rests must itself be international. It cannot be composed of men owing their whole personal allegiance to one particular nation. They must owe allegiance to a Government which itself is directly responsible to the citizens of many nations. There must, in other words, be both national Governments and an international Government.

American foreign policy since the United Nations was founded has been to pay lip-service to the notion that UNO must be developed into a world government without becoming a super-State[3]. By this is presumably meant a peace-keeping organization that can enforce law and order without having to go to war to do it! The only means by which this could be done would be to enforce international law directly on individuals (since this can be done by legal, peaceful means, whereas communities and governments can be coerced only by measures indistinguishable from war). Such a conception implies far-reaching changes in our notions of international law, and would involve an international law-making body or parliament.

American influence in the Nürnberg War Guilt trials contributed to the establishment of the principle that international law should be enforceable on individuals. This trend could be developed to ensure the enforcement of law on individuals before a war, instead of afterwards, when the damage is done, and to provide for the enactment of laws before people are punished for breaking them!

Nevertheless, it seems that offical American policy will have to make gigantic strides before we see the dawn of the era[4] in which there will be no need to deluge the world in blood in order to 'keep the peace'.

* * *

[3] It cannot be too highly stressed that this precondition is a vital element in the federal idea: the Union constitution as a guarantee against the super-state.

[4] Except in Boston, most Americans seem to pronounce this word: 'error', but this eera would be no mistake!

*Pax or Pacts?*
## WOMEN AND THE ATLANTIC PACT

I once treated English and German-speaking readers to the following article, an oblique attack on tracts and treaties, which I consider still topical!

### Women and the Atlantic Pact

Having been asked to write a topical article I have decided to make it doubly topical by writing about women and the Atlantic Pact.

Women all over the world will have heaved a sign of relief when the Atlantic Pact was signed, because now they no longer have to worry about whether the 'United' Nations are strong enough (or should it be 'is strong enough'?) to keep the peace. All they have to worry about now is whether the Atlantic Treaty is adequate to prevent a war.

Women who have been well brought up, and ladies, will know that they should not trust promises made by men, which is just what a Pact is. The reason why they can trust a government to keep law and order is that governments do not owe their existence to promises of Cabinet Ministers, but are able to reach quick decisions, translate them into action before disorder gets the upper hand, and to enforce the settlement of disputes without having to go to war to keep the Peace of the Realm. This is significant of something important in international affairs – I can't quite think what at the moment.

Women who have, or had, husbands and/or children, will remember that we have been having, for some time now, bigger and bigger wars, but on the other hand we have also been getting better and better pacts, treaties, protocols and promises of non-aggression and eternal friendship (usually in instalments of twenty years). We have now improved upon the Kellogg Pact, the Pact of Locarno, the Covenant of the League of Nations and even the 'Untied' Nations Charter. Statesmen (not the stateswomen) have promised 200 years of peace as a result of the Atlantic Pact. The year 2150 A.D. will thus be a trying year for us all, particularly the women who will have to stand in the queues when it is all over. Fortunately it will all be over quite quickly.

The Atlantic Treaty will protect all who have signed it, so if you have not yet signed I would suggest you do so right away. It will also

## The Parliament of Man

protect those who – like Sweden – have not signed, whether they like it or not. Prompted no doubt by their wives, some prominent men in America and elsewhere have suggested that it might be a good idea if the people in the countries that have signed the Atlantic Pact were to elect a Parliament to discuss and decide the matters arising under it (but keep their separate Parliaments for their own private affairs), and to have an international Government to carry out the decisions, and make a single army, navy and air force under one command. This might be better than to have several separate defence forces, often cancelling each other out. Some people even asked Mr Bevin if he would help with this sort of idea for United Europe, but he decided to make a Council of Europe, a kind of little League because – apart from the war years – Leagues have been so successful from the diplomatic point of view.

I do not propose to say much more about the Pact because taken by itself it is apt to be boring. On the other hand, women, taken by themselves, can be quite delightful. A foreign lady named Olga Offskova once told me she was interested in international affaires, but the Foreign Office recalled me just about that time and I was unable to pursue the acquaintance. Women, however, can sometimes be almost as deceptive as Pacts, owing to their unfortunate habit of shaving off their eyebrows to look insane, then painting them in again to look sophisticated. Some paint their lips and nails to look like heart disease, or their cheeks to simulate galloping consumption or half-concealed leprosy. The effect is fairly good if viewed across a wide road, but there is seldom enough traffic for this purpose.

Whilst writing I have remembered why it is that a government can keep the peace in its own Realm, whereas Leagues cannot. I think it is because governments enforce their laws directly on individual citizens, whereas Leagues try to enforce treaties on entire nations. They try to keep the peace by making war, which seems rather dangerous and silly.

*  *  *

*1992 note:*
Since the Americans were in Arabia for Desert Shield and Desert Storm, there has been a marked change in the treatment of women by the Arabs. Previously, the man walked ahead and the women and

## *Pax or Pacts?*

animals trailed behind. Now the women are permitted to walk ahead – in case there are any mines left behind in the sand.

## DRAGONS' TEETH

The following, which was written in answer to suggestions that Germany should be rearmed against Communism, also appeared in English and German. Incidentally, if the Allies had allowed Germany and Japan to rearm, this would have prevented them from becoming the two most wealthy nations in the world.

For those unacquainted with the fable, the title alludes to the crop of armed men who spring from the sowing of dragons' teeth.

### Dragons' Teeth

On 4 March 1997 the Franco-British Pact of Dunkirk, aimed against the resurgence of German militarism, expires. On 26 May 1992 the Anglo-Soviet Treaty of Friendship, providing against the same contingency, legally terminates. It is hardly worthwhile looking up the various other treaties aimed against German rearmament; those between the USSR and France, Czechoslovakia, Yugloslavia, Poland, Roumania, Hungary, Bulgaria and Finland; between Yugoslavia and Poland, Czechoslovakia, Albania, Bulgaria, Hungary and Roumania; between Czechoslovakia and Poland, Roumania and Bulgaria; between Bulgaria and Albania, Roumania, Hungary and Poland; or between Hungary and Roumania and Poland. A pact is apt to become a dead letter before the ink is dry unless one or other of the parties wishes to invoke it in moral support of some diplomatic or military escapade.

If it were wise and politic to enlist the aid of German military authoritarianism to dispel the bogy of Communist totalitarianism no paper promises would stand in the way. But this time there is no need to invoke the questionable morality of diplomacy as an argument against the resuscitation of the German Wehrmacht. The present West German Bund Government should cease to worry whether it is constitutionally authorized to recruit. Those German nationals who are so urgentlly needed to defend Germany and Europe against the Führerprinzip – whether operating through the O.G.P.U. or a revived O.K.W. – should be enrolled directly into a European army by a European government deriving from a European parliament directly elected by the people of Western Europe as a whole.

*The Parliament of Man*

Unthinking people, particularly Americans with itchy trigger-fingers, take the view that it is better to do something quickly, even if it is wrong, than to be slow about doing the right thing. But this is not the choice. Our problem is how to do the right thing quickly enough. The French are not the only people who reject the notion of staving off Communism by methods that would leave a French and a German army to fight over the ruins of Europe.

A German army enlisted by, paid by, and controlled by a German government would inevitably become not the guardian of liberty but — after shrewd bargaining — its captor; the mercenary neither of America nor Russia, nor of a United Europe, but the scourge of them all.

This is not an argument for delaying German participation in the defence of Europe, but one for hastening the federation of all those peoples who are prepared to pool their arms under a common authority and submit to the rule of law in their common affairs.

\* \* \*

## MANDATE MADNESS

Incensed by the politicians' breaches of promises made at the General Election held after Mr Ernest Bevin's famous pledge to re-examine the U.N. Charter, I wrote the following article which won wide circulation, and which may become relevant to current blabberings on the 'New World Order'.

This reprint of the article has been curtailed where indicated, to avoid repetition of matter contained in Chapter 3.

**Mandate Madness**

In November 1945 — wise after the event — Mr Ernest Bevin stated in the House of Commons:

> 'I am asked to re-study San Francisco. I have not only re-studied it but, when it was being developed I was gravely concerned whether we were finding the right solution . . . We need a new study for the purpose of creating a World Assembly elected directly from the people of the world. I am willing to sit with anybody, of any party, of any nation, to try to devise a franchise or a constitution for a

## Pax or Pacts?

World Assembly. Once we can get to that stage, I believe we shall have taken a great progressive step.'

Mr Bevin has been constantly reminded of that pledge. Indeed, there is evidence that he has never forgotten it; nor will he be allowed to. But the story that continually comes back is that the Government has no mandate to carry it out.

At the recent General Election both the Government and the Opposition had the opportunity to ask for such a mandate. The chance was thrown away. A few days before the electors went to the poll, Professor Lancelot Hogben, FRS, a member of the Labour Party for thirty-two years and connected with the Fabian Society for thirty-six, resigned from the Birmingham University Labour Party on the issue of World Government, saying:

'Our bi-partisan politics assume the aspect of backchat between the March Hare and the Mad Hatter. ... Great Powers make pacts to limit weapons of total warfare and then break them, and an inspectorate without the backing of an internatioanal police force armed with the authority of government is a charade fit for exhibition at a children's party.'

Professor Hogben quoted the Archbishop of York's sermon of 5 February:

'Our party politics are the games of children playing on the sands.'

In the intervening years, by his sins of omission, Mr Bevin has betrayed the promise he made in 1945. During that time, however, world federalists have not been idle (here I gave details of the samples taken of the electorates in many countries, showing between 60% and 94% of support for the plan of the Crusade for World Government. I also referred to the Tennessee State Parliament having passed a law providing for the election of delegates to the World Constituent Assembly, and similar bills having been introduced or prepared in twelve other states throughout the world).

Foreign Secretaries should bear in mind that their job consists in meddling in the affairs of other nations. In Britain, a Foreign Minister is chosen from among Members of Parliament who have received a mandate to govern British subjects. It follows, therefore, that − paradoxically enough − a Foreign Minister has a mandate to do, every day, things that he 'has no mandate' to do. The Government has a mandate to govern in the interests of the country. No government, no statesman, no politician, worthy of the name has the right to say that he is prevented from doing the right thing because he has not obtained a mandate to do it. He may perhaps ask himself whether he is pledged not to take a certain course, but no-one has yet dared to suggest that Parliamentary support must be denied to the World Constituent Assembly idea for any reason such as that. It is up to Mr Ernest Bevin and the present government, if they wish to justify their present lack of foreign policy, to prove that the peoples to whom they are responsible are forbidding them to take the only realistic step towards peace with justice – a first step towards world government.

If the British Parliament were to pass legislation along the lines of the Tennessee Bill, it could not be accused of exceeding its mandate. Even if such a step were harmful, it could always be remedied before any damage had been done, for no Constitution of supra-national government could bind any nation that did not ratify. Supporters of the World Constituent Assembly are offering to lead the horses to the water, not to compel them to drink.

Time must be found, and right soon, for the introduction of such a Bill in Parliament. The Government cannot pretend that it cannot spare the time, for in the present precarious balance it must of necessity limit its measures to non-controversial issues. Before the election the leaders of the three main political parties pledged themselves to make lasting peace their paramount objective. There is no controversy here. The 'United' Nations, designed to keep the peace can – by its design – do so only by making war. Preparation for war is not only ruinous; it is destroying our morale. Let us hope it has not yet quite destroyed those qualities of leadership, initiative and courage for which British statesmen were famous in less decadent times.

\* \* \*

### THE BRITISH MINISTRY OF PEACE
Incensed by the shallow thinking behind the Foreign Minister's assertion that his ministry was the Ministry of Peace, I wrote an open letter which was published not only in the UK but (in German) on the Continent:

## Pax or Pacts?

### Open Letter to Rt. Hon. Herbert C. Morrison[1], PC, MP, Secretary, Department of Peace, Whitehall, London SW1

3 February 1951

Dear Sir,

In *The Times* this morning you are reported as having made yesterday at Dudley the welcome announcement that your department is the Department of Peace. As one who believes in the necessity of a World Federal Government, however, I am puzzled to know how the mere re-naming of a national Foreign Office can bring us any nearer to peace. It would be reassuring if the public were to be told how much money your new department is prepared to spend during the coming budget year on research into the causes of peace, and to see how this sum compares with the amount to be spent at the War Office.

You are reported, too, as having said that if we could have peace for 100 years, you were sure there would be no more wars. 'Peace would become a habit.'

Do you not consider, Sir, that peace is a by-product of government, and that without an international government we shall never have the 100 years of peace we all desire? Do you believe that we in this country are habitually law-abiding, or is it because we live our national life within a system of government and law? As a first subject for your research, may I suggest the question whether peace comes first, and then government, or whether government is the prerequisite.

So long as the maintenance of peace depends on the precarious efforts of statesmen to patch and tinker with the obsolete system of peacekeeping-by-warmaking, we shall be like the tight-rope walker who is told that if he can keep his balance for a hundred years it will become a habit, and he will then be able to sleep peacefully in the same posture and find himself still up aloft when he awakes.

Is it not a fact that if, for 100 years, we keep the peace by our present methods of war-preparations, war-mongering would become a habit? You cannot hope to inculcate peaceful habits by means of a century of war-preparation. The 'Untied' Nations, that League to

[1] Gave his name to a type of domestic air raid shelter. See also Chapter 8 (Anderson).

*The Parliament of Man*

Keep the Peace by Making War, will, in any case, collapse long before your century is reached.

Now that Korea has shown us that if England is attacked the United Nations will punish the aggressor by laying waste the whole of our land, north to south, we are told that 'now is the time to end the war.' But the time to end a war is before it starts. Mankind will not become habitually peaceful except within a system that keeps the peace by peaceful means.

As a second item for your research, may I remind you of the words of your predecessor who, through frailty of one kind or another, was unable to implement them:

'We need a new study for the purpose of creating a World Assembly elected directly from the people of the World. I am willing to sit with anybody, of any nation, to try to devise a franchise or a constitution for a World Assembly with a limited objective, the objective of Peace ...'

Now that you have taken up the torch, federalists and others throughout the world will hope you will carry it far and fast, and ensure that this country will not remain unrepresented at the Peoples World Constituent Assembly (for World Law) when it comes to take the first real step forward in the march of mankind towards enduring peace.

Yours truly,

Harold S. Bidmead
(World Citizen No. 12,345)

Acknowledged by Foreign Office 14 February 1951, Ref.OP 295/1
This was also published in German.

* * *

**OPEN LETTER TO GENERAL EISENHOWER**

Worried by the appointment of a Supreme Commander for a coalition of allies lacking any united political will, I published an 'Open Letter' to General Eisenhower in *Freedom & Union*, USA. Here is the text of the correspondence:

## *Pax or Pacts?*
### Open letter to General Eisenhower

General Dwight D. Eisenhower
SHAPE, Hotel Astoria, Paris, France                     May 1951
Dear General Eisenhower,

When General Washington had the task of holding together the separate State armies in one Confederate army in the League of Friendship, he was, of necessity, obliged to concern himself with politics.

Your view that the military should always remain subordinate to the civil authority enhanced your great popularity in Europe at the time when you were asked to run for President of the U.S. (Public bickering on this topic recently underlined your wisdom.)

Great was my astonishment, therefore, when I learned that you had accepted a military post which cannot fail to embroil you in politics, a post as Supreme Military Commander who can never know for certain what is the precise civil authority from which his orders will come. Greatly though you may differ from General MacArthur, your position is ominously similar; you are like a gun in the hand of a monster which cannot be expected to make up its mind rapidly enough in an emergency, nor indeed to give the 'open fire' or 'cease fire' at the appropriate times.

Such a situation can please nobody but the enemies of peace, law and order, the partisans of anarchy and chaos. You cannot hope to attain the right ends by the wrong means, yet there seems to be no public evidence that you are striving to have established a civil authority to which you could properly give your allegiance.

If you wish to avoid embroilment in politics, your best course would be to resign your present post. If, on the other hand, like Washington, you accept the task of statesmanship that has been thrust upon you, your duty compels you to invite the peoples whom you have to protect, to set up a common government to ensure their common defence.

You have a great opportunity to lead the world out of the valley of a tragic shadow; speak out while you may still be heard!

Walsingham House, 35 Seething Lane, London EC3.          HSB

\* \* \*

*The Parliament of Man*

**ALLIED POWERS EUROPE
OFFICE OF THE SUPREME COMMANDER**

26 May 1951

Dear Mr Bidmead,

General Eisenhower wishes me to acknowledge your recent letter and to thank you for the interest which prompted you to write. The General is always pleased to receive the views of those individuals who are personally engaged in the promotion of the causes for World peace.

Sincerely,

C. CRAIG CANNON (signed)
Lt. Colonel, ADC
Aide to General Eisenhower

\* \* \*

Here let me cite some later declarations by General Eisenhower, when ex-President of the U.S.A:

*3 October 1956:*
There can be no peace without law.

*4 April 1965:*
The era of armaments has ended, and the human race must conform its actions to this truth or die.

The world no longer has a choice between force and law. If civilization is to survive it must choose the rule of law.

\* \* \*

**VOTERS OF THE WORLD, UNITE!**

I feel somewhat diffident about re-publishing the following effusion, which also appeared[1] in German in a Belgo-Luxemburg paper (circulating also in USA and France), but it contains many 'purple pass-

[1] Several of my articles were broadcast on 'Free Europe' radio, then operating from Strasbourg, I believe. I think this formed the basis of one of them.

ages' which might serve as a 'do-it-yourself' assembly kit for future federalist agitators. I leave it as a free bequest to humanity!

I drafted it as an unofficial manifesto in support of the Campaign for a People's World Constituent Assembly. I have no record of its having obtained the approval of the organizers.

### Voters of the World, Unite!
### A Challenge to Diplomats and Politicians

WE VOTERS OF THE WORLD, are determined that the peoples of Earth shall no longer be obstructed in their rightful strivings to save this and succeeding generations from the scourge of war.

We share the general concern at the steady, rapid and world-wide encroachment of totalitarianism in its various guises, not least within those lands that profess to be most jealous of their liberty. All over the face of the Earth, men and women are oppressed by excessive interference from their national governments, excesses largely caused by the complete absence of governmental institutions in the international sphere.

WE DEPLORE the incompetence and criminal folly of those blind leaders of the blind who make a show of combating totalitarianism by methods that only aggravate the danger and weaken our powers of resistance to it, devices that delight none but the enemies of peace and of law and order, and encourage the partisans of anarchy and chaos.

WE CHALLENGE, on our own behalf and in the name of those for whom we are called upon to speak, the 'right' claimed by national governments to levy taxes for 'defence' which they mainly dissipate on measures that demoralize their subjects, debase the value of what remains of their money, undermine national prosperity, whittle away their material power to defend themselves, destroy confidence at home and abroad, and leave to the people little that is worth defending. We hold these truths to be self-evident :

◆ Governments exercise sovereignty only as agents for the people from whom it is derived, national sovereignty being thus a conditional trust, not an irrevocable right.

◆ The citizens have an inalienable right to be consulted in the conduct of international affairs, particularly on issues of peace and war, and to have their due say in formulating legislation at world level. This can adequately be done only through the medium of a supra-national parliament, consisting of representatives directly mandated by the sovereign people.

◆ Good ends cannot be achieved by bad means.

◆ Human progress cannot result from submission to organized violence, nor therefore from a system that depends on the organization of warfare for the maintenance of peace.

◆ Instruments such as the atomic bomb are not police weapons, nor can war be described as 'police action'.

◆ Men and women, not States, are the only proper objects of government, and the only subjects from which an international authority can justly derive its powers.

We register our GRAVE REMONSTRANCE against the establishment, in flagrant violation of the principles of democracy, of gigantic international military systems not subject to proper political control.

WE DENY THE AUTHORITY of diplomats and politicians who behave as though they were the masters instead of public servants accountable to the people for their stewardship.

WE OPPOSE TYRANNY no matter where it may raise its head, remembering that the Mother of Parliaments was born in sedition and that the glorious Magna Charta was a revolt against outmoded authority; liberty cannot be won or defended by timid hearts.

WE CONDEMN as spurious the Charter of the 'United' Nations in that it falsely purports to be an agreement between 'the peoples of the United Nations', whereas it was in reality a pact between their respective governments, acting without consulting (even for the purpose of ratification) the only rightful source and fount of all political authority, the sovereign people.

WE DENOUNCE the 'United' Nations as just one more example of a league, a multilateral alliance to keep the peace by perpetuating the war system, a solecism in theory and a monstrosity in practice. Its system of representation and voting power is undemocratic, inequitable, unjust − and unworkable. So far as its Security provisions are concerned (and our condemnations should not be assumed to extend beyond this vital issue) they cannot be remedied except by reforms which in honesty could be described as nothing less than the creation of something new and the simultaneous abolition of the old. In this sense, talk of 'transforming' the 'United' Nations would be mere cant and humbug.

WE IMPEACH the 'United' Nations, as at present constituted, as a cynical betrayal of a sacred trust; we shall take no part in any action that might condone or camouflage that deception.

We deny the 'right' which the 'United' Nations has arrogated to itself to speak for the peoples of the world.

WE REJECT IT AS AN USURPER of our rights, as illegal, as illegitimate, condemned by its own experience and by that of its predecessors, and doomed, by the very nature of the pernicious principles on which it is constructed, to ignominious and disastrous failure.

We proclaim that no law-abiding, self-respecting citizen anywhere in the world can owe allegiance to the so-called 'United' Nations so long as it continues to be based on the evil notion of keeping the peace by making war.

WE REAFFIRM THE RIGHT TO ALTER OR ABOLISH any political system that has become a menace to the survival of the human race.

WE BELIEVE THAT:

◆ The dignity of the individual and his inalienable rights to life and the freedom to practise the arts of peace are among the highest aspirations of man everywhere.

◆ Until such time as all men are saints and governments shall have withered away, governments — deriving their just powers from the consent of the governed — are needed to protect these rights.

◆ Warfare has become so destructive that these rights are universally endangered.

◆ Just as national governments were created to secure those rights that local governments were unable to guarantee, so must we now create a supra-national government to afford the protection against war which national governments can no longer effectively provide.

◆ A world government must have powers adequate to enforce disarmament of all nations, to prevent aggression and to maintain peace.

## The Parliament of Man

◆ A world government must have direct jurisdiction over the individual in those matters within its authority (but in those matters only).

◆ A world government must be federal in form, exercising only those powers that have been specifically granted to it.

◆ All powers not specifically granted to a world government must be reserved to the national governments, or to the people, thus guaranteeing to each nation full internal sovereignty in the conduct of its domestic affairs.

◆ War is not inevitable; it can be prevented by our strivings towards world government.

WE SOLEMNLY SUMMON all men and women of good will to sign and publicize this Manifesto, and to rally in support of THE PEOPLES' WORLD CONSTITUENT ASSEMBLY, to the end that it may speedily be made adequate for the task of drafting, for the approbation of the peoples of the world, the Constitution of a supranational authority based not upon the totalitarian principle of government of states, by states, and for states, but on the ideal of government of the people, by the people, and for the people, so that Mankind, under God, shall have a new birth of freedom, and shall not perish from the Earth.

H. S. B. World Citizen No. 12,345.

# CHAPTER 10

# I MEET AN ATOMIC BOMB MAKER

My talk with Professor Urey was published in eight newspapers, in English and German, including the U.S.A., under the heading:

**One World or None**
Interview with Professor HAROLD C. UREY, Vice-Chairman of American Emergency Committee of Atomic Scientists, Director of War Research on the American Atom Bomb Project 1940-45.
Winner of Nobel Prize in Chemistry

Professor Harold Clayton Urey has the advantage over most of his fellow human beings in realizing to the full that we are on the threshold of a new era.

'There is no technical defence against atomic bombs, neither by way of interception nor by retaliation.' he told me, 'The only defence is a World government.'

Asked his opinion of the United Nations Organization he replied that UNO was incapable of preventing a third world war, or of developing into anything like a world government in the short breathing space that still remains. When I pointed out that many people attributed the failure of UNO to the bungling of diplomats, Professor Urey declared, weighing his words, that neither American nor Russian mistakes made any real difference. UNO was doomed to failure right from its inception.

'Talk of strengthening UNO is nonsense, unless by this is meant its conversion into a world government. I believe, however, that such conversion could not be achieved in time.'

'Do you mean, then,' I asked, 'that pressure to convert UNO into a genuine government is futile, and should be abandoned?'

'Do not get me wrong,' the Professor replied, 'I naturally hope that such attempts will succeed, and so long as there is life there is hope; somebody ought to keep trying. But I believe they will fail, and that some other approach must be made. Maybe the ideal of world government will never be realized. It is conceivable that the time has arrived for the disappearance of mankind from this earth, as other species have disappeared before him.'

'But,' he hastily added, 'I see a ray of hope in the scheme put forward by my young friend Henry Usborne, and his colleagues in your House of Commons.'

During the conversation I elicited the information that the USA could, if it so desired, produce anything from 10,000 to 100,000 atom bombs costing some one million dollars each, and still spend less than the last war cost America, and that super bombs may be made such that the radioactivity from twenty such bombs would be sufficient to destroy every vestige of life in the United States, human, animal, insect, everything.

Professor Urey considers that it is idle to speculate about Man's vast future, because it will never arrive unless we speedily abolish war from the world.

'There are many causes of war,' he says, 'but only one cure, namely, the establishment of a government over all possible warring elements, with the ability to settle disputes without any possibility of appeal to war or even to civil war.'

When I reminded him of the natural human objection to a super-government with wide powers of interference, he hastened to reassure me:

'I mean an authority with full governmental powers in the matter of keeping the peace, but having its operations confined to that field only. It need not bother itself very much with economic matters. Such problems will be nine-tenths solved as soon as war has been abolished from the earth.'

\* \* \*

## I Meet an Atomic Bomb Maker

My interview with another atomic scientist whom I met received equal and similar publicity, under the English title:

### The Chain Reaction of Peace
### Interview with Dr Daniel Q. Posin of the U.S.A.

Dr Daniel Q. Posin, now back home in America, gave up his holiday this year and went on tour of the British Isles, speaking and lecturing on 'What the atom means to you'. Dr Posin is a true universalist. Born in Russian Turkestan, travelled through Siberia, China, and Japan, reached San Francisco, and graduated at the University of California. He has written textbooks in Spanish and a novel in English. He is now Chairman of the Department of Physics at the North Dakota State College. In this special article our correspondent tells our readers something more about this remarkable man.

Every pair of eyes in the large audience seemed to be fastened upon the speaker during the whole of his ninety-minute talk on 'What the Atom Means to You.' But although he deals realistically with the horrors of atomic warfare, the concentration of his audience is not that of the terrified rabbit hypnotized by the snake, but rather the fascination that comes from having a mystery made so plain that a schoolchild can understand.

Dr Posin has brilliant new technique in oratory, and the dramatic use of the microphone. Speaking with fire and obvious sincerity, he yet contrived to avoid all overstatement, and in words seldom exceeding two syllables he conveyed his message of warning and hope with the impersonal objectivity of a scientist.

Having described the Oak Ridge Atomic Factory as a sort of madhouse[1] where the more rational kind of lunacy had its home, he proceeded to 'click-click-click' like a Geiger counter, and to 'whoosh' in semblance of an atomic bomb, until his spellbound hearers were completely in the mood to hear his appeal, in the name of his scientific colleagues, to support the Crusade for World Government.

This new prophet is somewhat slight of stature, so that one marvels at his having given over 300 of these lectures in America, speaking in the evenings after his work as Professor of Physics at the State

---

[1] Two-thirds of the scientists who, independently, chose 'secret' codes to lock up their confidential documents adopted the *same* number, the atomic weight of the uranium allotrope in which they were all interested.

## The Parliament of Man

College of North Dakota, if it does not involve more than 200 miles of motoring each time, or at the week-ends. For three years he has not rested in his personal crusade to carry the facts about atomic energy to every village square (as Einstein expressed it).

All this I had gleaned from reading Professor Posin's book *I have been to the Village*. It was therefore the realization of a new ambition when I shook him by the hand. Resisting the temptation to inquire whether the handshake would make me 'clicky' (Dr Posin's term to describe radioactivity), I asked him a question which I thought he might not have cared to answer during the public discussion:

'Do you really believe that World Government is possible?'

'I am a scientist,' he said, 'Economics and politics are too difficult and complicated for me to understand. Science is the really simple thing. But science has convinced me — and you can put this on record — that World Government is possible. It is not contrary to nature. It is desirable, since there is no other defence against atomic and still more terrible weapons — no defence *whatever*. It *must* be brought about, but it can be done in time only if we set up what I call a "chain reaction" of peace.'

Asked to explain, he went on:

'For many years now, scientists have known they could split the atom; the practical problem was to know how to do it on a sufficiently large scale. The solution, the chain reaction, is really quite simple. It is the old, well known "snowball" principle. You know, a little ball rolls and collects twice as much; rolls again — four times as much; rolls again, sixteen times as much — and so on.

Federalists discovered more than a hundred and fifty years ago how to organize a peaceful society consisting of many different autonomous states. It was done in my country (USA), in Switzerland, Canada, Australia, and other countries, but not enough people believe it can be done for the world. Or perhaps it would be more true to say that if people knew how much popular support there is for world federation they would all act together to achieve it. That is where the "chain reaction of peace" comes in. Many scientists in America and our many friends affiliated with us in the World Movement for World Federal Government, believe that if we can convince a sufficient number of intelligent and energetic enthusiasts, they will be able to influence and persuade vast multitudes, so that in a very short time the world should be ripe for the

## I Meet an Atomic Bomb Maker

election of the Peoples' Constituent Assembly to draft a Constitution of World Government.'

Turning to a member of his audience who still lingered, listening avidly, Dr Posin said:

'If you come in with us now, it may mean thousands of votes for world Government when the time comes. Then, when we can be sure that atomic energy will not be used to kill millions of people, we can get down to the real job of helping to use it for the benefit of mankind.'

# CHAPTER 11

# BOOK REVIEWS AS PROPAGANDA

Book reviews constituted another useful channel of propaganda, though my use of the word must not suggest that I consciously allowed myself to be unfair to the authors. When reviewing a book I always considered it my duty to give the reader an idea of its contents. I disliked book reviewers who seemed to urge readers to reject or select a work solely on grounds of style or quality, but leaving them in ignorance of the subject matter.

Preaching that goodness, beauty and truth are eternal virtues, Professor Joad used to remark that in persuading the populace, federalists must not lie to them (neither should politicians).

But he used to joke that:

'... the great (here insert your own nationality) public is a goose, and one needs a proper goose to propagate a proper gander.'

His fellow federalists were well aware that the 'spontaneous and impromptu' jokes he perpetrated during his antics on the BBC 'Brains Trust' (often in company with his federalist sparring partner Barbara Wootton, J.P.) were always well rehearsed among his friends before going on the air. He used to advise us to try to leave the point of any joke until the very last word, otherwise it will be lost to the slowest members of the audience, drowned by the guffaws of those who get the point before you have come to it.

History relates that this agreeable fellow spent his last moments telling humorous stories to his friends and students surrounding his bed.

## Book Reviews as Propaganda

I cannot remember whether this limerick is his, but it serves to emphasize his point:

> There was a young bard of Japan
> whose poetry never would scan.
> When someone pointed this out,
> he said: 'I don't doubt,
> but I always like to put as many words into the last line as I possibly can'.

The reviews in this Chapter are arranged roughly in chronological order, depending mainly on the dates when I received them from the publishers or authors.

### *Psychology and World Order*
### by Ranyard West, MD; MRCP (Lond.), D.Phil. (Oxon.)
### Pelican Books

The child is father to the man. The little boy who blames the cat for pulling its own tail when he is 'only holding it' grows up into the self-styled realist who clings to the opinion that the old League of Nations did not fail; the world it was that failed the League.

War came again upon earth because the sons of man did not desire peace earnestly enough. Tinkerbell can be cured of mortal poison if a sufficent number of children can be found to believe in fairies; world peace is assured if enough people will kneel down and wish for it. This is the logical conclusion to the argument that 'it is the spirit that counts, not constitutional machinery.' On this reasoning, a parasol is as good as a parachute on a trans-Atlantic flight.

It is refreshing to find a book that combines the optimistic view of human nature; scientific reasoning in support of its optimism; and serious proposals for world constitutional machinery and institutions through which it can become effective in the service of world peace.

> There seems to be enough friendly human nature throughout the world to enable all normal men and women to live a life of very great freedom and happiness. What is required in the psychological ... field is an organization which is based upon our knowledge of the facts.

Dr West's argument continues inexorably towards the conclusion that:

> ... all law, municipal and international alike, should be founded upon a single concept: The law of any society should represent the best selves of the majority of that society put into a commission of execution. The executive body must never include a party to a dispute.

## The Parliament of Man

The book is an argument for a World democratic electorate behind a world legislature and government.

How to attain it? Here again, Dr West is an optimist.

> No power on earth will preserve the sovereign nation states of the world if men once become convinced that they can see a better way of securing their lives, their liberties, their estates and their welfare.

The attack upon the existing international 'order' is specific, detailed and well documented. 'Everybody knows that all is not well with 'International Law', Dr West considers. 'Austin, one of the greatest of our British law writers of the 19th century, was categorically clear; it is:

> not law at all, but a branch of positive morality ... International law *asks* us to keep *ourselves* in order. It can never control us as long as "we" are sovereign states.

The author clearly shows the impossibility of predicting what types of dispute an international authority will be required to resolve in its task of upholding peace.

> 'Those who point to economic conflict between proletarian and capitalist point to one instance only of the source of human disorder.'

The weakness of the book reveals itself when Dr West turns from the rôle of psychologist to that of constitutional lawyer. For some obscure reason he shies at the conclusion towards which his own logic has driven the reader, and suggests, albeit half-heartedly, that a World Confederation might achieve his purpose.

Though he gently rejects this alternative in favour of a federal scheme, the idea reappears in his 'World Charter':

> 'Pending the introduction of a wider democratic initiative, access to the World Court shall be open to all democratically-elected governments of states as such.'

A well-meaning but impracticable piece of idealism is the suggestion that:

> 'Where equity conflicts with any other "law", equity shall prevail.'

One is left with the feeling that if the author had prescribed the cure with as much care and attention as he devoted to the diagnosis, this would be a brilliant book.

\* \* \*

## Book Reviews as Propaganda

The following review even reached Pakistan (*Pakistan Horizon*):

**The World at the Crossroads**
Blaine, Cassels, Embree, Waymack, Wright
World Citizens Assn. Chicago. 1946

Unthinking optimism pervades this naive eulogy of the United Nations Organization. The authors suggest that:

' ... if the benefits anticipated from the functioning of international co-operation ... materialize, a great power contemplating aggression might hesitate to deprive its people of these benefits by shattering the organization, a probable consequence of persistence in aggressive behaviour.'

This they piously call 'a powerful deterrent to aggression.'

The booklet argues that 'the sovereign rights of nations and the powers of the United Nations were augmented by the San Francisco Charter.'

This recalls Alexander Hamilton's verdict on those of his contemporaries who similarly sought mutually irreconcilable ends:

'They cherish with blind devotion the political monstrosity of an "imperium in imperio" ' (*Independent Journal* 1787).

The Charter itself is included, and shows the extraordinary care taken to deprive the Organization of the ability to perform its task: to 'maintain international peace'. The Assembly has the power only to 'make recommendations.' The 'Security' Council cannot make a decision, let alone take action, unless the Big Five are all agreed and two stooges vote with them. If they disagree, UNO is paralyzed.

The authors apparently imagine that Oklahoma lives at peace with Texas merely because they know of a peaceful way to settle disputes. They forget that the American Federal Government enforces a peaceful decision by operation directly upon individual citizens, and not on States as such. The world is indeed at the crossroads: it must choose international Government or U.N. Organization.

*\* \* \**

The following was published by, among others, the *Commonwealth Review*.

## The Parliament of Man

### *Soviet Policy toward Disarmament*
**Marina Salvin (Instructor in Government, Columbia University)**
**Published by Carnegie Endowment for International Peace.**

Miss Salvin asserts in her opening sentence that 'from its inception, the Soviet Union has been a vocal advocate of disarmament,' and proceeds to quote chapter and verse from diplomatic documents covering the period from the Genoa Conference of 1922 until the recent hagglings of the United Nations Organization.

The work is of interest mainly because it shows the clash between two schools of thought: the one that believes that insecurity breeds armaments, and the one that maintains that armaments cause insecurity. The fact that both are right does not assist in breaking the vicious circle.

It has long been regarded as the orthodox view that men will not surrender the means of asserting their 'rights' except to a superior agency which they believe to be capable of defending them more vigorously. It is thus difficult to follow the Russian thesis that the mere destruction of weapons will itself create the security that will render them superfluous.

Judging from the speeches quoted in this book, the Russians believe that the Western nations cling to their crushing burden of armaments out of a perverted love of self-impoverishment. The Russians, on the other hand, are suspected of plotting the destruction of warships and similar ostentatious weapons, relying on overwhelming numbers and arms more easily assembled in secret.

What the documents mainly illustrate is the criminal folly of statesmen of all fifty-seven nations, who ask us to put our trust in a world 'security' organization that can maintain peace only by waging war.

\* \* \*

### *The Great Rehearsal*
**by Carl Van Doren (Viking Press, New York 1948)**

This is the story of the making and ratifying of the U. S. Constitution. The title implies that 'the situation (in 1787) was . . . much like that of the sovereign states of the United Nations.'

The author admits, however:

## Book Reviews as Propaganda

'Nor do those citizens of the world who desire to see a federal world government created assume that the process would have to follow the example of the United States. The Federal Convention did not follow any single example. Neither should a General Conference of the United Nations be expected to.'

The fruits of painstaking research, the book records the contentions for and against a constitution for the United States and purports to provide a criterion by which to judge arguments advocating or opposing a general government for the United Nations. Whatever our opinions on this point, the book should help us to decide what sanctions should enforce the decisions of an international authority. It appears that the American Constitution suceeded because, in the words of Madison, it established a federal government that could 'directly operate on individuals, and would punish only those whose guilt required it.'

As Ellsworth[1] reasoned:

'We see how necessary for the union is the corrective principle ... The only question is, shall it be a coercion of law, or a coercion of arms? I am for coercion by law – that coercion which acts only upon delinquent individuals. This constitution does not attempt to coerce sovereign bodies, states, in their political capacity.'

Would that such wisdom had prevailed in 1919, or at San Francisco!

### Peace or Anarchy
### Cord Meyer, Jr. (Atlantic Monthly Press, Boston, USA)

The author made a name with his letters home from the Pacific war, published in the *Atlantic Monthly*. As one of the War Veteran observers at the San Francisco Conference, young Meyer:

'... watched, with growing concern, how the victory was squandered at the conference table, ... an organization created ... even weaker than the old League.'

---

[1] Oliver Ellsworth, delegate for Connecticut at Philadelphia Convention, 1787.

## The Parliament of Man

So thoroughly are the defects of the U.N. Charter analysed that it looks like a palace founded on shifting sands. The reconstruction he prescribes is so radical that the new text would have nothing left except: 'We the people ... '

'Two principles are indispensable.' he says, 'The first is the concept of enforceable law that binds individuals. The impractical and unjust notion of collective security must be repudiated since the only method of enforcement it provides is the waging of war against entire nations. It is essential that security rest on a legal structure of effective prevention and individual penalization rather than on collective measures that are merely another name for war. Secondly, national governments will never submit themselves and their citizens to the rule of law unless it is limited by the concept of federalism.'

\* \* \*

## The Last Trump
### Denis de Rougemont, Doubleday & Co.Inc. N.Y.

At first perusal this book, by a Swiss delegate to the Congress of Europe at the Hague last May, might be dismissed as a frivolous piece on a serious subject. However:

'When I observe that our entire world has changed since Hiroshima, and that, nevertheless, those responsible for the common fate go on behaving exactly as usual,' the author explains, 'I smile; that's my new way of being serious.'

The title is from St. Paul[1]:

[1] 1 Cor.25:51-52. My Norwegian bible, one of these popular popular translations — called *Good News* — when translated back into English, reads: '... in a now, in a blink, when it sounds blast in the last trombone.' As a translator I had always admired the majestic poetry of King James's authorized version, and this *Good News* reinforced it!

This raises the question of the effect poor translations may have on international relations. One recalls that the Old Contemptibles adopted their name in defiance of what they had been led to believe was an insult by Kaiser Wilhelm, who admired the courage of Kitchener's 'contemptibly little' army. Of course the propaganda-minded translator could not resist the temptation to change 'contemptibly' to 'contemptible'!

'... we shall all be changed in a moment, in the twinkling of an eye, at the last trump.'

'Do you know what the Greek text says where the French translation reads "In an instant"? It says *en atomo* – in an atom!'

Concerning the atom bomb as a trump card, he suggests:

'The militarists, may as well dedicate themselves to sports from now on ... There will be no more war in the classic sense of the word ... The stout-hearted captains and armies in fine array advancing undaunted against the atomic bomb would return after a few moments in the form of light vapour.'

Nevertheless, he inquires:

'Could it be that peace perished along with war?'

He develops the theme that the atomic bomb has no secrets that will not soon be discovered by other powers, and that catastrophe is imminent unless something drastic is done.

Monsieur de Rougemont then smiles his way through to the moral:

'A simple vision of ... world union ... This solution has all the marks of fate, and sooner or later it will be forced upon us.'

\* \* \*

### The North Atlantic Pact
Marina Salvin, Carnegie Endowment for International Peace, N.Y.
**Forerunners & Future of Atlantic Pact**

If any treaty between sovereign states merits study, this handbook can be commended, in the words of James T. Shotwell's preface, as an 'open-minded examination.'

It includes the text of the Atlantic Treaty, comparative sections from the Brussels, Rio and Soviet-Bulgarian Pacts, and relevant extracts from other official papers.

In a well-documented review of the antecedents of the Atlantic Pact, Miss Salvin points out that from the enunciation of the 'negative' Truman Doctrine, barely twelve months elapsed before the more positive Marshall Plan was approved by Congress; exactly a year later politico-military underpinning was provided by the North Atlantic Treaty, signed on 4 April 1949.

## The Parliament of Man

All this is traced against the background of Western Europe's own efforts: closer political and economic integration, the Dunkirk Treaty of 1947, the Brussels Pact of March 1948, 'Uniforce', and the Council of Europe. The 1947 Conference establishing the Cominform is not overlooked!

Perhaps of most interest is the author's appraisal of the pact. She admits the shortcomings of diplomatic scraps of paper. Decisions to give assistance will remain in national hands, each State having an equal vote and taking 'such action as it deems necessary.' Miss Salvin adds:

> 'For the purpose of restoring and maintaining the security of the North Atlantic area ... according to the terms of the treaty ... any measure that would serve this end would be permissible, even, at some later and more isolationist date, the appeasement of an aggressor if that seemed more convenient and less costly.'

In the author's eyes it is significant that the signatories of the Atlantic Treaty have recognized that the Security Council of the U.N. cannot provide security, and — shelving the idealism which hoped for Great Power agreement — have, more realistically, accepted the possibility of violent disagreement.

After considering the danger that rearmament will cause such impoverishment that Western economy will collapse, Miss Salvin declares that 'permanent security and peace have never in the past resulted from systems of alliances.'

She hopes nevertheless that the North Atlantic countries:

> '... by working together, through the Pact, on the creation of ... common political forms, may one day find themselves far along the road toward ... supranational organization ... and by chipping away at the structure of nationalism ... may lift their eyes to a broad horizon, and counter the ideological challenge of communism on its own plane.'

\* \* \*

### Searchlight on Peace Plans
**Edith Wynner and Georgia Lloyd, E. P. Dutton & Co. Inc., N.Y.**

If this concise and illuminating catalogue of peace plans since the year 1306 had not been compiled, it would have had to be one of UNES-

CO's first tasks. It should be in the library of every organization interested in peaceful international relations; indeed, it is a reference book which many a student of foreign affairs will consider an indispensable addition to his own shelves.

In the new and enlaged edition just published there is much new and up-to-date material on the United Nations and its specialized agencies, summaries of the federal constitutions of Austria, Burma, India and Yugoslavia, and particulars of the constitutional changes in Argentina, Brazil and Venezuela, studies of the Arab League, the Atlantic and Brussels Pacts, Western European Union, and other official projects, all of the same high quality as the earlier studies.

Dealing with developments since Dumbarton Oaks (October 1944) the authors say:

> 'From this momentous decision (i.e. to repeat the League experiment) the subsequent disintegration of United Nations unity was predictable with fatal accuracy. ... The confederation ... would have nothing to administer because the national governments retained all jurisdiction. It had nothing to enforce but peace – and it could attempt to enforce that only by means of war, and that after wholesale riot and arson were well under way. ... The United Nations has already reached the crossroads: forward to federation or backward to disintegration .. '

These criticisms are all the more remarkable since they occur in a work that gives the general impression of studied impartiality, and the authors' desire to let the facts alone speak their own case. In their detailed analysis of the United Nations Charter, the authors make some constructive suggestions. For instance, they argue that UNO should have effective legislative, executive and judicial authority over world affairs *applicable also to individuals*. This view is also developed in the section dealing with the War Crimes Tribunals.

The specialized agencies, it is pointed out, perform the functions of government departments under a parliamentary system, with the vital difference that each must submit its proposals not to one parliament but to over ninety. Their work, they conclude, is seriously jeopardized by the continued failure of the peoples of the world to establish an effective world-wide political authority.

The international authority should have 'sources of revenue independent of national governments,' which criticism should be read in conjunction with the fact that the UNO system of voting is undemocratic and unfair. Military and financial power will not be given to a body that cannot be trusted by its constituent members.

While the federal solution is still denied to us, the 'United Nations hobbles along on a budget under 44 million dollars. ... The cost of the entire U.N. system is under 234 million dollars. In 1949 the United States alone had earmarked over fifteen billion dollars for purely military purposes. The peoples of the world ... want peace ... at bargain rates. ... Since 1914, Humanity has been spending much of its time in wholesale murder and destruction and in poking among the ruins for scraps of sustenance, covering and shelter.'

It is obvious why the sub-title of the book is *Choose your Road to World Government*.

\* \* \*

### The World must be Governed
### Vernon Nash, Harper & Bros. N.Y.

Most of the American arguments in favour of world government have been so woolly and timid that there was grave reason to fear that American federalists, particularly the giant 'United World Federalists' movement, would degenerate into a mild and ineffectual echo of the United Nations Association, just one more straw prop for the idol with the feet of clay. But this book by Vernon Nash is original, vigorous, provocative and obviously written by a man who 'thinks things, not words,' who knows what he wants and precisely how to get it.

The usual American argument has been that the United Nations is a first step towards world government. Dr Nash adopts a more virile, more European attitude:

> ... propaganda which suggests that the U.N. is to some degree the beginnings of world government has obscured the essential fact that the U.N. is powerless. ... Put down a list of the powers lawfully exercised by any government under which you live, and you will find that the U.N. does not possess a single one of these powers. It has functions, but not power. ... The U.N. has no military forces of its own, and there is no prospect that contingents will ever be made available to it under present conditions. The U.N. has no police to arrest individual criminals; it can enact no laws that are binding upon its members; it has no courts with

compulsory jurisdiction. Hence it is not even a partial or quasi government. ... It is therefore not enough to say that the U.N. must be strengthened and improved. It must be *transformed* into a world government of limited but adequate powers.

In reply to those who urge us that 'anything is better than nothing,' that we should continue to put up with ramshackle makeshifts, he remarks:

In both war and peace, anything less than enough soon proves to be the equivalent of nothing ... The mere existence of a world organization, however inadequate, may cause too many to trust it just one day too long, and we may never have another chance.[1]

None of the classic pleas for world government appears to have been overlooked, yet there is no air of staleness about them; they are presented in a novel and pleasing guise. Dr Nash emphasizes the paradox of a league, 'designed to keep the peace — which, by its design, can do so only by making war.'

Dealing with the reluctance of statesmen to learn from history, he points out that the past has proved the impotence of confederations, and remarks that:

'We do not have to jump off a cliff again and again in order to know that the law of gravity works at all times.'

Answering 'those who repudiate any useful parallel between the formative period of the USA and our present struggle for the United States of the World,' Mr Nash adduces facts to prove that the Americans of 1789:

'... were not one people; they did not speak one language, nor did they have a common culture to any such degree as is now so widely assumed ... No one is entitled to claim an informed opinion on this issue until he has read a representative collection of the diaries, letters and other documents of our 1780s ...'

One might legitimately expect each new book on world government to be better than the previous ones, since each author has the advantage of studying earlier literature on the subject. *The World Must be Governed* is the best I have read, and I shall be surprised if a better one appears for a very long time.

*  *  *

[1] 1992: Precisely my attitude to the UN. Has this 'one day' arrived?

## The Parliament of Man

### The Pilgrimage of Western Man,
**Stringfellow Barr MA (Harcourt Brace & Co. N.Y.)**

The author is the President of the Foundation for World Government. But this book was begun three years before he realized that 'the system of sovereign nation-states was dead but not yet buried.'

Consequently, Stringfellow Barr's review of the history of the past four hundred years is an objective and dispassionate approach to the inevitable conclusion: that Man's pilgrimage toward the City of God upon Earth is a search for one world under one Government. This work, the result of thirty years of historical study, he intends to be regarded as a programme of action for the future.

This is not a book for those who are interested merely in tactics. But the intelligent reader will find in it the broad strategic outlines for the next and important revolution in the history of the world, the revolution in human thinking that must pave the way to world government.

Mr Barr studies and analyzes power with the objectivity of a scientist, which indeed a good historian or political strategist must be. Yet this is an immensely interesting human document, adorned with colourful and humorous stories of political intrigue, diplomatic scheming and shrewd[1] deals in the royal marriage market. He reveals to us the nature of sovereignty, shows how power has been acquired and wielded in the past, and suggests with prophetic insight how the monster could be tamed.

Barr does not blame Roosevelt for his share in the creation of the new league, the United Nations, but does condemn President Wilson for forgetting that:

'... all previous leagues in history had failed. Wilson could not grasp the force of Hamilton's argument that the price of peace is justice, the price of justice is law, that the price of law is government, and that government must apply law to men and women, not merely to subordinate governments.'

In stark distinction to the restrained, scholarly style of the rest of the book, Mr Barr's indictment of the high priests of national sovereignty stands out in vivid contrast:

---

[1] The original print-out said 'shrew'. I was tempted to leave it!

## Book Reviews as Propaganda

Under the ghastly new pressure of the system of sovereign nation-states ... every institution of Christendom underwent a profound perversion. Love of home became hatred of the foreigner. Protestant christianity ... sometimes appeared as mere religious tribalism ... Catholics became fanatical clericals, attacking anything that appeared to weaken the power of the Papacy. The nation-state became a kind of church itself; it had its flag ... its rabidly nationalist newspaper press ... its hysterical determination to impose the common national tongue ... The human race broke up into curious, new, and imaginary entities called 'races'.

The fact that Hitler could even momentarily gain control of Europe was evidence, the author argues, that Western civilization was intellectually and morally sick. 'By not federating, they came as near as men can come to guaranteeing another war.'

Political unity for Western Europe would not, Mr Barr admits, fulfil the necessity for '... a common government for the world-wide civilization that had sprung from Europe's womb. But it would be perhaps a step towards such government ...'

The reader will close this book with the conviction that the time for dreaming is past. It is no longer sufficient to pray 'Thy Kingdom come'. We must resume without delay our 'long and arduous pilgrimage' towards the fulfilment of our destiny: that we may build, upon Earth, the Kingdom of God.

# CHAPTER 12

# UNCLE SAM

In 1948 the USA's efforts at world leadership were still in their 'teething' or 'running-in' stage. Some gentle remonstrance seemed to be called for, and editors at home and elsewhere in Europe were inclined to agree with me, as the following article, several times printed, may indicate.

Incidentally, it may be as well to bear in mind that when the article was written, 'queer' meant 'ill', 'poorly'.

The American League of Friendship was converted into a federal union in 1789, the Constitution bearing thirty-nine signatures. So successful was it that the population increased forty-fold from 1790 – 1950 (1790 – 1991 more than sixty-fold), and the area of the Union increased fourfold.

Those who begrudge Uncle Sam a whole chapter to himself may console themselves with the thought that readers who are bored with the long chapters might turn in relief to this shorter one.

### Please, Doctor, Uncle's Queer

I've come to see you about my Uncle Sam, Doctor. I think he's alright in himself, really. He's got a very strong constitution, and powerful arms and wings. He's forty times as heavy and four times as big as when he was born. Being so big and wide and heavy he would normally be a very poor Life risk, the insurance people say, but he's got just the right kind of constitution to keep him hearty for ages yet, they tell us.

No, doctor, he never had a mother – he was just the result of a peculiar friendship – but he had thirty-nine fathers. They hardly expected to rear him. Even a hundred years ago, when he was only

## Uncle Sam

about forty-nine, an eminent specialist Mr de Tocqueville[1] said he couldn't be expected to last much longer. When he was seventy-two he had some trouble in his lower regions, doctor. We think he had swallowed some foreign bodies, so he got himself one of those Mason-Dixie belts. Nasty, dangerous things they are — nearly cut himself in half, he did. But he recovered after about four years, as hale and hearty as ever. Except that now he is frightened to death about germs and microbes — thinks people are plotting to spray them all over him. Silly, I think. He tries not to quarrel with the neighbours, so he's always lending them money, and never getting it back.

Yes, doctor, he does make love now and again. You'd die laughing. He gets the girl by the throat and yells:

'Love me, darling. Love, me, doggone you, or I'll bash your head in with this stick.'

Now you ask me, Doctor, I do recall that Uncle is rather allergic to red. Even red, white and blue annoys him sometimes, but red makes him see red, if you see what I mean. He is always having purges[2] to eliminate all the red corpuscles from his blood, but I think this does him more harm than good. He says red corpuscles engage in antiavuncular activities, but I don't think he knows enough about medicine to doctor himself; don't you agree?

I do hope you can do something for my Uncle, Doctor. I feel sure something awful will happen if he isn't cured soon.

What's that you say, Doctor? He ought to be treated with World Government? You say we all ought to have it? Well, I never! I might have known a psychiatrist would say something potty. If you expect us to pay you a fee for that, you can just whistle for it. Good day!

---

[1] Alexis de Tocqueville, 1805 — 1859, French author of *Démocratie en Amérique*, etc.

[2] McCarthyism.

# CHAPTER 13

# SOME OBJECTIONS ANSWERED

Perhaps one of the reasons why the federalist ideas from World War II had such a disappointing lack of support was that they met with so little opposition. Progress seems to be more secure when one has had to struggle for it.

In the hopes of driving my message home more convincingly, I shall try to recall and answer some of the objections that are raised, and — where these are lacking — think up some of my own.

*Objection:*
*Federation will strengthen capitalism at the expense of the common man.*

The recent world-wide triumph of market economics over communism might have persuaded many former socialists that capitalism confers benefits they had not hitherto realized. Though unbridled capitalism may be a bad thing, one of the chief criticisms levelled at it seems to be that capitalism is already internationally organized. The proletariat[1], however, is not internationally organized to the same degree of efficiency. In a federal parliament, Labour would vote across national frontiers against Conservatives, in contrast to the bloc voting (nation against nation, depending on which party is in power in each state), which we find in a League.

Federation would no more strengthen or weaken capitalism than it would strengthen or weaken socialism. The argument is actually

---

[1] Most of us are now 'workers of the world.'

## Some Objections Answered

irrelevant, since federation would benefit all who participate in it, and would tend to equalize opportunities.

It should also be remembered that a league system completely disenfranchises the opposition parties in every state, whereas in a federal parliament, being directly elected, they would be duly represented in international affairs.

*Objection:*
*The richer nations would have to lower their standards of living, perhaps to the level of the poorer participants.*

This argument is usually advanced by those of little faith and little imagination, of the type who believe that equality is achieved by cutting off the heads (or feet, or both) of those who are taller than average. Federalists are realists, not mere idealists, wishing to bring about federation by consent. Men will federate for the sake of the benefits it will confer; many will try to sacrifice nothing, so long as they can be better protected by a federal government than they are by their national state. It follows that the immense financial resources liberated by federation will be used to raise the standards of living of our less happy brethren. Though the rate of increase in living standards in the richer countries might thereby be slightly delayed, any time lag may pass unnoticed save by a few observers. In any case, there would be no need for any fall in anyone's standard of living, and therefore there is no probability that such a fall would occur.

*Objection:*
*The federal parliament and government would be a brain drain on the states members.*

This would not be an unmixed blessing. The best brains and talents would no doubt be attracted to the Parliament of Man. There, instead of having their thoughts constantly interrupted with domestic and local worries, federal civil servants and political and legal intellects could devote themselves exclusively to world affairs, and thus tackle them more efficiently. Similarly (and this is almost equally important) national politicians and public servants could devote their energies more efficiently to social reform, without the constant interruptions and worries of world affairs to distract them. There are only twenty-four hours in a day, seven days in a week, and only a limited number of years in a lifetime.

## The Parliament of Man

Also, it must be borne in mind that a federal system is the kind that can be run by normal human beings. Not even a superman can run a League system, not even when assisted by hordes of supermen, who, of course, do not exist.

Without wishing to flatter the reader, I would go so far as to say that even he or she, if fortunate (?) enough to be elected to the task, would be capable of running the federation, with the assistance provided. A federal constitution can withstand the strains imposed upon it not only by a weak or incompetent president, but by a dishonest one, and still survive without suffering mortal damage. Admittedly, a nation benefits from having a president of high calibre, but it would hardly be a disaster if the President were a Harding, a Coolidge[2], a Nixon, a Tricky Dicky or a Waldheim. It is the system, not the man, that is the essence. And in any event, a man is replaced eventually by election or by death. The Constitution endures.

A further safeguard might be that, instead of one titular head, the federation were headed by a Praesidium. Here, as in other matters, such as whether to adopt the British cabinet system or the American executive method, we cannot anticipate the decisions of the Constituent Assembly; it might emulate the famous assembly of 1787 and invent some superior method not yet known to mankind.

*Objection:*
*This country would be flooded with pauper immigrants from the poorer members of the union.*

Admittedly, there are some advocates of federation who either propose or assume that the federal constitution would permit free migration across inter-State borders. I doubt very much whether the Constituent Assembly would agree to such a provision being written into the Constitution. Nor can I conceive of a sufficient number of nations ratifying such a provision to bring it into force.

It cannot be stressed too strongly that federal union must be voluntary, and must not be imposed.

Similar arguments apply to the question of free trade.[3]

[2] Dorothy Parker, U.S. columnist, on hearing the report of President Coolidge's death, asked 'How can they tell?'.

[3] 'There is nothing a tariff can do that an earthquake cannot do better.' (Curry, *The Case for Federal Union*)

## Some Objections Answered

Nevertheless, in all honesty, I must here place on record that it is my own personal conviction (not in my capacity as a federalist) that free trade and free migration are ideals to be striven for, as bringing immeasurable long-term benefit to all concerned and only short-term disadvantages, if any. The aim is to create a federal union in which all citizens are happy, most of them content to live where they were born, among their friends and relatives and in their native habitat. It would be a union in which those who emigrate – specialists, experts, artists, cultural envoys – do so because they can be more useful abroad, where they would be welcomed by those whom they will benefit. In it, there need be no refugees, except from abroad.

It is my view that in due course, when the new union eventually realizes what boons are free trade and free migration, the citizens will amend the Constitution to conform to their more enlightened philosophy and better experience.

There are doubtless many critics of a very simple initial Constitution who would like to include federal guarantees to all citizens of the union not only of free trade and free migration, but also of certain hard-won liberties that exist at present only in some of the federating states, such as leave of absence from work because one's wife has given birth.

It is very probable that the initial Constitution will guarantee a minimum of Human Rights to protect citizens of the least favoured member states, but it must be remembered that the respective member states would thus be left full powers to protect the rights already enjoyed by their own citizens.

We would not lose any rights by federating, though we may gain federal defence of rights already won.

Those who wish to give the federal authority the widest possible powers should also remember what league supporters and some self-professed federalists so frequently forget: One does not confer more power on an authority by loading it with more duties. Man does not acquire rights merely by proclaiming them. They must be defendable, and be defended.

It is the essence of federalism to confer a power on that government (federal or state) which is best qualified to wield it in the interests of the citizens. Consequently, we do not give the federal government the power to decide, e.g. what colour to give the facade of our town hall.

Though I have proclaimed myself a supporter of free migration as an eventual ideal goal, that does not mean to say that my ideal federation is one where every nationality is inextricably mixed in one great omelette, even though this has been a comparative success in the USA. It would hardly be an improvement if each State in the USA contained exclusively Hispanos, Italians, Germans, Irish, Poles, or Greeks, etc., even if there were enough States for the purpose. Though this might make the USA an even more colourful community (and happier?).

*Objection:*
*A federal union would be a super-state, bossing us about.*

Federation is an antidote to the super state. Did the advent of the orchestra abolish the violin?

*Objection:*
*The federal power to tax would increase our burdens still further.*

So economical would a federal system be that it would be quite feasible to insert a clause in the Constitution to the effect that the sum of federal and state taxation shall never exceed the present level of taxation in any member state, or even that it shall never exceed (say) 80% of the present level. In practice, however, such a stipulation might be inadvisable, since legislators would be apt to regard it as a mandate to tax up to the specified limit!

It should also be borne in mind that, for technical reasons connected with tax collection, most serious drafters of Federal constitutions for the new world order propose indirect taxation to finance the federal government. I am no tax expert, and would — as in most matters — have to rely on those more competent than myself to advise on federal taxation, but my own feeling is that a small tax on, e.g. sugar might suffice to finance the federal government. Everything depends, of course, on the range of powers entrusted to the federal authority.

Lionel Curtis[4] suggests that both taxation and representation should be proportionate to taxable capacity. Any state that appealed

---

[4] *World War, its Cause and Cure.* Note that Curtis proposed federal taxation of states, not individuals. This is a compromise of federal theory.

## Some Objections Answered

against its tax assessment would therefore have to be prepared to see its representation quota cut if its tax appeal succeeded! Under the Curtis scheme, federal tax would be a first charge on the consolidated fund of every member state.

*Objection:*
*The Soviet Union is breaking up, and it is a federation. The same could happen to your proposed nucleus world federation.*

The USSR is a federation only on paper. It is collapsing not because its constitution is nominally federal, but because it is communist. A 1992 vintage joke is the proposed new name for the Soviet: UFFR, the Union of Fewer and Fewer Republics. Eastern Europeans have an explanation why the change to a market economy is so difficult. They say the reds made fish soup out of an aquarium, and now the blues are trying to make an aquarium out of the soup. This applies with particular force to Yugoslavia at the present moment.

*Objection:*
*War is inevitable. You cannot change human nature.*

This is a fallacy. Human nature can be changed by the laws under which we live. The human temperament varies according to our environment. This environment partly depends on the laws we ourselves have made to govern our conduct.

Duelling ceased in most countries when the law laid it down that men do not have the divine right to bear arms at all times and in any circumstances. There would be fewer murders and other crimes of violence if this fact were more widely recognized by the less civilized nations (this includes many nations who claim to be more highly civilized than any other).

Gun-carrying, by both criminals and police, would become less common in a world where war and preparation for war between states had become almost unthinkable. Television 'entertainment' would no longer show so many incidents where the 'hero' does a 'Pearl Harbour' on the villain by punching him on the nose without warning!

In a world where we had more time, money and brainpower to devote to social reform, terrorism, gangsterism, hooliganism and indeed petty crime would be easier to deal with and – in some instances – eradicate.

## The Parliament of Man

*Objection:*
*Why bother? (a) Politicians are crooks and will diddle us anyway. Besides, (b) the world is not worth saving.*

This is hardly a valid argument, being based more on sentiment than on reason. A person with such a misanthropic philosophy would be of little use to any campaign to improve the world and would be wasting his time in reading this book.

However, in the hope of persuading waverers, I shall try to answer both objections.

(a) In an imperfect world there will always be self-professed public 'servants' who try to misuse positions of trust. Federation is no universal remedy to be sprayed indiscriminately upon the world to cure all its ills. However, in a world less obsessed by fears of war and preparations for war we would have better opportunity and greater legal powers with which to deal with criminals of all types, including political and commercial racketeers and hoodlums.

(b) This objection deserves a Chapter to itself; see Chapter 14.

# CHAPTER 14

# A HOUSE OF MANY MANSIONS[1]

In the previous chapter I undertook to answer the objection that 'The world is not worth saving.' This should perhaps have been the first chapter to follow Chapter 1 'Definitions', since before setting out on any undertaking of any magnitude one should first have decided what is the purpose of life, what are we here for? Otherwise, how are we to know in which direction progress lies?

As I see it, there are two main schools of thought: those who believe that everything we experience around us is the result of a prodigious accident, and those who feel sure it is the result of something akin to design, intention. This latter belief is, in my view, based on reasoning.

Admittedly, some of those who reason that life must be the result of a grand design carry their belief still further into the realms of faith and conclude that life must therefore be indestructible. This philosophy of course gives the believers in the 'accident' theory a stick with which to beat those who refute them.

I incline to the 'design' hypothesis because it seems to me that to believe that our miraculous surroundings are the result of some tremendous accident requires a prodigious amount of faith which my rational mind is quite unable to swallow.

---

[1] Jesus said: 'In my Father's house are many mansions'. (John 14:2) Did he mean that the Commonwealth of God is a federation? (This implication is often lost in translation).

## The Parliament of Man

Look around at the teeming life on this planet, extending down to the utmost depths of the sea and up into the uppermost layers of the atmosphere, into the snowy wastes of the polar caps and spread profusely over the apparently sterile sands of the hottest desert. Life exists and persists on the brinks of volcanoes, even those under the oceans, and it exists in the form of bacteria, viruses[2], fungi, plants and animals. Whether animal or vegetable, living organisms use a common program, the DNA molecule, to develop and proliferate. It is not surprising that George Bernard Shaw believed in some sort of divine 'Life Force'.

Note that the adherents of the 'accident' hypothesis believe that all these finely adjusted and coincident phenomena are fortuitous, as though life were a sexually transmitted disease, a vast restaurant in which the guests eat each other. If a rational being from outer space were to be shown how to use a computer it would assume that the machine, and its program (a DNA ?) had *designers*. Unless it had *boundless* faith in the 'accident' theory, it would not believe either the hardware or the software to have been devised and assembled by chance. (But remember, I called it a 'rational' being.)

Yet when faced with a brain, human or animal, or indeed any other living organs (all far more complex and miraculous than a computer), the human adherents to the 'accident' theory blithely assume such miracles to be the result of mere hazard, created and designed automatically by blind chemistry and physics (and, of course, alchemy, which is now practicable).

Does it not dismay them to know that swimming in the oceans of the world are innumerable dolphins whose IQ is far superior to theirs?

Time may be a mere invention of man, whose life span is long enough to contain a myriad of generations of, e.g. the fruit fly. Time probably passes at different speeds in the life of a man and that of a fruit fly – a corollary to Professor Einstein's relativity theory which I gladly donate to society.

Eternity, too, may be a mere invention of man. But if we believe in it (think about it for too long and the concept seems unbelievable),

---

[2] A Nobel prizewinner, debating in Stockholm 'What is life', professed to finding distinct evidence of intelligence in viruses. Scientists have recently found that there are millions of viruses in every drop of clean water.

we must agree that there is time enough within it for anything to happen an infinite number of times. Indeed, there is time enough within it for *everything* to happen an infinite number of times — time enough, in fact, for an *infinite number of things* to happen an infinite number of times.

It follows, therefore (and I concede this to believers in the stupendous 'accident') that there would be sufficient time in eternity for our present universe, in all its bewildering variety, to have happened just now by accident. Indeed, there is time for it all to happen an infinite number of times.

However, and here is the main point, the fact that something *could* happen is no guarantee that it *will* happen, despite the engineer's dictum that if something can go wrong it will. And the fact that something *could have* happened is no guarantee that is has happened. Here we see a difference between reason and faith.

Take the theory that if a word processor were to be operated by a monkey for an eternity, at some time or other the monkey would be bound to produce, at random, the complete works of William Shakespeare, containing only those spelling mistakes that the bard himself had made. Reason tells us that such a 'miracle' is possible.

However, this, to my mind, is no guarantee that it would or will happen. Otherwise, we are bound to accept that all the other literary works by every author who ever existed, of any nationality, would also be produced by this prolific monkey. If this were so, the question arises: What was the point of Shakespeare producing Hamlet if a monkey could write the play by accident? And what kind of miracle would be required to enable all the literary works contained in all the libraries of the modern world to appear by chance *all at the same time*[3]?

Also, would not the world already be flooded out with ape-made 'masterpieces' that were imperfect duplicates? Do not misunderstand me. Reason leads me to believe in a great designer(s), but only faith would lead me to believe that He or She or They (black or white or yellow or ...?) is or are omnipotent (except by comparison with our own puny abilities) or eternal.

If our own blood corpuscles could communicate with and argue

---

[3] Measured by geological time, man's life on earth is as 'short as the watch that ends the night before the morning sun.'

among themselves, some of them would surely assert that there is a divine being, and go on to describe the human body as experienced from the inside. Some of them would no doubt also attribute eternal life to this divine being, giving Him a throne to sit upon, thus presuming that divine beings have the same anatomical equipment that requires us to have some means of support before we can be comfortable.

All this notwithstanding, if you believe in the 'accident' theory you may conclude that life begins and ends on this planet and that no matter whether our experience here will be repeated an infinite number of times *or not at all*, any attempt to improve life on earth for ourselves or for our fellow sufferers is just a waste of time and effort.

Surely, however, if this life is all we have and all we shall ever have, it would be more reasonable to try to make the best of it. This might be a good reinsurance if, after all, we find that in the end we have to give an account of what we did with Life. It may not suffice merely to say 'I passed it on.' (Some of us may even have had to leave this pleasure to others!)

If, on the other hand, life on earth is merely a preliminary to something different[4], it would be wise to use the opportunity it gives us to better ourselves and to try to improve the lot of our fellows.

Therefore, dear reader, join us in our work to create a nucleus federation that will be so powerful that none will dare to threaten it, so just that none will wish to challenge it, and so successful that all outside it will clamour to join in.

\* \* \*

Federalism still lives on, and can be contacted through the following addresses: (These organizations do not necessarily endorse all policies advocated in this book.)

*Netherlands:* World Federalist Movement, International Secretariat, Leliegracht 21, 1016 GR AMSTERDAM.

---

[4] The optimist believes we live in the best of all possible worlds. The pessimist is afraid the optimist is right.

## A House of Many Mansions

| | |
|---|---|
| U. K.: | *Association of World Federalists*, 158 Buckingham Palace Road, LONDON, SW1W 9TR |
| | *Federal Trust* (This is educational only), 158 Buckingham Palace Road, LONDON, SW1W 9TR |
| Australia: | *World Federalists of Australia*, 212 Watts Road, WILSON, W.A. 6107 |
| Bangladesh: | *WAWF – Bangladesh*, 13-A/1-A Babar Road, Block B, MOHAMMEDPUR, DHAKA 1207 |
| | *WAWF National Youth Organization of Bangladesh*, Marathon Trading Ltd., 15/18 Sher Shah Suri Road, MOHAMMEDPUR, DHAKA 1207 |
| Belgium: | *WAWF – Belgium Section*, 50 Corniche Verte, BRUSSELS 15. |
| | *Young European Federalists (JEF)*, Rue du Trône 98 Bte.8, B-1050 BRUSSELS. |
| Canada: | *World Federalists of Canada*, 145 Spruce Street, Ste.207, OTTOWA, ONT., K1R 6P1 |
| Denmark: | *FN-Forbundet*, Skindergade 26 I, DK 1159 COPENHAGEN K. |
| France: | *Les Fédéralistes Mondiaux de France*, 142 Avenue de Versailles, 75016 PARIS. |
| Germany: | *Bund Deutscher Föderalisten*, Postfach 120447, D-W-5300 BONN 1. |
| India: | *Indian Nat. Organization of World Federalists*, World Federalist Chambers, 115 Park Street, CALCUTTA 700 016 |
| | *World Federalist Youth of India (WOFYIN)*, 115 Park Street, CALCUTTA 700 016 |
| | *Asian Youth Centre – India*, 127 Dr. Radhakrishnan Rd., MYLAPORE, MADRAS 600 004 |
| Italy: | *Movimento Federalista Mondiale*, Via Porta Pertusi 6, I-27100 PAVIA. |
| Japan: | *Japan Association of World Federalists*, 2F Daiichi Fujikawa Bldg. 4-23, Yotsuya Shinjuku-ku, TOKYO. |
| Korea: | *Korean League of World Federalists*, POB C.252, SEOUL. |
| Netherlands: | *Wereld Federalisten Beweging Nederland*, Leliegracht 21, 1016 GR AMSTERDAM. |

## The Parliament of Man

*Norway:*     *En Verden*, Uranienborgveien 26, N-0258 Oslo 2.
*Russia:*     *Centre for Study of Federalism,* Kirovogradskaya 20-1-88, 113587 MOSCOW, Russia.
*Senegal:*     *African Federalist Movement*, B.P. 200, Saint-Louis.
*Sweden:*     *Sveriges Världsfederalister*, POB 224, 10122 STOCKHOLM.
*Switzerland:*     *Verein der Weltföderalisten der Schweitz*, Postfach 2640, CH-3000 BERN 8
*U.S.A.:*     *World Federalist UN Office*, 777 UN Plaza, N.Y.10017
    *World Federalist Association*, 418 Seventh St., S.E., WASHINGTON, D.C.20003

# BIBLIOGRAPHY

1942, *Action*, Lionel Curtis; Oxford University Press.
1946, *The Anatomy of Peace*, Emery Reves; Geo. Allen & Unwin.
1991, *A New World Order*, R. Hudson et al.; World Federalist Organisation; Washington D. C.
1939, *The Case for Federal Union**, Dr. W. B. Curry; Penguin, UK.
1989, *The Charter of the United Nations and Statute of the International Court of Justice*; United Nations, New York.
1991, *Common Responsibility in 1990s*, W. Brandt et al.; P.M., Stockholm.
1954, *The Commonwealth, Federation and Atlantic Union*, (Sir Ted) E. M. G. Leather, M.P.; Federal Union.
1941, *Decision*, Lionel Curtis; Oxford University Press.
1940, *Economic Basis of a Durable Peace*, J. E. Meade; Allen & Unwin.
1941, *Economic Aspects of Federation*, Lionel Robbins; Macmillan.
1939, *The Ending of Armageddon*, Lord Lothian; Federal Union.
1943, *Faith & Works*, Lionel Curtis; Oxford University Press.
1939, *The Federal Idea*, H. N. Brailsford; Federal Union.
1943, *Federalism and Freedom*, Sir George Young, Bt.; O.U.P.
1787-8, (reprinted 6 times between 1911 and 1937) *The Federalist*, (Ed: Prof. W. J. Ashley), Alex. Hamilton, John Jay, Jas. Madison; J. M. Dent & Sons.
1940, *Federal Europe*, R. W. G. Mackay; Michael Joseph.
1940, *Federation for Western Europe*, W. Ivor Jennings; C. U. P.
1944, *Federate or Perish*, John S. Hoyland, M.A., F.R.H.S.; Federal Union.
1990, *Federal Union:The Pioneers*, Mayne, Pinder & Roberts; Macmillan.
1959, *Freedom in a Federal World*, E. L. Millard; One World Inc.
1948, *The Great Rehearsal*, Carl van Doren; Viking Press, N.Y.
1946, *If Men Want Peace*, Eds: Harrison, Mander, Engle; Macmillan.
1948, *The Last Trump*, D.de Rougemont; Doubleday, USA.
1947, *Man and the Atom*, C. E. Vulliamy; Michael Joseph.
1949, *Must We Hide?*, R. E. Lapp; Maddison Wesley, Cambridge, Mass., USA.
1949, *The North Atlantic Pact*, Marina Salvin; Carnegie End.

1941, *One Anglo-American Nation*, George Catlin; Andrew Dakers Ltd.
1947, *One World or None*, Eds: D. Masters & K. Way; Latimer House.
1940, *Peace by Federation?*, Sir William Beveridge; Federal Union.
1948, *Peace or Anarchy*, Cord Meyer Jr.; Atlantic Monthly Press, USA.
1941, *The Philosophy of Federalism*, C. E. M. Joad; Macmillan.
1949, *The Pilgrimage of Western Man*, S. Barr; Harcourt Brace, N.Y.
1988 *PlanetHood*, B. B. Ferencz & K. Keyes Jr.; Vision Books, Coos B., Ore., USA.
1938, *Power*, Bertrand Russell; George Allen & Unwin.
1947, *Psychology & World Order*, Ranyard West M.D., M.R.C.P., D.Ph.; Pelican.
1946, *Searchlight on Peace Plans**, E. Wynner & G. Lloyd, E. P. Dutton & Co.
1941, *Socialism and Federation*, Barbara Wootton, Macmillan.
1947, *Soviet Policy toward Disarmament*, M. Salvin; Carnegie Endowment.
1947, *The State of the World*, A. de Hegedus; Cape.
1943, *Studies in Federal Planning*, Ed. P. Ransome; Macmillan.
1944, *Summary of the World Federation Plan**, Ely Culbertson; Faber.
1939, *Union Now**, Clarence K. Streit; Jonathan Cape.
1945, *The United Nations Charter*, Ed: N. M. Butler; Carnegie End.
1992, *U.N. & New World Order*, H. Kochler et al.; Int. Progr.Org., Wien.
1944, *The Way to Peace*, Lionel Curtis; Oxford University Press.
1941, *What Federal Government is*, K. C. Wheare; Macmillan.
1944, *A Working Peace System*, Prof. D. Mitrany; R. Inst. Int. Aff.
1947, *The World at the Crossroads*; World Citizens Assn., Chicago.
1950, *The World must be Governed*, Vernon Nash; Harper Bros., USA.
1980, *World Unification Plans & Analyses*, H. Newcombe; P. R. I. Dundas.
1944, *World Unity*, C. F. Spence; C.N.A.J., Johannesburg.
1945, *World War, Its Cause & Cure*, Lionel Curtis; O. U. P.

(* containing draft federal constitutions)

# INDEX

Adler, Ota, C.B.E. 65
Afghanistan 30
Allard, Baron Antoine 74
Allenbrook, Ruth 73
Anderson, Sir John 164
Armenia 28
Ashley, Prof. W. J. 136 *
Auschwitz 64

de Baer, General Marcel 60, 61
Baltic States 28
Barr, Stringfellow 224 *
Bavaria 18, 29
Bennett, Air Vice-Marshal 168
Bentley, F. H. 121
Bentwich, Prof. N. 63, 121
Bernadotte, Count 89, 98
Bernhard, Prince 163, 173
Beveridge, Lord 44, 64, 109, 110, 111, 124, 127, 192
Bevin, Ernest 10, 83, 107, 159, 188, 196, 198
Bhutto, Benazir 23
Bicanic, Dr Rudolf 60
Bidmead, H. W. 43, 159
Bloom, Claire 57
Borgese, Elisabeth Mann- 180, 182
Boston Tea Party 63, 133
Boult, Sir Adrian 171
Boyd Orr, Lord 51, 89, 179
Brailsford, H. N. *
Brandt, Willy    ix, 23
Brent, A. R. 73
Breton, André 51
Bretton Woods 23, 81, 144
Brugmans, Henri 167
Brundtland, G. H. 23
Bryce, Lord 187
Bush, George, US President    ix, 4, 91, 103, 184
Butler, R.A. 44

Cameron, Evan 73
Camus, Albert 51
Carr, R. 47
Carter, Jimmy 23
Catlin, Prof. George 64 *
Cecil, Lord 158
Chamberlain, Neville 47
Charlotte, Grand Duchess of Luxembourg, G.C.V.O. 174
Chatham House 107
Chelmsford 107
Chiang Kai-Shek 106, 189
Churchill, Winston S. 44, 60, 84, 106, 121, 140, 146, 148, 158, 163, 165, 167, 173, 192
Citrine, Sir Walter 156
Clarin, Anders 55, 71, 74, 75
Clements, G. E. I. 19, 84
Coll, John, F.I.L. x
Collin, Jean F. 177
Collins, Victor 161
Cominform 159, 220
Constantin, Prince 171
Coolidge, Calvin 230
Cooper, Duff 44
Cosyn, M. R. 73
Coudenhove-Kalergi, Count Richard 166, 170
Crusade for World Government 160
Culbertson, Ely *
Curie, Prof. Juliot- 180
Curry, Dr. W. B. 8, 15, 17, 43, 57, 64, 77, 230 *
Curtin, P.M. Australia. 142, 143
Curtis, Lionel, C. H. iv, 105, 106, 118, 120, 140, 191, 232, 233 *
Czechoslovakia 28

Daladier, Edouard 170
Davies, Lord 143, 153, 186
Davis, Garry 50, 55, 68, 71, 73

*243*

Devos, G. B. 56, 73, 177
Diedisheim, Jean 73, 182
Disington, Terje x, 66
Donat, R 57
Doren, Carl Van 216 *
Drese, Belgian M.P. 182
Dumbarton Oaks, 1944   81, 221
Dunkirk, Pact of 1947   220

Edward I, King 151, 152
Einstein, Prof. Albert 46, 48, 49, 51, 236
Eisenhower, General Dwight 200-2
Ellsworth, Oliver 217
Engle, Nathaniel H. *

Farmer, Fyke 47, 48, 52, 53, 73, 182
Felix, Prince of Luxembourg 174
Ferencz, Benjamin B. *
Fiske, John 134
Fleming, Peter 171
Franco, Gen. Francisco 103
Franklin, Benjamin 14
Frazer, P.M. New Zealand 142
Friendship, League of 41, 113, 134, 201
Frisell, Sven, 176

Gafencu, Grégoire 171
Geesteramus, Max 166
George III, King 133
George VI , King 157
Georgia 28
Gevaert, Edgar 17, 73, 74
Gevaert, Marie 73
Gevaert, Thérèse 75
Ghent, WMWFG Congress 181
Girard, Prof. 161, 162
Goedhart, Dr G. J. von Heuven 171
Gorbachev, Michael 30
Grant, Ulysses Simpson 190
Greenwood, Arthur 44
Grenfeld, Arthur J. 73
Grieg, Sir Robert 64

Hague, Congress 80, 163

Halifax, Lord 142
Hamilton, Alexander 5, 6, 9, 14, 113, 134, 135, 136, 144, 155, 224 *
Harding, Warren Gamaliel 230
Harrison, Joseph B. *
Havel, Vaclev 23
Heath, Sir E. 23
Heydecker, Joe 180
Hiroshima 35, 180, 218
Hogben, Lancelot, FRS 197
Hogg, Quintin 117
Hore-Belisha, Leslie 171
Hoyland, John S. *
Hugo, Victor 67
Hungary 28
Hussein, Saddam 4, 103
Huxley, Aldous 33

Ickes, Harold 45
Inagaki, Morikatsu 180
Iraq 29, 79, 91, 102-4, 184

Jaksch, Wenzel 65
Japan 123
Jay, John 6, 14, 134, 136, 137 *
Jeans, Ursula 57
Jenkins, Lord, of Hillhead 42
Jennings, Dr W. Ivor *
Joad, Cyril E. M. 64, 212 *
Juliana, Princess 163, 173

Kerstens, Senator Pieter 171
Keyes, Ken, Jr. *
Keynes, Lord 112, 145
Kimber, Sir Charles 58
King-Hall, Stephen 171
Kleffens, van 101
Koch, Henri 73, 177
Korea 68, 70, 121, 154, 200
Kowarski, Dr 180
Krupp, Bertha von 66
Kuwait 6, 7, 102, 184

Lang, Rev. Gordon 161
Lapie, P.O. 166

## Index

Larmeroux, Jean 174
Larsen, Brit-Eline x
Last, Jef 171
Law, Richard 171
Leather, Sir Ted 66 *
deLeon, Jack and Jean 57
Lie, Trygve 35, 68, 91, 139
Lindsay, K. 167
Lindsey, Robert 73
Lindsey, Treska (neé Gevaert) 75
Lippmann, Walter 184, 191
Lloyd, Georgia 220 *
Lloyd, Mary 73
Lothian, Lord 44, 105, 106 *
Luxembourg WMWFG Congress 69, 174

Machiavelli, Nicholas 93
Mackay, R.W.G. 44, 163, 167, 169 *
McNamara, Robert 23
de Madariaga, Salvador 35, 171
Madison, J. 6, 14, 134, 137, 217 *
Maine, Richard *
Malleson, Miles 57
Mander, Linden A. *
Marc, Alexandre 168, 175, 180
Marshall Plan 219
Masefield, John 171
Meade, James E. *
Meston, Lord 110, 121
Meyer, Cord, Jr. 217 *
Millard, E. L. *
Milner, Lord 106
Mitchell, Dr M. J. 73
Mitrany, Prof. David 38, 40, 169 *
Monroe, James 187, 189
Montreux WMWFG Congress 159
Moore-Brabazon, Lieut.-Col. 44
Moore, Cyril 64, 121
Moore, Dr. G.    x
Morgenthau 112, 144
Morrison, Herbert C. 124, 199
Munich 123, 187

Nagasaki 35

Nansen, Odd 180
Nash, Vernon 222 *
NATO 80, 219
Newcombe, Dr Hanna (Peace Research Institute, Dundas) *
New York 7, 46, 134, 157
Nielsen, Knud 73
Nixon, Richard 230
Nürnberg 54, 164, 166, 192
Nyere, Julius 23

Oak Ridge 209
O'Donnell, Jean 50
O.P.E.C. 185
d'Ormesson, Marquis André 170

Palestine 70, 90
Pankhurst, Sylvia 141
Paris Conference 35, 84
Parker, Dorothy 230
Pearl Harbour 123, 188
Philadelphia Convention 1787    134
Pierre Abbé Grouès 93, 174, 175, 180, 186
Pilsudski, R. 171
Pinder, John, O.B.E. *
Pitt, William, the Elder 63
Poland 84
Poncet, Francois 170
Popper, John 73
Posin, Dr. Daniel Q. 209
Procope, Hj. J. 171
Prussia 29

'Q' Theatre 57

Radhakrishnan, Sir S. 176
Ramadier, Paul 165, 166, 167, 170
Randini, Nicoló, Count Dr. 167
Ransome, Patrick 58*
Rawnsley, Derek 58
Rawnsley, Violet and Noël 73
Reves, Emery 162, 174 *
Reynaud, Paul 168, 169, 170
Robbins, Prof. Lionel *
Roberts, John C. de V. *

245

Roberts, Justice Owen 45
Roosevelt, F. D. 106, 154, 188, 224
de Rougemont, Denis 218 *
Russell, Bertrand 19, 88, 171 *
Russia 28

Sainsbury, Lord 64
Salazar 147
Salter, Sir Arthur 171
Salvin, Marina 216, 219 *
Sandys, Duncan 47, 163, 172
Sarrazac, Robert 50
Saudi Arabia 103
Selassie, Haile 141
Shawcross, M. 161
Shields, Sir Drummond 64
Shotwell, James T. 219
Sigurdsson, Ingvar 73
Sim, Alistair 57
Sinclair, Sir A. 44
de Smedt, Jan 73
Smuts, Field Marshal 115, 121, 138, 142
South Africa 106, 123, 157
South-West Africa 90
Spaak, Paul-Henri 81
Spence, C. F. *
van den Sprenkel, Prof. Berkelbach 171
Stapleton, Dr Olaf 64
Stettinius, E. R., Jr. 153, 154
Stockholm, WMWFG Congress 176
Streit, Clarence 41, 42, 57, 134 *
Sweden 29, 75
Swing, Raymond 180
Switzerland 18

Teitgen, P. H. 170
Tennessee 197
Tennyson, Alfred Lord 5
Thompson, Dorothy 93
Thorndyke, Sybil 57
Thirring, Prof. Hans 162
de Tocqueville, Alexis 227
Trevelyan, Sir George Macaulay 117

Truman, Harry S. 190, 191

Ukraine 28
U.N. Military Staffs Committee 79
Urey, Prof. Harold 187, 207
Usborne, Henry 45, 46, 47, 73, 160, 161, 180, 182, 208
Ustinov, Sir Peter viii

de Valera, E. 122
Van der Eecken, V. E. 73
'Vercors' 51
Versailles Treaty of 1783  134
Vulliamy, C. E. *

Wachtel, Ludwig and Mary 65
Warsaw Pact 5
Washington, George 14, 23, 108, 113, 134, 151, 152, 187, 188, 201
Wedgwood, Lord 60
Wells, H. G. 150
West, Ranyard, MD, MRCP, DPh 213 *
Westminster, Statute of 92, 122
Wheare, K. C. 15 *
Williams, Francis 64
Wilson, Woodrow 23, 154, 187, 224
Wingate, Monica M. 64
Wingate, General Orde 64
Wofford, H. 162
Wootton, Lady Barbara 22, 64, 112 *
World Federalist Press Association 56
World Movement for World Federal Government 13, 159, 174, 179
Wynner, Edith 220 *

Yalman, S. Ahmet Emin 171
York, Archbishop of 197
Young, Sir George *
Yugoslavia 28

van Zeeland, P. 170
Zeidman, Leonard 132

* also in Bibliography